FOREIGN BABES
IN BEIJING

W. W. Norton & Company
New York   London

FOREIGN BABES
IN BEIJING

*Behind
the Scenes
of a
New China*

Rachel DeWoskin

Copyright © 2005 by Rachel DeWoskin

All rights reserved
Printed in the United States of America
First Edition

For information about permission to reproduce selections from this book,
write to Permissions, W. W. Norton & Company, Inc.,
500 Fifth Avenue, New York, NY 10110

Manufacturing by Courier Westford
Book design by Anna Oler

Library of Congress Cataloging-in-Publication Data

DeWoskin, Rachel.
Foreign babes in Beijing : Behind the scenes of a new China / Rachel
DeWoskin.— 1st ed.
p. cm.
ISBN 0-393-05902-2 (hardcover)
1. China—Social life and customs—1976– 2. DeWoskin, Rachel—
Travel—China. I. Title: Behind the scenes of a new China. II. Title.
DS779.23.D48 2005
951'.156059'0820973—dc22

2005000939

W. W. Norton & Company, Inc.
500 Fifth Avenue, New York, N.Y. 10110
www.wwnorton.com

W. W. Norton & Company Ltd.
Castle House, 75/76 Wells Street, London W1T 3QT

1 2 3 4 5 6 7 8 9 0

For my family:
Judith and Kenneth
Aaron, Jacob, Melissa,
and Adam Hunter

And the loves of my life:
Zayd and Baby Day

Contents

Author's Note

There is a Chinese expression for the blindness brought on by inside perspective: *jing di zhi wa*, "frog in the bottom of a well." The frog looks up and sees only a single circle of the sky; he thinks he sees clearly, but "he doesn't know how big heaven really is."

Since the 1600s, Westerners have journeyed to China and preserved flashes of the middle kingdom they saw. Beijing served as the empire's capital for more than eight hundred years, but was never pried open like the treaty ports of Shanghai, Canton, or Tianjin. Instead, it stayed shrouded in the center of gates and concentric walls. At the middle of the great throne halls of the Forbidden City, Beijing was the essence of China, rarely seen.

Now the city is on display. The Forbidden City itself is open to locals and foreigners; the tangled confusion of *hutong* alleys that ringed Beijing's center has been carved into boulevards and expressways. Skyscrapers have shot up over the squat, bureaucratic buildings that lined once-empty avenues, and street stalls have been sacrificed for sleek boutiques, cafés, and sushi bars. Aging with grace and hesitation, the city embodies all the contradictions of the modern world, offering dizzying lessons on the intersections between an antique past and a global present.

I lived in Beijing for over five years, peering at the patches of China visible to me. I was, even inside China, an outsider watching as the world's longest continuous civilization lurched inexorably into the twenty-first century. My notes from Beijing are about the people I knew, as well as the language and frameworks with which we came to know each other. Against the advice of cautious friends, I kept diaries of hundreds of Beijing discussions. Chinese are generous with time, praise, and conversation. Any foreigner who speaks even a shred of Chinese is a friend, encouraged to say and hear more. Grateful for the years of language lessons and insights, I wrote them down.

At the core of all my Beijing interactions, both the successful and the not so successful, was language. The Chinese language has density and ambiguity, made richer by my evolving but always uncertain grip on its edges. Much of the interface between my Eastern and Western friends was revealed in the elastic span between our words and the entertaining process of connecting Chinese and English. We came to speak in what we called Chinglish, an efficient hybrid of English and Chinese, importing the most expressive components of each language into the other. Beijing's hip, globalizing population converses and identifies itself almost entirely in this mixed language, a representation of some mixed feelings and selves. Our best tool for creating communication that worked was *pinyin*, which means literally "spell sound."

Author's Note

A Romanization system for Chinese characters, *pinyin* made it possible to decode the sounds of the language, and so speak and understand it. Major street signs in China are written out in *pinyin*, as are the Chinese names in this book.

The great and whimsical Daoist philosopher Zhuangzi once said, "Language is like a fish net. Once the fish are caught, you can throw the net away. Once the idea is caught, you can throw the words away." This book is the record of what I picked up, from friends whose city and company I cherished. It is their story more than mine: of one round corner of Beijing's transformation, where some insiders and some outsiders were changed forever.

FOREIGN BABES
IN BEIJING

From *Foreign Babes in Beijing* Theme Song
(The whirring of pigeons can be heard over the music)

Man's Voice (Chinese)
They all come from different countries.
They're all in love with Chinese culture
and green vegetable snacks.
Their lives are carefree and fun.
Because they're all old foreigners!
But they can all speak Chinese.
They are beautiful and poised.

Man's Voice (English)
Foreign girls, foreign girls in Beijing, Beijing!

Man's Voice (Chinese)
They give their hearts and souls, everything to Beijing!

ONE

脱裤

Tuoku

Drop Trou

learned the Chinese for "drop trou" on the set of a nighttime television drama called *Foreign Babes in Beijing*. It was Director Yao who gave the order: *"Tuoku."* Perched on the edge of a bed in Beijing's five-star Great Wall Sheraton Hotel, I thumbed through a red, laminated dictionary that looked suspiciously like a Mao primer from the Cultural Revolution. I found the *pinyin*: *tuo*, "peel off," *ku*, from *kuzi*, or "pants."

"You must be kidding," I said to no one in particular.

I was playing Jiexi, the manipulative American hussy who seduces a married Chinese man, falls in love with him, and then sacrifices everything for true love when she agrees to marry him. The acting job was supposed to be a lark, an adventure. Fresh out of undergraduate school in New York City, I'd been in China for two months, working for an American public relations firm, exploring Beijing, and trying to make use of limited and nerdy college Chinese. Now I was half naked and surrounded by a crew of Chinese men, with an open dictionary on my lap. I tried to remember how I'd arrived at this moment. Could "peel your pants off" be slang for something other than "strip"? I turned to Wang Ling, as if he might be able to help. He grinned and started on his belt buckle.

Wang Ling played my love interest. He was unstoppably macho, six-foot-two, and chiseled, designed by producers and personal trainers to turn the tables on Hollywood stereotypes of wimpy Chinese men: Charlie Chans, inscrutable Orientals, and Asian houseboys. My role was to play the exotic, mysterious femme fatale, relieving Eastern women momentarily of that chore. Jointly, Wang Ling and I would establish a contemporary counterpoint to a tense historical reality: that intercultural romances in China were primarily between Western men and Chinese women. There were 106.6 males for every 100 females in China in the 1990s,[1] and no Chinese man liked to see beautiful marriage prospects plucked from the pool. But China could spare some of its most strapping men to foreign women. Chinese producers would not have dared show a Chinese woman seducing a Western man on TV. It was safer to depict China penetrating the West.

In some ways, Wang Ling was like his scripted character, Tianming. He was protective, sexy, and soap-opera romantic. He tutored me in Chinese pronunciation and held my hand on the cast bus. He asked questions I could not answer about American girls. I asked questions he did not answer about his wife. We carried dictionaries and cultivated a delicate flirtation.

"Jiexi is a good girl in the end of the show," Director Yao had frequently assured me. I didn't need reassurance. Bad girls were more interesting. And after all, this was Chinese TV, bound for censors; I figured it had no chance of being racy by my American standards.

The day before our rendezvous in the Great Wall Sheraton, Wang Ling had tried to warn me. "Tomorrow's scenes . . ." He coughed. "Do you understand?" I nodded and smiled provocatively. And then I ran home and called Teacher Kang, my Chinese tutor. She was grandmotherly, and wore a short cloud of poufy hair and layers of clothing she never removed even inside my duck oven of an office. She helped me with the *Foreign Babes* script as many times a week as I had to film. We had hundreds of panicked tutorials. As soon as I knew what scenes we were filming, Teacher Kang worked through each one with me, correcting everything from my tones to the placement of my tongue in my mouth to my body language and facial expressions. She was conservative, patriotic, and overly generous with advice. She was horrified the day she read the sex scenes.

"Love business!" she whispered to me urgently. I wasn't worried: I'd never even seen anyone kiss on Chinese TV, although I hadn't watched enough to warrant my confidence.

"Do we kiss?" I asked her, smirking.

She flushed. "Yes, you even sleep!"

Sleep? I imagined a scene in which we woke up together, my naked, pale arm glowing across his chest. I unearthed my bathing suit and by the next day had it all under control: makeup on every freckle.

I also had one directive. "I'm embarrassed to request this, Director Yao," I said from the bed. "Trouble you, but perhaps we don't need any media in the room for this scene."

Director Yao held up a hand, palm flat out, at the journalists. "*Zou ba!*" he said. Go!

Reporters slunk away in droves, leaving a cast of dozens: lighting technicians, makeup artists, Assistant Director Xu, costumers, prop boys, and script consistency staff.

Wang Ling and I were front and center, unable to make eye contact. He had just carried me from the door to the bed, dangling my head. The karaoke soundtrack blared in the background. He set me on the bed.

"Begin your dialogue," said Director Yao.

"I love you! What are we waiting for?" Jiexi cried. And in this line, she hurled her Westernness at Tianming; he and the audience would instantly understand her lacerating style of seduction and wanton disregard for the sanctity of marriage as typically American.

Tianming stood quietly, digesting this unpalatable pass, perhaps mourning his male weakness and the inevitable betrayal of his wife, son, and country. Jiexi was an import, after all, and with her came all kinds of temptation and corruption.

Wang Ling and I waited for direction. Director Yao said something incomprehensible and Wang Ling took off his shirt and tie and then began unbuttoning my shirt. This was it, the stripping down of every awkward cultural mistake we'd made in the months of filming, every misunderstood conversation, tone, suggestion. We were going to get down to the naked basics. Or at least a fair imitation of them, made-for-TV.

While acting the foreign babe, I puzzled at how little art imitated life. This scene was where all the obsessive divides of life in Beijing became more apparent than ever, only to vanish into the thin air of sex and love: Chinese and non-Chinese, directness and indirectness, modesty and boldness, virtue and vice, cloaked and stripped down. Jiexi and Tianming were about to act out a beautiful metaphor for success in Sino-U.S. diplomacy. My shirt was off. Wang Ling had his jeans unbuttoned and his belt loosened. The cameraman was three feet away. And suddenly, after weeks of sly glances and electricity, all attraction vanished. His skin was rubbery; I was dripping with sweat; I noticed him noticing my freckles, which Chinese people think are ugly. His hair was sticking up in clumps. Mine was glued to my forehead. Around the bed, cameras buzzed like mosquitoes. The only sizzle came from the lights. I could taste my makeup.

I slumped back against the pillow, flushed from the heat. The makeup staff descended upon me with hair products. Then Director Yao interjected a quick, "*Tuoku! Tuoku!*"

Wang Ling watched me look the words up and then, with an amused glance, dropped his pants to the floor. His belt hit the bed frame and clattered. He was wearing tighty-whities. He was hairless and tan, flexing a stomach that looked like several bricks stacked on one another, and puffing out his chest. His sweat was festive, like that of a calendar boy. Under normal circumstances, I'd have thought he was fabulous. He was watching me. My hair had fallen out of the preposterous up-do the make-up team had managed, and Wang Ling pushed some of it back from my face. I took the hair clip out and let the rest fall down. In ancient Chinese literature, the removal of hairpins or jewelry signified that a woman was guilty of sin or crime and awaited punishment. I set my hairpins on the bedside table.

"Are you embarrassed?" Wang Ling asked me; a spotlight made him squint.

"Why do you ask?" I was desperately embarrassed, but wanted to save face. I didn't want Wang Ling to think I was inexperienced, either in love or TV. And I had a bikini on, at least.

"You have to take those straps off," said Director Yao, interrupting. "They'll show." I took the straps off my shoulders, trying to leave the actual bra cups on. Not possible.

Now we would kiss and sleep. I prepared myself for our first illicit kiss. Wang Ling! I pursed my lips. Wang Ling craned his neck down to kiss me, but Director Yao shouted, "Roll around on the bed!"

I paused to consider what that might mean, but before I could ask, Wang Ling, jumping forward and tilting me back with his thumbs, pinned me to the bed, opening his mouth as wide as a gate and stretching it over my head. This was a soap-opera kiss?

"No laughing!" Director Yao said when I shouted out. Wang Ling stopped the frantic grinding and became a huge, dead weight on top of me. "Rub his back," said Director Yao.

Dutifully, I began to massage Wang Ling's back, starting at the shoulders, while he kissed me enormously with his mouth still open. My bikini top was somewhere near my waist. I shrank back, wondering if he might swallow my head, and continued gently rubbing my fingertips in small, even circles.

There was an awkward silence in the room. At the time I pondered whether the scene might be exciting for our immediate audience. Now I know they were just astonished, wondering whether Western girls do it like that.

Wang Ling peered down at me, worried for my reputation. "No, no," he said. "Like this." He faked a split-second version of clawing orgasm, grinding his tighty-whitey hips and shouting. Director Yao nodded.

"Yes!" he said. "Reqing yidian." More passion, a bit more "hot emotion."

I was supposed to be writhing in ecstasy, but I had missed a vocabulary clue and given a chaste backrub. I sat up, naked to the waist. "Cut," called Director Yao. I crossed my arms over my chest. The makeup artist rushed over to repair my lips with a tool kit of lipsticks. I thought surgery would be the only way to put them back together.

"You know," I said, "I'd be more comfortable if Director Yao were also naked." Wang Ling inhaled sharply. The lip-gloss brush retracted. It was a request born of desperation. But later, when I tried to convince everyone that Jiexi and I were not in fact the same person, I would regret asking Director Yao to *tuoku*.

I turned to Wang Ling and grinned. "Are you embarrassed?"

He smiled and I felt slightly better. Everyone's focus shifted to Director Yao.

"We're all professionals here," he announced. And in a gesture of tremendous camaraderie and allegiance, Director Yao unbuckled his pants and dropped them to the floor. He, too, wore bikini briefs. I wondered whether they sold boxers in China.

"*Xie xie, Yao Daoyan,*" I said. Thank you, Director Yao. "Let's try the scene again."

"No problem," he said. "I can understand this request. Now we are *dou yiyang.*" All the same. I waited until he said, "Action," and then tried to redeem myself by grabbing Wang Ling and clawing his back with enthusiasm. The director of photography whispered to the assistant director: "You see what I mean? Foreign babes are tigers."

Funny, I had always thought that was a stereotype of Eastern women.

The story of *Foreign Babes in Beijing* still shapes Beijing for me. It is the tale of two American students, in love with China and Chinese men. The trailer for the show puts it eloquently: "These foreign babes! When they meet our Chinese men, they dare to love, dare to hate!" In the background, a squeaky babe voice sings out: "*Wo ai Beijing!*" I love Beijing!

Produced in 1995 by Beijing's central television studio, Beiying, the show was a follow-up to the huge hit *Beijinger in New York*, about a Chinese man who moves to New York and experiences the horrors of modern life in the West. *Foreign Babes in Beijing* was a patriotic and optimistic sequel: instead of losing its best assets to the West, China was gaining some beautiful, admiring babes. In the same way that *Beijinger in New York* had given the "Chinese view of New York," so *Foreign Babes in Beijing* would give a "foreign view of Beijing." Except that it was written, directed, produced, and marketed by Chinese to Chinese. It gave the Chinese view of the foreign view of Beijing. The only truly Western aspects of the show were the babes themselves, and our makeup and hairstyles, which appeared to have been dreamt up by Hollywood and propagated by shows like *Dallas*.

The plot of *Foreign Babes* is true to a yin/yang sensibility of cosmic balance: each of the two American babes finds her equal in a Chinese love, and her opposite in the other babe. There are also Russian and Japanese babes, but they are given fairly little screen time, likely the result of historical resentments against their home countries. There are no European babes in the script. The focus is on the American girls, who, much like America itself, both shine and wither under the scrutiny of a hot spotlight. Louisa is the blond China hand, full of angelic patience for crowded public buses, profound interest in Chinese culture, and everlasting love (at first sight, no less) for Li Tianliang, the Li family's young, unmarried son. In spite of the fact that Louisa was to be a "typical American," she was played by a German girl named Sophie. In the same way that Westerners often cannot distinguish Chinese from Japanese or Korean, many Chinese think all Westerners look and sound alike.

I played Jiexi, Louisa's classmate, the brunette vixen: sassy, liberated, and infatuated with Li Tianliang's older brother, the married Li Tianming, whose model life includes a precocious and adorable little son.

The imported babes find themselves in an instant culture clash with the traditional Li family, who live in an old-style courtyard house right in the middle of the new China. Their house, a traditional *siheyuan*, or four-sided garden, features four adjoining living quarters, built around an inner courtyard full of potted plants, trees, cabbages, live birds in cages, and ropes of garlic and red pepper. The house is designed to hold centuries of family members, expanding to include new generations and, in the case of *Foreign Babes*, new cultures.

With the Li family live their eldest son Tianming's wife and child; a bitter, divorced neighbor and her expensive lapdog; Grandpa Lu, a puppeteer; and Grandpa Lu's son, a modest pedicab driver. One big, happy, unrealistic family, the courtyard cast represents a flattering range of the levels of Chinese society, from the elderly traditional parents to the wealthy but unhappy divorcee to the laborer. The Li sons, like the babes, are models of virtue and vice.

The *laowai*, as the theme song calls them, infiltrate Beijing, the Lis' courtyard, and the hearts of the Li brothers. *Laowai* translates roughly as "old foreigner," but carries a delicate scent of the word "buffoon," the oldness suggesting an edge of dementia and foolishness. The expression is widely used and celebrated by Chinese and *laowai* alike.

The *laowai* Louisa courts Tianliang in a traditional and demure fashion, tutoring him in English by whispering, "Here is a pencil! This is a pencil! Here is a pencil!" on a date in her dorm room. Then she rides horses with him across a dust-caked landscape outside of Beijing and writes an essay for her Chinese conversation class about her love of the city and Tianliang's family, whom she describes as "average Chinese people, like the ones you see on the street, selling vegetables." To celebrate her new, increasingly authentic Chinese life, Louisa walks around Beijing's Houhai Lake dreaming of Li Tianliang, and learns to steep tea and roll dumplings. After four short episodes and an accidental kiss (Louisa is leaning on the door and when Old Man Li opens it, she is thrown unwittingly into Li Tianliang's arms), Louisa and Li Tianliang kiss at their virgin wedding. On their wedding night, they sleep in Old Man Li and Mrs. Li's bed. The generous in-laws, tucked away in the living room, have sacrificed their space so that the new couple may have what privacy there is to be had in a crowded courtyard house.

A princess of a daughter-in-law, Louisa has made a long-term commitment to China, where she will live forever in the courtyard, trying to roll attractive dumplings and eventually giving her in-laws a grandson to embrace. She will continue to express her foreignness with inappropriate gifts, including a clock for her father-in-law, which suggests impending death. He screams upon receiving it, creating the opportunity for other characters to instruct Louisa and deepen her understanding of China.

The darker Jiexi is more of a taker. She meets Li Tianming through Louisa, takes a thirsty look, and then gives a double thumbs-up to her classmates. When Tianming comes to the dorm to ask the exchange students if they will help him find clients for his tour-guiding service, Jiexi offers herself. She appears at his office. "I helped you find clients," she says, licking her lips.

"Great!" he says. He looks around. "How many?"

"Me!"

Since he has asked for help, it is too awkward to turn her away. She hires him to teach her about Beijing.

"First," she dictates, "I want to try Chinese food. What shall we eat today?"

"Small Chinese snacks," he says.

"What about tonight?"

"Oh!" he cries. "Tonight, too? You need a guide tonight?"

"What will we eat tonight?" she asks lustily.

"Big Chinese snacks?"

Enticed by Jiexi, Tianming is lured into the destruction of his traditional marriage and the end of his commitment to China. She teaches him not only the meaning of true love and sacrifice, but also useful English phrases, including, "I love you. What are we waiting for?"

Jiexi's love is, as Director Yao liked to put it, "true"; she demonstrates this by resisting financial pressure from her American parents, racist patriots who threaten to disown her over her love for Tianming. They describe Tianming (without having met him) as "lazy and uncultured." This was to me a fascinating example of a Chinese view of foreigners' views of Chinese. Before the *Foreign Babes* script, I had never heard the stereotype that Chinese are lazy. But Chinese believe that Americans believe it.

Louisa's parents are expatriates in China; they speak Chinese, go bowling and dancing with Louisa's new in-laws, and help the Li sons become crafty businessmen. Louisa's dad, Jack, calls the Great

Wall great. The show explores genetic logic, depicting the most obvious of connections and disjunctions between young people and their parents. All of the characters both resist and become their own parents, modern-style. In this way, the show dimly reflected reality. I watched my friends in Beijing adapt to China's new geography and ideology in ways that cleaved them from and to their families. As Westernized and wild as my Chinese friends were, they became (as we all do) increasingly their parents' children.

In the final episode of *Foreign Babes*, Louisa and Tianliang stand in the courtyard, set to carry on the tradition of the Li family. Louisa wears a red padded Chinese jacket and *bu xie*, cloth shoes worn primarily by old Chinese men. She and her husband and mother-in-law wave good-bye to Jiexi and Tianming, who are Westward-bound. Jiexi wears a floor-length fur coat and carries a suitcase, which she sets down for long enough to embrace Tianming's father and exclaim, "Baba!" in Chinese. Old Man Li has realized that Jiexi's love for his son is true, and has forgiven Jiexi for stealing his son. In the Chinese family, Jiexi is redeemed, even as she exports their son to America. It is, of course, ideal to have one son stay in Beijing to *yanglao*, care for the parents in their dotage, and one son go to America to seek great wealth, even if the way to that happy ending is a bit scandalous and unconventional.

Tianming further burnishes the ancestral tablets by falling to his knees in a final traditional kowtow to his father. He is, in a last-ditch gesture, following the filial scripts and putting all back in order. Jiexi does not bow. She follows the ugly ways of her predecessor, Lord Macartney, a British diplomat who famously did not get the kowtow idea and refused to bow to the Chinese emperor, stalling the advance of Sino-British trade for five decades and bringing on the Opium Wars.

And yet, in the final moments of *Foreign Babes in Beijing*, the lovebirds carry their suitcases off into the horizon, bound for a glistening life in the West. The whirring of pigeons provides a natural soundtrack to their exodus. Firecrackers light up the night scenes. Regardless of what the producers, censors, or media later claimed the message of the show to be, *Foreign Babes*, with its fur coats, *laowai* gaffes, and knowledgeably global chic, took its pitiful place among China's most famous ancient stories of love and sensuality: *Dream of the Red Chamber*, the *Peony Pavilion*, and *Romance of the Western Chambers*. Breaking the frame and following their hearts, finding and indulging in freedom, Jiexi and Tianming were envied and beloved in Beijing and across every province in China, where the twenty-episode drama played repeatedly to an estimated six hundred million viewers.

Wang Ling and I were not the only ones who found ourselves stripped down in a struggle to find common ground. The 1990s were a confusing time for Chinese, who were living in a disjunctive culture where suddenly, in spite of everything their parents and China had believed and taught them, getting rich was glorious, Western images, products, and tourists were everywhere, and familiar ideologies (embodied in model workers) evaporated from the public mind and left a dazed, excited, and disoriented population.

Chinese learn from models; China's historical record and literature are filled with exemplary biographies, model workers, diligent scholars, loyal widows, good officials, bad last emperors, foreign babes. People are appropriately titled, not so much by how they were born as how they have acted. A son can lose the title "son" by being un-sonly. A part of this system is the penchant in public culture for classification and counting: "one country, two systems," "three represents," "four modernizations," the Confucian "five relationships," and so on, up to the *wanli changcheng,* the ten-thousand-*li* Great Wall.

This mode of thinking does not allow for sweeping personal transformation. But the stripping away in the 1990s of Chinese models of good citizenship, moral participation in society's collective goals, and marriage in service to state made for a lot of searching in that decade. In 1989, five years before I arrived in Beijing, an ambitious but brief taste of political and cultural freedom had been abruptly crushed during the democracy movement in Tiananmen Square. That movement, organized by students and joined by workers, writers, artists, and even some government officials, ended with a military attack on the square during the week of June 4, 1989. This landmark moment is known in China by its numbers, 6/4.

Everyone in the world who watched the news that week remembers a solitary Chinese man standing in front of a column of oncoming tanks. Models do not need names. In the context of China's frantic-paced modernization, June 4 was a brutal reminder of the potential for repeating history, or worse, moving backward through it. My Western friends who were in China in 1989 said they felt betrayed, that they had believed China was modernizing, changing, and opening, and that June 4 had slammed the door shut and pushed China back into its own isolated past. Foreign business, whether driven by the risk of bad publicity or genuine outrage, pulled out of China after 1989. Activists and artists were arrested and modernization seemed, from the outside at least, to have halted, even retreated. Sister-state relationships collapsed, and the international community loudly condemned the Chinese government's behavior.

When I arrived five years later, the search for freedom was alive, maybe recently reborn, but the politics had been removed. It was as if an unspoken compact had been reached between the government and its citizens: we do the politics the old way; you do your lifestyles any way you want. When my Chinese friends talked about June 4, they took a view long enough to drain the passion and make the date an abstraction. By 1994, the event suggested decade-long cycles and echoes of a century of Chinese rebellions: the 1919 May Fourth Movement; the 1949 rise of the Communist Party; the late 1950s Anti-Rightist movement and break with the Soviet Union; and the 1960s Cultural Revolution.

Only slightly less than three years after June 4, Deng Xiaoping took a southern tour of Shenzhen, China's so-called Special Development Zone near Hong Kong, and China's most liberalized city. There, he uttered with imperial brevity: "All China should follow this example." And so ended the post-Tiananmen uncertainty about China's direction. Foreign investors, businesspeople, scholars, and students flooded back in. By 1993, businesses were coming back with confidence; by 1995, the ingress was in full force. China felt reasonably stable, growth was surging, and everyone wanted to invest. Western companies wishfully calculated sales. If just half or one-third of China's 1.3 billion people bought one can of soda, a shoelace, a button, or a car, then a company could make millions of dollars. It was an upward moment, filled with enthusiasm, investment, and attention. Consumerism became a religion; companies arrived like missionaries, converting employees, testing advertising strategies, and seducing the average Zhou Schmoe with products he had never known he needed.

One of China's main dilemmas was, and still is, the question of how a country can stay closed politically or socially if it opens economically. *Foreign Babes in Beijing* is an apt if tacky example of this problem. Jiexi and Louisa were offering up certain kinds of products: hard currency, the freedom to travel, liberated sex, international business opportunities, and air-conditioned condominiums. The question is, can such pleasures be enjoyed without compromising China's spiritual essence and moral integrity? The Chinese government and its state-owned business enterprises were working hard—both to open up to foreign partners and projects, and to keep control and compete. International firms, frustrated by China's unpredictable regulatory environment, were frantic to understand what the rules were, to predict what they were likely to become, and to have an impact on shaping them. (Following them was a separate matter; in China, rules are made to be interpreted.)

Also open to interpretation was the question of what the opening of some doors and locking of others would mean for China's cultural landscape. Deng Xiaoping promised that reform would open China, even at the risk of "spiritual pollution" of China by Western forces. As he put it, when China opened its doors, some "flies would come in."

Tourists and expatriates carried a dual and heavy weight on our shoulders; we were representatives both from the promised land and from a country Chinese called "the world police." America used its iron-fist foreign policies to boss, attack, and contain other countries, and our pop culture exports to deflower them. The East, many maintained, had been innocent until the festering spread of capitalism and AIDS (believed by many to be a Western import) had destroyed its virgin values. Images of Western wealth, sex, and beauty had compromised Eastern citizens' sense of self. Others argued the opposite: that it took capitalism and Western images beamed all over Asia to give villagers a sense of self at all. My Chinese friend Anna often said that the West had given Chinese women the right to be individuals, albeit slowly. Her friend Xia Ning, desperately seeking a Western husband, once told me that if she had not been exposed to Western freedom and European men, she would have "dried up and died of repression."

From the moment any foreign babe set foot in the vast, concrete chaos of Beijing's old Capital Airport, we were believed to be importing American dollars, spiritual pollution, libido, and disease. Chinese both embraced us and recoiled; our ways were as foreign and terrifying as those of any of the barbarians who had invaded and conquered China in the preceding centuries. And yet, we were also representatives from the land of the free, ambassadors from TV, delegates from the movies. Any white woman in China looked more like Pamela Anderson or, as I heard countless times, Vivien Leigh, than Chinese women themselves did. And with our curls, eyelashes, and wide, light eyes, we might as well have stepped straight from the giant screen into the streets. Moreover, we had chosen to be in China. This was acknowledged by Chinese as an obvious truism, and yet analyzed quietly as a surprising reality.

On the one hand, China housed the world's longest civilization, biggest population, and greatest treasures and traditions. Of course the less cultured would want to visit the Great Wall, the Giant Buddha, and the proud northern capital. Naturally, Americans, with our meager two-hundred-year history, wanted to enrich ourselves by catching glimpses of a culture steeped in tradition, and buildings in which emperors had dined and negotiated.

On the other hand, why were so many of us choosing to leave the world's greatest affluence and luxury to live in dusty, difficult

Beijing? Some interpretations were cynical: Westerners who came to China did so in order to capitalize on the country's development and make American dollars. One cabdriver complained righteously that it was outrageous that I should be able to make American dollars in China, working for an American company, while the presence of so many Westerners did not relieve him from being paid in local currency.

All Westerners in Beijing during the late 1980s and 1990s, whether we magnified the vision by televising it or not, were models for imports and U.S. dollars. Western food, toys, shoes, and cars multiplied on the streets and in "Friendship Stores," so named in spite of the fact that until more than a decade after they opened, Chinese were not allowed to shop in them. They sold luxury goods "suitable for foreigners," a distinction that did not inspire friendship. By the 1990s, *laowai* and Chinese shopped together at Friendship Stores all over China. Ceramic Ronald McDonalds sprung up with clown hair and smiles, and Penguin Classics went on sale in select bookstores, along with international magazines.

Beijing's new Levi's, pinstripes, Nikes, and perms were Western cultural side effects, both causes and effects of a change in language. Political discourse in China was shifting from the enforced discussion of making sacrifices to that of making money. New words stretched Chinese stroke marks: *Maidanglao* was a melodious Chinese version of McDonald's, and Burger King became *Da Wang*, the "Big King." *Kekou Kele*, Coca Cola, contains in four beautifully transliterated syllables both a mimic of the original and a meaning that the sound doesn't have in English. Chinese *Kekou Kele* is *palatable* and *pleasurable*. Its homonyms suggest thirst, delight, and quenching. It's a richer word than its English original, flaunting the compressed power of the Chinese language to contain multiple meanings in single syllables, even when the syllables are foreign. Every sound in Chinese has inescapable, numerous, and sometimes clashing meanings. The state-run media's vocabulary became one of consumerism and success previously not celebrated by party cadres and not allowed among citizens. There was suddenly a slang term for a peasant who *fa'cai'*ed, or made a fortune overnight. *Caifu* was a newly minted, quick term for a nouveau riche peasant.

The West was advertised not only in new words, but also on billboards and packages. A translated, aspirational world could be contained in a single can of Chinese *Kekou Kele*. In 1995 after a visit to China, Roberto Guizetta, then Chairman of Coca-Cola, called the soda "a symbol," and said that to "become more like Americans,"[2] people drink Coke.

The desire for foreign foods, partners, and products, if translatable into wanting to "become more like Americans," was complicated by love-hate ideas about consumerism and capitalism. The leadership was excited by the potential of consumerism to develop markets, satisfy the people, and convey messages. But they were also wary of the probable cost to the cultural fiber that distinguishes Chinese from outsiders, hedonists, and imperialists. China's own ancient self-conception as the "middle kingdom" has always relied on its sense of being surrounded in all directions by outside peoples. The Chinese word for China, *Zhongguo*, recognizes the distinction between China and the "outside." *Zhong* means "middle" and *guo* is "country" or "kingdom." *Wai* means "outside," and is half of the word for foreign places: *waiguo*, "outside countries." Foreigners are "outside country people."

As China swung its doors open wide to outside country people, Party leaders found themselves less charged to deliver ideology and more responsible for economic growth, consumer products, and better lifestyles.

Deng Xiaoping's famous statement "to get rich is glorious" took effect, resonating everywhere. Young Chinese tore off their Mao suits and adopted goals so starkly different from those of their parents that connections stretched precariously between the two generations. For the elders, Deng Xiaoping's policy signaled explicitly that the result of 1989 was not going to be a return to the Cultural Revolution. For my friends, opening up meant that instead of making steel for the state, they could send their children to college, travel abroad, open companies, and drive Mercedes sedans.

An axiom of Deng's statement on the glory of wealth was that some would get it sooner than others. This was a jarring shift for Chinese of all ages, who had been deeply versed in the virtues of a communal society, where advantage and class distinction were ostensibly erased.

Privilege and its trappings had long been closely associated with Western imports. Illicit movies, fancy cars, and frivolities in general were considered banes of Western civilization, but now became the new playthings of a Chinese politically advantaged class. Urban China sparkled; while most of its citizens remained poor, its cities were getting rich. Rows of proud skyscrapers with spectacularly strange "traditional characteristics" (including roof cornices in the style of the Forbidden City) flaunted the success of China's reforms. Chinese women stalked through China's cities in miniskirts and heels, pagers attached to their leather purses. They dyed their hair blond and had eyelid lifts to widen and "Westernize" their eyes. Northwest Airlines introduced a direct flight from Detroit to Beijing in 1995, marked by a live Beach Boys concert in the convention hall at the China World Hotel. Discos spread across

Beijing, lighting up Chinese nights. People all over China exploded out of previously held patterns of social understatement and repression, lurching into lifestyles that were once the central objects of ridicule in revolutionary operas and films.

Tianming and Jiexi were resonant symbols, fit for the new world because they were beautiful, fake, aspirational, in true love, and featured on a cheesy, prime-time soap. During the Cultural Revolution, personal love always gave way to love of the cause, and reform was demonstrated in the sacrifice of private feelings and redirection of youthful romance into passion to serve the state. In *Foreign Babes in Beijing,* genuine love was its own end goal: once realized, such love itself became a celebration of personal "truth," even at the cost of one's marriage, inheritance, or national identity. When producers wanted to make money for state-run TV, political baggage shrank conveniently to fit commercial appetites; by the 1990s, family, patriotism, and morality could be popularly sacrificed in the name of love.

In Li Tianming's search for personal freedom and an escape from the last stifling generation, he finds meaning, magic, and a ticket to the new world. And if that search for fulfillment requires a flight to America, who can blame him for leaving? Not the producers. Not the audience. Not even his own father, it turns out. And there *is* a certain truth in those love-and-exodus scenes; lots of urban Chinese found themselves naked and searching in the 1990s. I just happened to be a culture-shocked *laowai* among them.

From *Foreign Babes in Beijing*
Episode Nineteen

Jiexi and Tianming sit at a table across from each other. They are in a bar. Jiexi's father has threatened to disown her if she marries Tianming.

JIEXI
I decided what to do about my father's threat. I want you.
My love, for you, I can sacrifice everything.

TIANMING
Jiexi! It's because I love you that I can't accept this sacrifice.
We have to break up.

JIEXI
(Crying)
No! No! Tianming, no!

He leaps up and rushes from the restaurant. Jiexi pushes her chair over and follows him out.

TWO

随便

Suibian

As You Wish

I went to China to get a glimpse of the new China, and the more years I spent there, the more work that vision required. The silver lining was that I also saw America clearly for the first time, as well as my own, private Americanness, in the reflected views of the Chinese. China showed me America's place in the world; I saw it in Beijing's Marlboros, spiked haircuts, sunglasses, *Titanic* T-shirts, and violent protests after NATO bombed the Chinese embassy in Belgrade in 1999. I saw America on my Chinese soap opera. And I saw that what I had always believed to be "American" and true of America mattered less than what China's billion citizens saw, thought, and believed. Even if less accurate by my standards, their America was at least as meaningful as mine.

I moved to Beijing in October 1994. I had just graduated from Columbia University, where I majored in English and studied poetry. I wanted to be Frank O'Hara, writing urban verse about the world. But I had no idea how to be anyone other than the student I had always been. At graduation, I looked in the rearview mirror and saw seventeen years of American childhood and education. In front of me, a world map was opening up.

The possibilities of mediocrity or boredom panicked me; I wanted a fiery life. I sought out Columbia's career services, where a woman in pinstripes counseled me about banking and consulting, jobs for which I knew I was grossly unqualified. In fact, the meeting reminded me that I was not qualified to do anything other than write academic essays. Feeling frantic, I went to three interviews for an executive job at a headhunting firm, and did not get the job. The twenty-five-year-old who had recruited me wrote me a personal letter saying he was disappointed, but that some of the employees had found me "too unusual for this line of work." I cried.

I moved to Beijing because I wanted an adventure and was too weird to get a real job, and because I felt connected to China. My father, who was a sinologist for thirty-five years before retiring from the University of Michigan to be a China consultant, had been taking my family to China since my brothers and I were tiny. My parents, rounding out our privileged edges, had treated us to years of overnight train rides across internal China, and had served us thick, warm beer, since they could never be sure water was clean, even when it was bottled.

"This is just like Disneyland," my mother laughed, "except authentic. If we were at amusement parks, we'd be on rides, too! Without the views." Soot blew in the windows and glued streaks across our faces.

My mother brushed her teeth out the train window, rinsed with beer, and read us *Charlotte's Web* in hard sleeper bunks. We longed for summer camp, fireworks, and ice cubes. But my parents loved China, its cracked summer landscapes passing like centuries outside our train windows. They had moved to Taiwan themselves, freshly married at twenty-two, and then to Japan, where my mother taught and my father studied China before China opened its doors to foreigners. My older brother Jacob and I were born in Kyoto, and spent our infancies in a one-room teahouse, Jacob asleep in a drawer and I in a suitcase.

Our childhoods were a collage of infinite staircases to Chinese walls and temples, drivers revving engines over roads that melted in rain, blaring their horns at darting pedestrians, chickens, and cattle. We wandered lost through villages in Sichuan, slept in military guesthouses allegedly in beds once used by revolutionary heroes, and trekked up holy mountains over paths pressed in the ground for thousands of years by pious pilgrims. We were shown bones of the Buddha, mummified remains of Han princesses, and wax renderings of Three Kingdoms warriors. My father stood in front of armies of bronze bells, stones, and Xian's terra-cotta soldiers, ecstatic that each clay warrior was carved with enough precision that he could gauge its hometown from its bone structure.

My parents gloried in the decrepit boats we took down the Yangtze River, eclectic communities of tourists bonding as we rushed downstream, mountains rising on either side as if from the water itself. We scanned the famed Three Gorges, looking for the nine horses, the shaman goddess of the cliffs, the hanging coffins, and the golden monkeys the tour guides promised. We studied bits of Chinese language and ate sea slugs, turtle, and "horse whip" soup. We stayed awake late, swathed in mosquito nets, cracking sunflower seeds and spitting sharp shell piles into our palms.

When Jacob was twelve, I was eleven, and Aaron was six, we

climbed down a dangerous staircase over swirling water to peer up at Leshan's Giant Buddha, more than 230 feet tall. Carved into a cliff wall, the statue gleamed out at us from huge stone eyes. Each of his limbs was larger than our whole skinny family combined. Back at the clifftop parking lot, we turned our attention to a "microcarver," who carved Chinese characters on single strands of human hair. China held for me, even then, the possibilities for what was biggest and smallest; it gave me an image of myself in the world. China's billions of people, miles, mountains, and stairs made America a tiny Monopoly board in my mind. And yet, the difficulty of daily life, travel, and interactions in China made America loom clean and convenient by comparison. Being so far away from America—our house, time zone, language, friends, and framework—let us feel the thrilling mix of terror and freedom I will always associate with China.

So in some sense it was no surprise that at twenty-one I went to Beijing to reinvestigate and plant roots. My father was delighted when I went to Beijing, where he traveled regularly. He and my mother, a high school English teacher, called constantly with good news: "You have a billion potential friends, and there are only seventy-seven thousand known Chinese characters," they said. "How's progress?" Progress was turtle-slow, but I euphemized and doubled my efforts.

I was hardly equipped for a life abroad, but felt optimistic. Based on my undergraduate understanding of the Western canon, I imagined cultures were contained in their languages, and miscalculated slightly. Once I was fluent in Chinese, I reasoned, I would speak and live smoothly. I would read Chinese literature, which would provide the insight I needed into Chinese imagination, history, and modernity. My favorite ancient Chinese book remains the useful *Biographies of Model Women.* Compiled during the Han Dynasty (A.D. 212–206) by scholar Liu Xiang, *Biographies* is the first Chinese book devoted entirely to the subject of women. The biographies begin with illustrations of the "Correct Deportment of Mothers," and work their way from "Chaste and Obedient" wives and widows to the climactic final chapter, the "Biographies of the Pernicious and Depraved." The bad girls in the biographies are the most interesting, as are the lessons they offer up. *Biographies* warns that for women to bare their bodies and shout is a terrible curse.[3] Needless to say, when I moved to China, it did not occur to me that such an opportunity would present itself. I thought I'd be exemplary.

With no plans to bare anything other than my college transcript, I faxed résumés all over Shanghai and Beijing and got a single interview—with an American public relations and marketing firm in Beijing. The position was that of an "account executive." My boss Charlotte, a voluptuous blonde from Arkansas, had worked in public relations for over a decade. Beijing had been her home for several years, but she spoke no Chinese; she spent twenty-four hours a day running a big American public relations firm's small Beijing office. She hired me next to Gate F12 in the Detroit airport, where she interviewed me while en route back to Beijing. She said life in Beijing was chaotic, that the public relations industry there was "pioneer-style." I cultivated an image of myself arriving by covered wagon. I told Charlotte that I was diligent and proficient in Chinese, words I had learned for the occasion of writing a cover letter.

"You're hired," she said, and "can you return my rental car?" I was to move to Beijing in three weeks and be an account executive; I drove her rental car back to National and emptied out the junk food wrappers and stiff fries.

Within three weeks, I was in Beijing. My father, there on a business trip when I arrived, met me at Beijing's Capital Airport. I came down the ramp from the arriving flights terminal into the waiting area and picked him out in a sea of hundreds of faces. The owners of the faces were carrying signs, either with the names of business associates they had never met or with welcome messages to their friends. My father held a handmade sign, printed tidily in English affecting the cadence of translation: *"Rachel, you are warmly welcome to live forever in Beijing."*

I was to live at the Chinese Huarun Hotel, the "China Resources," a mammoth state-run building on the unfinished Jingtong Highway. Night had draped the city by the time I arrived, and my exhaustion and disorientation made Beijing's lights streak outside the cab windows. I thought of combination snow cones, all the sweet summer colors melting into a mess. It was October 20, already frigid in Beijing. My father dropped me off at the Huarun, which I could not pronounce correctly, and presented me with a welcome gift. It was a silver bike, which he said I would need. "It will help you localize," he suggested.

After he left the hotel that night, I floated about the carpeted room. The walls, curtains, bedspread, and towels were hotel beige. There were two lamps above the bed, and a television set, which I turned on. The shows were Peking Opera and vaudeville; they featured characters shellacked in white face paint, wearing tiny red lips in the middle of their faces and ornate silk costumes. People on prime-time TV in China sang and spoke in high-pitched voices. On the news channels, politicians smiled with mechanical faces and shook hands in front of red banners with white Chinese characters I could not read, in spite of my college efforts. The TV was painfully bright and unfamiliar. I slept diagonally across the bed for an hour, and then sat up, eating airplane peanuts while I watched the sun rise out the window.

Beijing also woke predawn with a start. First thing, vendors called out their offerings: fried dough, soymilk, newspapers. The vowels and unfamiliar sounds rose over the Huarun's awnings into my windows. I was electric with jet lag, flipping through a dictionary for words I thought I might need at work: *strategy, account, executive.* I practiced saying my Chinese name, *Du Ruiqui,* in the mirror in my first-ever business suit, a maroon one my mom had bought me at Ann Taylor the week before I left. "*Nihao,*" I said to the mirror, " I'm *Du Ruiqiu." Du* is Chinese shorthand for DeWoskin, and *Ruiqiu* sounds as close as Chinese will permit to Rachel. I loved the name, mostly since I admired the Chinese professor who had given it to me. Of course, I had yet to learn what it meant. Finally, I clicked downstairs in heels, my heart bouncing around in my rib cage.

Outside, the sky was whitewashed. Real life in Beijing looked like an old photograph, Technicolored to include pagodas perched atop skyscrapers, Coca-Cola awnings, and billboards screaming the lit language of global advertising. Factories woke first, so the city was already getting smoky, even though it wasn't even six A.M. Only on weekends or public holidays, when the factories had been closed for a day or two, did the skies clear to blue. When international events took place in Beijing, factories were shut down in favor of producing smokeless skies. But even dingy, Beijing offered its own sets of colors. The metal stall covers rolled open to expose rebellious vegetables, fruit, and blood-dark meat, purple eggplants alive against the instantly familiar Beijing gray. I saddled up my bike with a briefcase and some bottled water, and rode to the office for the first time.

Beijing's workforce rushed by on bicycles, dark hair slicked back, purses and briefcases stuffed into baskets. There were men in suits, women in knee-high pantyhose and short skirts. Laborers rode side by side with executives and schoolchildren. Whole families rode on single bikes, wives on back fenders and children on handlebars. Fancy women wore full pantyhose, heels, and long skirts they pulled up and tucked underneath their seats. I tried for modesty, too, but eventually simply hiked my skirt up far enough that it wasn't in danger of twisting in the spokes or attracting gear grease. I felt anonymous in traffic; I could rush away from any impression I might leave behind. I had yet to learn that this feeling informed much of the way in which expatriates lived their lives in Beijing. Knowing they'll leave a city gives people a feeling of impunity, a meeting-strangers-on-the-plane energy. And almost every Westerner who moves there eventually leaves Beijing. Even celebrities are happy to shed their faces and Western images as soon as they're far enough from home. Arnold Schwarzenegger has been all over Chinese DVD billboards and boxes since the early 2000s, ads his public relations team would have been unlikely to endorse back at home. What American fans or voters will see bad ads so far away? And what hometown familiars will witness bad expat behavior?

I had studied a map on the plane. Beijing was growing in circles, its roads expanding as if a stone had been thrown into its center, rippling out into Second Ring, Third Ring, and eventually Fourth Ring Road. Beijing was reinventing itself, as it had many times before, and yet keeping its foundation intact. The new ring roads encircled the same square capital Beijing had become in 1421. At the center were still the Forbidden City and symmetrical portals leading out of the center, creating an urban path between heaven and earth. Mao's portrait hung flat across from Tiananmen Square, where soldiers raised the flag each day and throngs of Chinese tourists gathered to peek at the Chairman's waxy, pickled body.

I took off, thousands of workers riding in a chorus of spokes and bells. The popular Flying Pigeon and Forever-brand bicycles were narrow and practical, black with small white cursive brand names on the bars. My *Tian Wang* was a chunk of a wannabe mountain bike with inflatable-looking letters on its fat bar. But I kept proud pace with the crowd, surging with glee and freedom as our giant mass of metal turned, braked, and whipped up dust. I was in China! Riders flanked the avenue by four feet, flashing toward each other.

The lanes of nonbike traffic were *luanqibazao*, "chaos, seven, eight, grains," or cleanly translated, "sheer chaos." Clattering taxis and sleek black Mercedes-Benzes honked furiously at clopping donkey-drawn carts. There were construction sites on both sides of the road, with cranes shuttling building materials up and down the skyline. Dust and cement grime wafted up from the ground, mixing with exhaust. Migrant workers used rickety carts to tote twenty-foot piles of bricks, wood, steel, glass, cabbages, and split pigs, strings of glistening innards visible.

The smells varied with shocking instancy and intensity: fried bread, tire rubber, industrial smoke, peppers, ginger, cigarettes, slightly sweet spoiled fruit, and oil. Children stood outside, brushing their teeth with water from metal basins; old ladies stretched, danced, and ate *mantou*, steamed buns. Vendors lined the streets, hawking underwear, dish racks, and sweet potatoes wrapped in newsprint.

After half an hour, skyscrapers jutted into view. They were almost the same color as the sky, shrouded in industrial and coal smoke. The fog was like marble; I could barely see the buildings until I arrived at the CITIC building, my office. I slowed down, dodging buses that screeched up to the curb to pick up passengers. Cyclists jumped up onto sidewalks, clanging bells and trying to dodge pedestrians, not always successfully. Ticket girls hung out the bus doors, shouting, "*Mai bu mai piao!*" Want a ticket or not? There's a nice symmetry in that question. Most Chinese grammar is set up this way; one has two choices when asked how are you. *Nihao bu hao?*" Are you good or not good? "*Ni chi fan le mei you?*" Have you eaten or not eaten? "*You mei you qian?*" Do you have or not have money? The answer must be either one or the other.

In slow motion all around Beijing's morning mania, old people exercised, practicing *taiji* calisthenics, jogging in place, and wrapping their arms and legs around trees. When they finished exercising, some set up small stools and spent the days chatting, playing Go, babysitting grandchildren, or birdsitting cherished songbirds. They seemed to me to watch the rush of the rest of us knowingly. I watched them, too, the diligent mothers, honorable fathers, virtuous wives. They had read the model bios, watched the Nationalist Party retreat to Taiwan, the rise of the Communist Party, the Great Leap Forward, and the Cultural Revolution. Modern Beijing may have seemed to them nothing more than an ephemeral fad. I couldn't imagine what we Westerners looked like, flying by on Chinese bikes.

Suibian, As You Wish

In the parks, "water calligraphers" streaked paths with wet brushes long enough to reach the ground. Mostly old men, they wrote out whole poems in water, backing up behind their words. As soon as the sun was hot, the water dried and the poems disappeared. Then the calligraphers chatted about whose characters were the best crafted, and therefore the hardest to watch go.

The firm's offices in the CITIC building were temperate and unscented, distinct from the world outside the building's door. My first day, I banged my head on the glass door when someone in front of me stopped, raising a red welt across my face. I had the perspective even then to think it was poetic that I should be literally dizzy, and that I should wear the red mark like a scarlet A, evidence that I was out of step. Mainly, I was amazed that Beijing could house both itself and this nether-corporate-world. I straddled the two universes, not realizing yet that Beijing would offer up many more, in increasing levels of unfamiliarity.

My colleagues at the company were Chinese, mostly women close to my age. When I arrived my first day, my Chinese colleagues said *nihao*, hello, to me, and then to each other, "She has a red mark on her head" and "She's thin!" with some emphasis. "Thin" was not a compliment, just a revelation of what surprised them, since in spite of what they saw on TV, they believed that all Americans, or at least those who traveled to China, were fat. I wasn't sure how to respond even when a comment was flattering, which put a strain on the conversation right away. I had learned the word "red" while studying the 1949 Communist takeover; I got "welt" from context and polite gesturing toward my forehead.

Later, after I no longer had a wound on my forehead and people still pointed, I would discover the useful expression *bertou* or "big foreheaded."

Americans are receptive to praise. It's courteous to say thank you, in appreciation of the kindness behind an accolade, not prideful acknowledgment of its truth. But my college Chinese textbook had suggested it is indecorous to accept praise. "Thank you," my textbook said, should be replaced with "*nali, nali?*" or "Where? Where?"

When my colleagues called me thin, I thought for such a long time that they thought I was mute. Then I tried it out.

"*Nali, nali?*" I asked, carefully clipping the syllables for clarity. They looked at me blankly, then smiled and went back to work. "Where, where?" it turns out, is an archaic and stilted expression, so nerdy as to be almost unrecognizable.

My blond boss, Charlotte, was the only other American in the office. She had a head of curls, a Southern lilt, tightly tailored pastel suits, and a lit string of menthol cigarettes. She also had a blue-hot temper, which was flaring when I arrived. She was standing tall in the doorway to her office, beckoning furiously at the driver to come in "this instant!" and then slamming the door once he had entered.

There was one other full-time expatriate in the office, a Taiwanese man named Gary. He never stopped moving, talking, managing, or criticizing. He and Charlotte immediately began vying for position as my mentor, walking me through the small maze of cubicles, introducing me to everyone in English, and then inserting me into a box with carpeted walls.

The firm was located high up in CITIC, and its ceilings were low, white, and stained with water damage, creating the feeling that they might collapse. I could see over my cubicle walls into other people's workspaces, and looked at everyone else through cigarette clouds. My colleagues were also peering over the tops of cubicles to see me. We popped back down once spotted. I wanted to ask questions, but I couldn't think of what they would be or how I would put them.

Charlotte's office was a mint smokestack, and the place was a madhouse. As soon as she had finished berating the driver, she called me in and assigned me my first big project, a stack of two hundred pages from which I was supposed to distill a "briefing book" for a CEO on his way to China.

"Make sure to give him valuable information about what he should and should not say," she advised. Gary was to assist me by giving me "boilerplate," another word I did not know. I thought of the hot plate I had kept under my bed at Columbia for making illicit ramen in the dorm. I was supposed to use boilerplate to give someone valuable information about what to say in China?

Gary took me to his cubicle and thrust at me a document called "Do's and Don'ts," by which I was advised of several key strategies. First, it said: be patient. It read: "The Chinese system is sometimes slow, but the Chinese can be fast or slow. Like all bureaucracies, Chinese systems run more slowly than most businesses. However, the Chinese can test your patience or surprise you at their speed in expediting matters." Of what country was this not the case?

The briefing book's second rule was: get in touch. "The Chinese dislike doing business with strangers. Set up a proper introduction by an intermediary known to both sides. If this is not possible, provide as much information about your company as you can during initial meetings." I decided to adopt the latter as my strategy for befriending colleagues.

The third rule, greet people appropriately, included advice about how to address people. Names are meaningful in China; there's a whole discipline of fortune-telling based on the characters in a person's name. Everyone in the office had an English name, as did our clients, including unusual choices like Satan Han and Weenie Wang, which I took to be either misspellings or cruel jokes played by English teachers. Of course, I was about to learn at lunch that my own beloved name, *Du Ruiqiu,* meant "Bumper Harvest Du." When Gary broke this news to me, I couldn't be sure it wasn't some sort of terrifying translation mistake.

I had studied the protocol document by lunchtime, but it did not save me from myself, and I had little hope that it would help a bewildered Western CEO in China. Each time I left my cubicle, a chorus of questions rose in my wake. They were directed not at me but at Gary, who, being somewhat of a foreigner himself, might be able to answer them. Where was I from? Where was I living? What was my salary? Weren't all Americans actually giant fat people with yellow hair? What did I think of Beijing? I asked Gary why no one asked me questions directly.

"Because it's rude," he snapped.

I decided I would talk primarily about food, since it seemed a safe and compelling topic. I knew, for example, that instead of "How are you?" people asked, *"Chi fan le mei you?"* Have you eaten or not eaten? And *"Chi bao le mei you?"* Are you full or not full? Food was a concrete sign of abstract values. What one chose to eat was a fairly reliable indicator of wealth and cultural and personal leanings. Food was delicious or bland, boring or varied, fattening or thinning, abundant or scarce, refined or common.

Xiao Li, Gary's assistant, who was often too terrified and harried to speak, ordered *hefan*, boxed lunches, and came to my cubicle to ask, quite shyly, whether I would join the staff for lunch.

"Of course!" I said, pleased to know a Chinese word past the simple but sufficient "yes." Xiao Li nodded, grinning. But immediately after I carefully enunciated my affirmation, Charlotte asked if I would join her in her office for lunch. She had ordered personal pan pizzas from the new Pizza Hut across the street. This presented a tense, politicized decision, since it would not be possible to be at the same table with hand-eaten pizza and chopstick-eaten *hefan*. I told Charlotte I was lactose-intolerant, the first of many such lies I would tell toward building social walls and digging ditches at the office.

When the *hefan* delivery came, the office filled with the smell of pepper and garlic. Everyone except Charlotte stood and rushed to the conference room. Styrofoam boxes were passed around, and each diner joyously tore off half of one and filled it with rice. Then we opened disposable chopsticks from plastic wrappers, rubbed them together to remove potential splinters, and took portions from various dishes, also presented in half boxes: ants climbing the tree, red dragon goes through the snow, twice-cooked pork, hot and sour cabbage, and home-cooked tofu. Everyone was obsessed with what everyone else ate. I was a vegetarian, but embarrassed to say so lest it seem unfriendly or finicky. I carefully picked ground meat off of noodles and hid it under my rice.

"So much rice!" Xiao Li called out when I took my portion. "And no meat! Don't be polite! Eat more pork!"

Not eating from the most expensive dish was ungrateful, so I took a small portion of pork, which I was careful not to eat. I suspected that the pig had ridden to work on the back of a bike like mine, splayed and unhappy. I thanked Xiao Li and moved myself closer to the cold salads with sesame oil and hot peppers, scorched bean sprouts, and red braised tofu. I later learned that Jewish populations in ancient China had been known as "those who pluck out the sinew."[4] I should have told the staff I was religious.

"Americans eat a lot of rice," said Xiao Li. "That's why they're fat."

Everyone looked at me politely. I put my chopsticks down. Charlotte's assistant, Anna, who spoke good English, changed the subject by reminding me of everyone's name, and asking each person to hand me a name card across the sea of food.

I diligently filed all of my colleagues' name cards. From my morning research into the protocol document, I knew to take each one with two hands, study it, and tenderly tuck it into my business card holder. Name cards in Beijing represented people, so stuffing one in your back pocket and sitting on it had a certain ugliness about it that wouldn't do.

I was quiet, watching for signs of rules number four and five in our protocol list, about understanding Chinese "actions" and "reactions." The book said, "Sometimes Chinese laugh at mishaps. This is an uncertain reaction reflecting embarrassment or discomfort, and should not be confused with amusement. Chinese are more comfortable with silence than Westerners. Things left unsaid are often as important as those spoken of directly. Silence can be a virtue, a courtesy, or a ploy to ferret out information."

As for reactions, it suggested the following: "Never force a Chinese to say 'no' directly to you. He/she will refuse in a number of ways, including 'inconvenient,' 'maybe,' 'being discussed,' 'requires consideration,' or 'under construction.' When being pressed, a Chinese may tell an obvious lie to avoid saying 'no.'

Often the lie is well-intentioned, usually to prevent a guest, friend, or colleague from "losing face."

"Face" is a favorite topic among experts on China. I have read accounts, including all of the briefing books our firm produced, that identify face as a Chinese construct. I may have become more Chinese myself over the years, since I dislike losing face, but I think it's more likely that nothing about face is particular to Chinese culture or physiology. The word says what it is and what it means; *face* is the part of ourselves we show the world. No one, in China or anywhere else, wants it disfigured, reduced, laughed in, or lost.

Everyone spared mine that first day. It was not until a year after our first company lunch that Xiao Li told me everyone had been amazed to meet an American who did not bring name cards and had grown up unable to afford meat.

I t took me one workday to know I needed help. So I hired a tutor. Teacher Kang would meet me twice a week for all the years I spent in Beijing, and teach me to speak "standard talk" and read simplified characters, including the *Foreign Babes in Beijing* script, a patriotic Chinese textbook she chose, and dozens of Tang Dynasty poems. A juicy compliment in China is that one's Mandarin is *biaozhun,* or standard, which in Beijing means the great achievement of a Beijing accent. My colleagues were relieved that Teacher Kang was a Beijinger; otherwise, my accent would not be "standard" or *haoting,* nice to hear. They said this within earshot of Gary, whose Taiwanese accent was a subject of fierce debate and gleeful ridicule. He had his corner of foreign power, his management responsibilities, and his enviable expat salary, but he would never have *biaozhun* Mandarin. So when Xiao Li asked why I had studied complicated characters used in Taiwan, rather than the simplified ones Beijing favors, Gary had his own investment in the question.

"Complex characters are more intellectual," he interjected, silencing the staff.

At my first Chinese lesson, Teacher Kang arrived carrying a jar of tea and a textbook. Xiao Li came into the conference room where Teacher Kang and I were seated, poured hot water into Teacher Kang's tea jar, and listened to our lesson. She returned every ten minutes to refresh the water, giggling. Teacher Kang spoke no English, but was able to communicate with me. She understood foreigners' Chinese, and we had vocabulary lists in front of us, so even if my tones were wrong, she knew what I was saying anyway. Her textbook worried me. It featured lessons about the Three States period and the superiority of chopsticks, "delicate extensions of human fingers," over more barbaric utensils such as forks and knives, with which less civilized people stabbed at slabs of food. I was less insulted than I was concerned with whether such vocabulary would prove useful. I felt with great urgency the desire to communicate to the people in my new life that I wasn't lobotomized. When our lesson ended, I asked Charlotte's assistant Anna for input. Anna spoke good English and I thought maybe she and I had had meaningful eye contact while I was hiding food at lunch. I couldn't be sure.

"I would like to study intellectual lessons," I told Anna, using the expression I had learned in college, *zhishi fenzi*, for "intellectual," not realizing it meant "intelligentsia." I hoped the request would not be offensive in any way. Anna smiled a beautiful wide grin and angled her face sideways to look at me. She said she would "consider that request," using bureaucratic language she suspected I'd be likely to get, since I spoke textbook most of the time. Later that afternoon, Anna passed me a book of Tang Dynasty poems with Post-It notes marking the pages she thought were *heshi*, suitable. I was delighted.

The first poem Anna marked was called "The Hard Road." In it, poet Li Bai writes: "Journeying is hard / Journeying is hard / There are many turnings / Which am I to follow." Its lines were shaved down and essential, making it not only clean and spare, but also easy to translate. I was poring over it, hoping Gary would not catch me, when Xiao Li and a group of women surrounded my cubicle to present me with "decorations" as a welcoming gesture. These gifts included a small ceramic pig in a hammock and a postcard of George Michael from his days with Wham!. I put the postcard away, but gave the pig pride of place on my monitor. "It makes you feel relaxed," said Xiao Li.

"Yes," I said. "Relaxed. Thank you."

The pig swung back and forth. "She likes the gift," Xiao Li said to all of us. *"Meiguoren xihuan siubian di dongxi."* Americans like casual things. *Suibian*, "as you wish," or "casual." *Sui* is "to follow," and *bian* is "convenience." Americans liked to follow convenience. We were casual in our language, negotiations, conversations, romances, eating habits, and clothing.

No one in the office was surprised when Charlotte instituted a "casual Friday" policy. To my colleagues, she was just showing off American messiness in a context that required reserve and formality. It made no difference to the staff's opinion that Charlotte never actually dressed casually. Charlotte was even made unhappy by my decision to enjoy and take advantage of the policy, which she had allowed only because all the other American companies in Beijing were doing it. She did not want to be a maverick in the American Chamber of Commerce community in Beijing, but also did not want me, her protégé, wearing jeans. I loved Fridays, and used them to showcase my connection to the staff by wearing T-shirts and platform shoes.

Much later, when Bill Gates wore jeans to a meeting with Jiang Zemin and horribly offended the Chinese president, I would think of my first week in the office and how little I had understood. By the time Gates made his faux pas, I had made enough of my own to know that most Chinese would not be surprised. Gates was just following convenience in the American way.

Faced with the ceramic pig, I learned that no matter what I said, wore, or did, it was common knowledge that all Americans *were* casual. My colleagues discussed my every move, whether I came to work with my hair wet, wore my hair up, rode my bike, took a cab, unbuttoned my suit jacket when I sat down, or neglected to wear long underwear "even when it is so cold!" I chewed the edge of a pencil, painted my fingernails, whistled, and wrote sideways, with the paper turned away from me. I typed fast, moved fast, drank bottled water from the bottle, was small, and was "like a boy" in some ways. Other women didn't whistle or laugh "so easily" or while they talked. I never covered my mouth when laughing. I did not like tea and did not chew leaves. I had a boy's bike, silver with a bar. Everyone surmised from my behavior early on that Americans "could talk," meaning could speak a little Chinese, "could eat," meaning were not birdlike in our appetites, "rode bikes," "didn't fear cold," and "didn't fear spicy." Walking through the office was like walking a runway.

In Beijing, even before I made a spectacle of it on national television, I was representing all foreign women. This fact made my footing rocky. I became unsure of which of my own qualities were individual and which were, in fact, "American." I wanted to figure it out so I could give Westerners a good name, at least in the small marble world of CITIC. And even though I was inclined to argue that no one American represents all of us, I wanted to prove, by representing all of us, that Americans are kind and open-minded.

I got off to a stumbling start, since I still imagined the word "open-minded" to be a good one. *Kaifang* was the official word China used to describe its opening up to the world. Americans went abroad, I thought, learned languages, made friends, opened doors, engaged. We did not all weigh too much, have blond hair and blue eyes, or indiscriminately lose our tempers. Chinese thought Western women were *kaifang*, or "open-minded," too, but the word in Chinese was used to talk about a lack of discipline, peppered with promiscuous abandon. When Anna asked me whether I agreed "with the Chinese idea" that American women were more *kaifang* than our Chinese counterparts, I nodded, flattered.

Anna invited me to go shopping with her. I had considered her an ally since she had given me the Tang poems, but did not know how to approach her socially without being too *suibian*, casual. I thought perhaps my colleagues spent enough time with me not to want to see me once we left CITIC. This would have been reasonable, considering we worked fourteen-hour days and I was, ludicrously, in a position of authority over most of my colleagues, even though I was younger, less experienced, and more inept in China. My status at the company was the result of ethnicity, a fact so obvious it did not warrant overt acknowledgment.

Resentment ran like a fatal undercurrent in the office, but most of it was directed toward Gary, rather than toward those outsiders the staff considered "real foreigners," Charlotte and me, who in some self-evident way represented the headquarters. Expatriate salaries were anywhere from five to fifteen times local salaries, a circumstance that did not inspire warmth or camaraderie in corporations.

When Anna approached me, she told me right off that she preferred to be called Anna, rather than her Chinese name. She was starkly pretty. Tiny and intense, she had shadowed eyes and square bangs cut straight across her face. She could look twelve years old or forty, sometimes shifting from one to the other in the instant of a facial expression. Her cheekbones were high and her smile broad and symmetrical. Anna exuded intellectual energy and frisk. Her face was lively; watching her, it was obvious that she was thinking about something other than what she was saying, a quality I found appealing. There was something hard to get about Anna, a forbidden fruit about her thoughts and insights. She was a master of vague language, able to pull off paragraphs of avoidance when she did not want to talk, and then blade-sharp whenever she wanted to cut to the point. Her ability to move from one way of speaking to the other made me appreciative of both. She always carried books, and was deeply tanned, unusual for Chinese girls, for whom dark skin is a sign of farmwork. Anna saved every *yuan* she made at work toward traveling, a practice her mother saw as selfish and her father encouraged. Anna was restless, fiercely independent, and always moving, from boyfriend to boyfriend, home to home, job to job.

Anna had been to boarding school in the countryside for much of her schooling, and had enjoyed a greater measure of freedom than most of our colleagues. The women in the office studied and envied her; she was aloof and hard to work with. She attributed their disregard to our friendship, but it was at least as much the product of her personal rebellions and ideas. Our connection, if it deepened resentment of Anna, did so only because it was a small symbol of the ways in which she opted to be different.

On our first outing, Anna took me to Wangfujing, a central shopping district in Beijing. I learned later that she hated Wangfujing, but thought I was likely to enjoy it. She was wearing a short skirt and blouse under a parka that covered her legs. Her hair was in pigtails held by lace scrunchies, and she carried a large black purse. Pressed into the bus, she turned to me, eyes flashing. "Wangfujing will be *renao,*" she said. *Renao,* the Chinese word for "festive," is composed of the words "hot" and "noisy." Even the quietest tourist sites in Beijing, including the fragrant hills and remote-access sites to the Great Wall, blast music over loudspeakers into the wilderness. Deafening noise is more fun than quiet is. To *kan renao,* or "look at what's hot and noisy," is to rubberneck.

When we arrived at Wangfujing, Anna and I squeezed out the bus doors into winter sunlight. The commotion on the streets created friction and warmth. Small interactions inspired large crowds to form and *kan renao.* As we got off the bus, I stood still for a moment to straighten my jacket and take a scarf from my briefcase, and people stopped to watch. Anna pulled me forward. The streets, mobbed with people, bikes, carts, and food, felt especially narrow. I could hear the blood pounding in my ears. As if reading my thoughts, Anna said, "Beijing is known in China for wide streets. Even Shanghai feels jealous—it's cosmopolitan, but most of Shanghai's money pays for Beijing's infrastructure."

I glanced around. Storefronts stuck out unevenly onto the sidewalk, some flaunting newly renovated glass and metal, others with makeshift boards for walls and countertops. There were pastel sky-scrapers, making way on the Avenue of Eternal Peace for the Bright China ChangAn Club and bureaucratic shoebox buildings. Anna and I jammed into the doorway of a Wangfujing department store. As soon as we were safely inside, she wove her way through the clothing racks and throngs of people, finally holding up a tiny, brightly colored dress. "Do you think it's nice for work?" She asked.

"Uh, yes," I said. It was outrageous for work. I wondered whether she was testing my taste. If so, she didn't let me call her bluff, since she had the dress on at work the following day. Anna wore sexiness in a way that struck me as oblivious, but then it turned out that the obliviousness was mine. I thought she was virginal, perhaps because she sometimes looked so young, or perhaps because I blindly thought of all the women at the firm as innocent. They denied having boyfriends, and I took everything at face value. They also had Bambi conversations at lunch, giggling over PG-13–rated jokes told by our male coworkers, and covering their mouths when they laughed. One such joke was about a girl who accepts a bike ride home, sitting on the bar of a man's bike. When she hops off the bar and thanks him for the ride, she realizes that the bike has no bar. My colleagues watched me for signs of amusement while this joke washed over the table. But since I didn't know the word for "bar," I stared blankly until the joke had snowballed into a disastrous explanation of why it should have been funny. If they had not had access to Hollywood depictions of Western girls, they would have thought I was a virgin, too.

Anna and I tried on outfits in the back of an outdoor market, shivering behind boxes of scarves and fake North Face parkas. I got a skin-tight sweater as a gesture of allegiance, and Anna led me to "snack alley," where I bought a sweet potato wrapped in newsprint. When the vendor gave me change, Anna corrected him. "You owe her four and a half *yuan,*" she said, pointing at the coins. The exchange rate was 8.3 *yuan* to one dollar. He owed me fifty-four cents.

"That's fine," I said. "Three back is fine."

Anna looked at me sternly. "The potato costs five *mao,*" she said. It should have been six cents. We all stood there. I didn't want the change; I just wanted to escape the conversation. Anna wasn't ready to let it go. "Give my friend the money you owe her," she said.

"I gave her the change," he said. "Why help the foreigner rather than a Chinese?"

I backed away, beckoning Anna over. I hoped we could drop the potato-surcharge topic. We both knew that China still operated under a two-tier system, that foreign airline prices, rents, and entrance tickets cost anywhere from two to ten times their local equivalents. It was my understanding that this was true elsewhere as well. Foreigners always got cheated; it happened globally, and in this instance, the margins were small.

"I'm sorry for that man," Anna said. "He tries to cheat you, but most Chinese are not cheaters. There are two prices for things in China: one cheap price for Chinese and one expensive price for foreigners."

"I know." I imagined telling her what my rent at the Huarun Hotel cost, but refrained.

"He asked me why I help the foreigner," she admitted.

"I heard that part."

"I don't think it has to do with foreigner or Chinese," she said. "I help you in this situation because you are right. The potato should be five *mao.* It's unfair."

She was right: it was unfair. But I didn't care about the extra pennies. I didn't want to make that point, because it seemed grotesque. I wondered what the difference between five *mao* and a few *yuan* meant to her, probably very little, and it was curious to me that she felt personally or culturally implicated by his and my interaction. If she had been a guest in New York City and a street vendor had cheated her, would I have fought so hard for her? Maybe. Would I have felt personally implicated by his antics? Probably not.

But she had lost face because the neighborhood she took me to housed cheaters and the vendor had kept his change. She bought two squids on sticks. "*Wo qing ni,*" she said. I treat you. Octopus Popsicle—I took it and ate the flailing tentacles from the stick. A beautiful woman in high heels and a long quilted coat stood bending like a dancer over a bowl of noodles. She was eating them delicately with chopsticks and gazing at her boyfriend in between bites. He reached chopsticks into her bowl and dangled a noodle into his mouth. Two old women in army hats rushed by eating egg pancakes with scallions.

Anna and I walked back toward the main avenue, window-shopping snacks: bowls of hot noodles, deep-fried kiwi slices coated in white sugar, barbecued beetles, fried dumplings, and tripe winding out of cauldrons. I asked Anna what the word for "tripe" was. When she told me, I wrote it in my journal.

"What is in that book?" she asked.

"Words," I said. "Vocabulary, notes, ideas, stories, and conversations."

She looked concerned. "Is it a diary?"

"Yeah," I said. I asked her how to say "diary" in Chinese.

She ignored the question. "I don't keep a diary," she said. "The

Cultural Revolution is too bad a memory. Do you ever write critical things about China?"

I said no, which wasn't true. I wrote whatever I wanted about whatever I wanted to write about. It had never crossed my mind that there could be any price other than a small personal one. This is one difference between growing up with parents who read you *Harriet the Spy* and growing up with parents sent away for political reeducation during the Cultural Revolution.

"The political climate can change suddenly here," Anna said, "and everyone can read each other's private documents. It's better not to write your secrets down. Or maybe Chinese people are just more private; maybe they're too conservative to have any secrets."

I wasn't sure how to interpret this, although later I knew unmistakably that she was testing me to see whether I thought Chinese were conservative. I put the journal away. I did not tell her that I wrote whatever I wanted, because to me such a declaration seemed to be a flaunting of personal luxury. I wondered whether she was envious, or whether my diary was actually evidence of self-indulgence and carelessness.

We walked out the mouth of Wangfujing to Changan Street, where the Beijing Hotel towered across from McDonald's. We turned and walked to Tiananmen Square, flanked by immaculately pruned trees and pink sidewalk squares. The red walls of Zhongnanhai, the government compound, rose up in the distance. Anna pointed them out to me. Those walls separate the city from its leaders, yet connect the past and future in a way that feels visceral. The compound is ancient and foreboding, a modern forbidden city, juxtaposed bizarrely to frenzied shopping districts and traffic.

Of course, Beijing has always been divided up. Originally, the city was like a *siheyuan,* like the four-box courtyard house of the *Foreign Babes in Beijing* Li family. It was composed of four sections: an inner city housing the imperial palace, an industrial eastern city, a walled southern city where the elite went for entertainment, and a western suburb with universities, hospitals, a zoo, and the summer palace. To me, it seemed both impossible and inevitable that the city could have remained so much the same for centuries, that the bound feet of concubines had traversed the same paths Anna and I now clicked across.

At the Forbidden City, we bought tickets without discussing the difference in entrance ticket costs. Stepping into this other world with Anna felt dangerous and significant, as if she might slip backward somehow into time and be lost to me. The palace was an old world, embedded in our new Beijing, and we were inhabitants only of the modern outer city.

We walked from courtyard to courtyard, each opening into the next, each more interior, private, and forbidden than the one preceding it. When we reached the inner sanctuary, where the emperor's concubines had spent their hours, Anna turned to me.

"Can you imagine that fat emperor coming to your room at night?" She tapped on the dirty window of one of the rooms, attracting the attention of a guard, who shook a finger at her. In the room, old silk covers were thrown over beds made to look as if they hadn't been altered since the emperor had slept on them. Cloisonné vases sat on tabletops next to combs.

"How do you know he was fat?" I asked.

She pointed out toward the stairs we had just climbed, each a double staircase with a wide dragon carved on a kind of driveway between the two sets of stairs. "The servants walked on either side of that dragon, carrying the emperor in a chair," Anna explained. "And the reason the two staircases are so far apart is because that's how wide the emperor's ass was. This happens if you keep a country's food for yourself and never walk anywhere."

At the end of our field trip, I was grateful and recklessly hugged Anna before climbing into the cab we had finally hailed. She stiffened like she'd been shocked with a prod. "Chinese girls don't really hug so casually," she said. "It's American, this hugging." In fact, I had miscalibrated. Chinese women held hands as they walked through the city and slow-danced in clubs, which I had almost never seen women do in America. Yet American women hugged freely and with abandon. The boundaries for intimacy were just slightly altered.

Anna poked her head into the window of my cab and told the driver to take me to the Huarun. Then she took out a piece of paper and made a show of writing his identification number down, in case he cheated me. The city was dark and bone-cold. The driver, perhaps insulted by Anna, did not speak to me. Or maybe her instruction of where to take me was evidence that I did not speak Chinese. Of course, "Huarun" was one of my very best expressions by now.

Embarrassed that I had hugged her, I wondered what Anna thought of our excursion. Beijing went by in the dark: the highway overpasses beaded with a line of white traffic lights, and restaurant facades, two-dimensional but for smoke pouring from their kitchen chimneys. The city's round roads wound around like tentacles in the cauldrons I had seen at snack alley. We sped back down Beijing's central Avenue of Eternal Peace, until the last bright building, the China World Hotel, had melted behind us. When the desolate Huarun finally appeared with a dingy facade, it looked to me like Transylvania, alone on acres of emptiness. All stalls were closed for the night. It would be hours before the factories, sun, and vegetable carts came alive. No one was around, except for me and a night guard. I wished for morning, Michigan, my family, snow.

From *Foreign Babes in Beijing*
Episode Fifteen

Tianliang sits with Lu Xiao Qing, a modest pedicab driver.
Lu Xiao Qing has just won a sports car in a contest held by
Louisa's father's American company. They are in the shiny car.

TIANLIANG

China is a poor country; we should help our nation make money.
It doesn't matter what business you're involved in, you always
have to consider and care for China.

LU XIAO QING

There will be a day when China makes its
own wonderful products.

They share a patriotic sigh.

THREE

小秘
Xiaomi

Concubines

W hen I first heard about *Foreign Babes in Beijing*, I was working fourteen-hour days under fluorescent lights and wrenching deadlines. Anna and my colleagues had taken to commenting that my complexion was turning tofu-toned. I did not look healthy, they said, and should eat coagulated duck blood to help balance my internal heat. They worried that I might be feverish or have flu, and brought me *ganmaoyao*, cold medicine, which I ate gratefully in order to distract from the possibility of bird-blood cubes.

I finally left the office one night for a party, where a young guy named He Jin told me about the TV show *Yang Niu Zai Beijing*. He Jin was from the southern province of Yunnan, and we were in the *siheyuan*, courtyard, of a localized expatriate.

"My friend is a director and is filming foreign *niu* in Beijing," He Jin said in Chinese. I heard most words unclearly; listening to people speak was like standing on my tiptoes and trying to catch their gists with a butterfly net. I was gleeful when I could pick single fluttering words from a sentence and get any meaning at all. I heard "foreign" and "*niu*" and "in Beijing." *Niu* sounded both like "cattle" and "girl," so I figured his friend was filming girls. Foreign Girls in Beijing. That made sense. It wasn't until I saw the characters inked onto a scrap of paper and taped to a door at Beijing's film studio the following week that I realized there were a few extra, sexy stroke marks in what I knew as the Chinese character for "girl." Those extra strokes changed generic "girl" into the vastly more particular "babe." By then, I was already at the audition.

When He Jin first tried to tell me about *Foreign Babes in Beijing*, it was in the context of his bragging, or *chuiniu*, "blowing the cow." He said he had come to Beijing to participate in Tiananmen, had been arrested, become a dissident, and only recently reemerged. Prior to that, he had been an Olympic track athlete and dated Chinese movie star Gong Li. Now he was going to open a hip bar in Beijing and call it Peking Chalet. I doubted this last part, since Beijing had only a handful of bars, all of which were either state- or hotel-run. There was Frank's Place, a *laowai*-owned greasy spoon and bar across from the workers' stadium. There was Charley's, in the Jianguo Hotel, with a Filipino band and salted peanuts. It was unimaginable to me that a young person would open a bar, or that any bar in Beijing could be hip. As for dating Gong Li, winning running medals, and escaping the authorities, for all I knew he was telling the truth. I nodded a lot.

The traditional courtyard house we were drinking at featured a giant tree growing straight out the middle of its central garden, surrounded by potted plants and ceramic statues. The inner walls of the garden were lined with frozen cabbages, bicycles, and boxes.

Such houses were increasingly scarce in Beijing, since they were being replaced rapidly by low-rise cement apartment buildings. The regulations surrounding ownership and upkeep were complicated enough to be nearly incomprehensible, so living in a courtyard house as a foreigner was a sure sign of having achieved Beijing insider status. There was tension in Beijing over reconstruction of the old neighborhoods and buildings into modern apartment complexes. The ancient neighborhoods housed beautiful traditional *siheyuan*, which were expensive to preserve and renovate, and for the most part had no running water, bathrooms, or heat. Some of the nicest ones were renovated by wealthy Chinese or expatriots. The most desirable, those on the edges of the Forbidden City, were eventually turned into art galleries and five-star restaurants.

"My friend is a director," He Jin was saying. He was speaking Chinese. I couldn't think of anything to say.

"Great!" I said. I could feel the blood flood up into my face. I was a bimbo in Chinese.

"Are you an actress?" He Jin asked. He had switched to English and I felt like crying with gratitude.

The territory was somewhat more familiar now. So his friend was that kind of director. Was He Jin flirting? I could still barely order food in restaurants; I certainly didn't have the confidence to respond to a pickup line. I was already exhausted by our five-minute dialogue and wanted to go home. I felt like a floating apparition, ghost of my confident college self. How had I ever known what to say?

He Jin must have wondered about my responses to his questions. They were ungracious and slow; I scrunched my face up a lot. Maybe he wondered the same thing I had about cabdrivers: did I not understand or just not want to go there? In any case, he bailed me out with, "Maybe you should meet my friend Director Yao! I think he likes you."

A Eurasian-American girl came over and looped her arm through He Jin's. He introduced her to me as his girlfriend, and she shook my hand, and said she worked for the *L. A. Times*. When she went to get drinks, I asked He Jin why she wasn't auditioning for *Foreign Girls in Beijing*. He said she didn't "look Western enough" because she was half Asian.

"Doesn't that make her even more appropriate?"

"No, they need average Western girls."

"Average?"

"Standard."

I excused myself, wandered off, and spent the rest of the night with a blond American woman who ran a metal and mineral company in Beijing. She spoke fluent metallurgical Chinese, and told me where to buy furniture and mittens, and that Frank's Place had iceberg lettuce salads. I hadn't had lettuce since the Northwest Airlines salad on my way to Beijing. I met a twenty-two-year old Chinese-American who was running the public relations department for the Gloria Plaza Hotel, a French computer programmer, and a ponytailed Italian guy who worked in the textile industry. At these parties, Beijing seemed smaller and less intimidating. Expatriate small talk ran a predictable gamut. There was "How long have you been in Beijing?" usually accompanied by the subtext "I've been here longer." Or the more direct "How is your Chinese?" which carried with it the thinly veiled "Mine is better." Finally, I dreaded most the "What are you doing in China?" and my embarrassed response that I was working in public relations. Many of the interesting foreigners I met were journalists who heard this and darted away, worried that I might try to badger them into attending content-free, corporate-spun events. Later, I came to admire and love many of the *laowai* I met in Beijing, particularly the women. In my experience, women who shipped to China alone had a certain bravado.

In fairness to all of Beijing's expatriates, it is hard to find a language in which to talk about someone else's country. Visitors to a country who get angry about the unsavory or unfamiliar aspects of that country will be perceived as racist, sometimes accurately and other times preemptively. One choice is to celebrate even the most backward parts of a place and name them exotic. And yet, if those parts don't serve the indigenous people or lack authenticity, then the celebration is pandering. If there is behavior you would never condone in your own culture, you condescend if you stand for it elsewhere. At the same time, it's necessary to approach and describe your love of a country's relics, energy, and habits with care, lest you turn orientialist or fetishist. There is a delicate balance to be achieved.

It wasn't until I ran into He Jin a week after the party that I agreed to go to the film studio with him and meet his friend Director Yao. The firm had just put on an aluminum company's ribbon-cutting ceremony. The CEO's scissors had been too dull to cut through the ribbon, so he sawed away for the duration of the photo op and then had to borrow the scissors of the Chinese joint venture partner. It was inauspicious, and I was in trouble with Charlotte for not hiding my amusement. As a suitable reprimand, she had sent me out to "source" a better scissors supplier. It was seven P.M. and I was wandering through the imported erasers and stationery aisle at the Friendship Store. The shelves overflowed with Hello Kitty.

He Jin called out my name, switching the "r" and "1," and erasing the "ch" so it came out "Leecer."

"*Nihao*, He Jin," I said. It flashed through me that I couldn't pronounce my own name in Chinese. And if He Jin called me "Leecer," instead of "Rachel," when his English was light years beyond my Chinese, then what did I sound like when I said "He Jin"?

In graceful, Cliffs Notes English, he said, "I will go to the Beijing film studio tomorrow. Will you come and meet Director Yao?"

Tomorrow. I would be wearing a suit and tearing my stockings. I kept extras in my file cabinet at the company. Charlotte kept Spray N Starch in hers, to keep her skirt from grasping at her thighs. We would move through the day in screaming fits of sending and receiving faxes. Our "teams" would make mistakes and Charlotte would call me into her huge office, where she would offer me menthols, spritz herself with Spray N Starch, and talk with me about bullet points and media plans. Once, through a cloud of smoke, she threw a fast-food hamburger at one of our accountants. It was a terrible and symbolic moment, a McDonald's missile hurling through the air. Tomorrow we would consider whether we were "adding value" to our clients' businesses, and I would wonder if we were subtracting value from the world, our lives, and China. I would write a recommendation to our automotive client and do a "postmortem" on the aluminum party. Had we gone over budget? Our billing rates were hundreds of dollars an hour and I spent hours trying to send faxes through broken phone wires, writing and rewriting cover notes to Chinese partners, striking an inoffensive tone while saying offensive things.

"I'd like to go," I told He Jin.

I packed Levi's, a white sweater, and cowboy boots in my brief-case the next morning. When I put the bag in my bicycle basket, I felt like there was an extra person accompanying me to the office. At four P.M., I slipped out of my cubicle, rode the elevator down to the first floor and changed in the lobby bathroom before meeting He Jin outside. It was icy.

We walked out under a group of workers stringing Christmas lights and a banner that read: "Marry Chritmas!" It is mysterious that Chinese organizations so rarely ask one of the hundred thousand Americans living there to proofread banners. Of course, NBA players and American teenagers rarely ask native Chinese speakers for etymology or proofreading services before they tattoo their bodies into scrolls. I have seen girls in American shopping malls tattooed with everything from the predictable "love, peace, and happiness" to the more surprising "girl vegetable."

"You look casual," said He Jin, his eyes moving from the angora to the boots.

I considered that. "Thanks."

We drove for forty-five minutes. Out the windows, apartment buildings stacked up like barracks. Frozen long underwear hung crisply from laundry lines. We drove the Avenue of Eternal Peace, past the ancient observatory, the Bright China ChangAn Club, and Zhongnanhai. The sun set as we wound into residential streets, and I looked up at apartment windows, each of which contained a whole family and private universe. So many families, compartmented into the smallest spaces possible. Balconies sagged with boxes, bicycles, and furniture. For the first time since I had arrived in Beijing, I was reminded of New York. This was just a city. It could be understood or cracked like any city—one just had to know the rhythms and the words.

"How do you like Beijing?" He Jin asked, twice.

"It's okay," I said. "I'm not totally used to it yet."

"So, do you like Chinese food or American food?"

"I love Chinese food, especially pickled vegetables!"

More minutes passed. Outside, groups of schoolchildren in uniforms, padded coats, and backpacks galloped along the edges of the streets, stopping at kiosks that sold shrimp chips, stickers, and sesame candy. I wanted to ask He Jin about his journalist girlfriend and recent reports of human rights violations.

Instead I said, "So, what do you do?"

"I sell furniture."

"What?"

"Office furniture. I can take you to the store on the way home from the studio if you'd like to see it. Maybe your company needs some office furniture." He Jin, like most of the men I met in China, was an entrepreneur. I shouldn't have been surprised; no one in the new China does only one thing. The Chinese system, ironically, doesn't lend itself to institutional stability. China's citizens still have *danwei*, or work units, but most now make their real livings by moonlighting in other jobs. *Danwei* used to provide everything to everyone: work, friends, sustenance, weekend entertainment, medical advice, family planning, education, career advice, political and thought development. The work units kept a file, or *dang'an*, on each employee's lifetime history, noting any black marks (political impropriety, usually) that might have accrued.

No matter where a person lives in China, he gets a residence card at birth, which documents his registered location, the most critical factor of affiliation in the huge Chinese population. It is a good setup in terms of managing the constant and growing flow of migrant workers into urban centers. If anyone moves, his residence card, *hukou,* might be "applied" to a new place, but he might also be forever an alien in another Chinese place. Without a *hukou,* one must seek under-the-table work in Beijing, in hivelike construction sites, sewing villages that ring the city, restaurants, bars, and other service venues.

But the work unit system is in decline; most of the state-owned sector is still organized into *danwei,* and every citizen has a file, but companies have given up their greatest measure of control, that over employees' after-hours lives and general welfare. Among the key unforeseen consequences of reform, Chinese nuclear families began to play the edges of this system. Keeping one spouse in a well-provisioned *danwei* job freed the other to be entrepreneurial, thus using the state to subsidize family entrepreneurship.

At the time, knowing nothing about the Chinese system or what it meant, I could not recover from He Jin's response. He was a track star, a bar owner, a dissident, and a furniture salesman? In a year, this conversation would not strike me as remarkable, and I would likely ask what else he did. But in the cab, I could not process it.

We arrived at the studio. There were two large stone gates on either side of the main entrance, pillars, and a sign for Beiying. Colorful flags hung from each pillar. An emaciated guard stopped us by jumping off his stool and thrusting his open palm at the cab-driver, who grunted. "You have to get out," he told He Jin and me. I reached to help pay for the cab, but He Jin ignored me. He asked the driver for something and got a receipt. *"Fapiao,"* he said. Receipt. It was a word I needed.

I took out my diary and wrote *fapiao* and *Beiying,* the name of the studio. *Bei* is "north," and *ying* is "shadow." Movies are "electric shadows," *dianying.* Beiying takes its *Bei* from *Beijing,* the Northern Capital, and *ying* from *dianying,* or "movie." It's satisfying that words in Chinese so effectively borrow syllables from other words, but *laowai* need healthy vocabularies to follow the flow. An English word like "telecharge" is an interesting equivalent, since it requires knowledge not only of the words telephone and charge card, but also a sense of what the combination might mean.

We walked down a winding path littered with cigarette butts and lined with trees. It was almost fully dark and the air was stark and dry. When we arrived at building number sixteen, He Jin gestured to me to walk in front of him. To the left of us was a tall wall, behind which Beijing's television world took shape. He Jin took me to an arched opening in the wall and pointed in. A giant two-story teahouse faced out, featuring a hot-lit balcony on which actors were staging a fight scene. They were dressed in white silk robes and had long braids hanging down their backs. I stared. Dozens of production people bustled around beneath the balcony, packed into down coats. I couldn't tear my eyes off of the actors.

"We should go," He Jin said. "Director Yao will be waiting."

I backed away from the arch, still watching the people on the set, imagining their lives. This was a small moment that felt large; simply put, it had never occurred to me that Chinese TV was filmed at all, that actors had to dress up to do kung fu movies or to make the incomprehensible programs I had flipped by on TV. I reminded myself that we were in China, and thought back to my house in Michigan, a tiny green Monopoly house, just as it had seemed during childhood trips to China. My world would have to continue to expand to include what China offered up.

He Jin led me to building sixteen, where I stood dazed while he opened the door. The hallway was like American project housing: green and gray cement, bare lightbulbs dangling from wires. There were rows of boxy offices furnished with metal cots and blond wood desks with overflowing tin ashtrays on them. We climbed the stairs to the second floor. A paper sign hung from the first door we saw: "*Yang Niu Zai Beijing.*" I pointed to the character for "*niu*," which I still thought meant "girl,"

"Why that extra stroke mark?" I asked He Jin.

"Not important," he said.

"Is it *nü*?" I asked, using the word for "girl."

"No, it's *niu*."

I heard the difference, just barely, and tried a new line of questioning.

"Whom would you call *niu*?" I asked.

"*Niu* is the kind of word you say about a girl walking on the street."

Did it have to do with walking? Walking on the street?

"For a pretty girl," He Jin added.

It dawned on me. He meant a call. Catcall! The word was a pleasant and distant memory. I wondered how many English words I might be forgetting. So, *Foreign Babes in Beijing*, even though the studio later translated it as *Foreign Girls in Beijing*, had a sexy "chick" or "babe" tone in its *niu*.

"It's not a thing you call your mother or your sister," I suggested.

"Not your mother."

"What about your sister?"

"I don't have a sister." Past-tense counterfactual hypotheticals were hard to discuss in China. I wasn't sure why this was so, but I knew from experience that my colleagues were literal. I turned the sentence forward.

"If you have a sister someday, will you call her *niu*?"

80

"I won't have a sister. My parents are too old," He Jin said. He knocked on the door.

"*Jin lai!*" shouted someone. Come in!

The first person I noticed was the young American, seated on a couch that was, except for the one cushion where he sat, covered with styrofoam boxes. It didn't occur to me until much later to wonder how I knew he was American. His posture, jaws, teeth, goatee, complexion, and jeans were all milk-fed and straight out of college. He looked like me, like my brothers, like guys I had slow-danced with in seventh grade, studied with in high school, dated in college. He had wide blue eyes and long lashes. At the sight of him, guilty relief soared into my throat. An American! He would know me, remind me of something I had forgotten, and save me from my stranger self. Perhaps he would explain the scene, the white silk robes, braids, balcony, extra stroke mark.

None of this happened. He introduced himself in Chinese, as *Bi'er,* a transliteration of "Bill," and I felt the first surge of a disappointment I would later know by heart and prevent through careful expectations management. The loneliest I ever felt in China was around other Americans, because they inspired mistaken hope that we would know each other intimately, instinctively. It took me years to accept the fact that American strangers are just as unknowable as any others. It was hard to decide whether to nod to, wave at, or in any way acknowledge other foreigners. Such gestures felt vaguely conspiratorial and racist; were we special friends because we found ourselves and each other in an exotic and uncomfortable land? And yet, not acknowledging other *laowai* was pretentious and dishonest, since I noticed every single one I saw (and usually stared unabashedly). *Laowai* who did not acknowledge each other were making a point, proving that they were old

China hands and did not get excited at the sight of aliens from their own planets.

When I met new Chinese friends, I knew I would be speaking across distances and was prepared for the Beijing feeling of disconnectedness and half understanding. It was harder to adjust to this distance with other *laowai*. I grinned widely at Bill, hoping to have meaningful eye contact in which we would express our agreement about the *Babes* office. I didn't know or care what that agreement would be. He smiled back. I noticed as soon as I looked away from him that the styrofoam boxes had chopsticks poked through them, a strategy I now know was meant to prevent their reuse by food vendors. Next to the blue-eyed, bearded Bill, the stabbed *hefan* boxes looked like an avant-garde art installation.

In a fish tank against the far wall, some thick fish splashed. An elderly Chinese man sat at a desk, smoking and writing. He stood up when we came in, and began introducing everyone in the room. A short fat man, also smoking, filmed the introductions. "I am Line Producer Zhu; this is Director Yao; this is Han Lei, the cameraman; this is Wu Jie, the executive producer and investor; this *laowai* is Bill (Bi'er), from America."

Everybody but the *laowai* Bill hung their cigarettes in their mouth corners for a moment to hand me name cards with both hands. I studied and placed each lovingly into my embossed holder.

"*Nihao*," I said. Wu Jie, the investor, was wearing a purple silk suit and smoking.

"This is Ruiqiu," said He Jin, gesturing at me. Bumper Harvest. Director Yao looked at me briefly and then nodded at He Jin.

"Does she have acting experience?" He lit a cigarette off the one he was smoking and smoked both for a second before crushing out the first and starting heartily on the second.

My mind flipped through productions of *Antigone, Free to Be You and Me,* and *Oklahoma!* I had played a lesbian with ovarian cancer in a Columbia production of a play called *Last Summer at Bluefish Cove,* and an embarrassingly suburban rendition of a shabop girl in *Little Shop of Horrors.* I wondered how to say "Bluefish" in Chinese.

He Jin looked at me. "Are you actress?"

"No," I said.

"Okay, let's start," said Director Yao. "You used to be in love with Bill, your American boyfriend," he began. "But now you have a Chinese boyfriend you like more than Bill. So you need to get Bill out of your room. Your Chinese boyfriend is coming over. You can begin acting now."

Bill got up from the couch. "So, what are we doing tonight?" he asked me in Chinese. He was posing next to me, arms akimbo. I looked at him.

"Uh, I have other plans," I said.

"What?" he shouted.

I remembered high school theater. How you learn to say "yes, and" in improvisation classes, instead of shouting, "No!" at your partner. And how that strategy made life in Beijing more livable.

"Yes," I said. "I'm sorry, but I have plans tonight with my Chinese boyfriend." I didn't know the right way to say it humanely. I hoped the improv would be over. Maybe Bill would cry.

He shouted with laughter. Director Yao interrupted us. "Now pretend that you are foreigners living in China." There was a moment of silence. It was the first time I had ever heard the word "pretend" in Chinese.

"Bill loves to take the bus," Director Yao continued. "But you," he said to me, "like to take cabs and live like a true foreigner." I thought about true foreigners.

"Let's take a cab," I said to Bill.

"No!" he said. "I want to take the bus!"

We stood there.

"You're hired," said Director Yao.

I didn't know the word for "hired." Bill translated for me. He Jin, who had been quiet for the duration of the audition, stood. "I'll take you back," he offered. He and Director Yao had meaningful eye contact. It's effortless to understand body language in your own cultural context. If I stood in an American classroom, for example, in which some students were winking, others were twitching, and some were mocking those winking and twitching, it might take me six seconds to figure out the dynamics. I know the difference between a wink, a twitch, a flipoff, a shake, a look, a flirt, a glare, a glance, a provocation, and a provoked response. I can tell actions from reactions, since the nuances of body gestures have a set of cultural interpretations we imbibe from birth. But in the *Foreign Babes* office, I was rootless. I couldn't gauge anything about or from their looks. It's one thing not to understand the flow of language. It's another not to understand anything at all.

Foreigners were allowed to live only in "foreign-approved housing," and most approved apartments were upward of U.S. $3,000 a month. All the journalists lived in one of three "journalist compounds," Jianwai, Sanlitun, or Taiyuan, where the Chinese government kept a close eye on their comings, goings, meetings, and phone calls. Students and young foreigners with internships or poorly paying jobs lived in dorms or illegal Chinese apartments. My housing allowance was $1,000 a month, which placed me in a nether land. One thousand dollars was more money than any of my Chinese colleagues could imagine spending on rent, but too little for a legal apartment. So when I moved from the Huarun into my first apartment, it had to be an illegal Chinese one. I picked a complex called *Fangzhuang,* "Suburban Farm," where my rent was $800 a month, because I knew of one other foreigner, a redhead who worked for Ford Motor Company, living there. She said that she and her American boyfriend, who studied pandas, had lived there for over six months and not been evicted. I was sold. Over the next two years, dozens of foreigners would move to Fangzhuang and life would take on a Melrose Place ambience. But initially, cab-drivers couldn't find the place at night, and I couldn't find my own building. I lived in fear of the apartment and the complex.

Fangzhuang was far from the office, and featured a barbecue meat restaurant called "Barbecue Meat Place," a carpet store called "Carpet Store," and a burgeoning local life. Next to my building was a park, complete with a small fountain in which children splashed, and a makeshift net for playing badminton. Across from the park were a bar called "Arcadia" and a bakery called "Sun-flower," which never had more than a few lonely cakes in its display cases, but always managed to exude an overwhelming smell of sugar and starch.

The compound itself was a sprawling maze of gates, construction zones, and identical government-issue high-rises growing from the ground like chalky plants. I lived on the eighteenth floor of building number four. Apparently, the number four had decreased the amount I paid in rent, since *si*, four, is a homonym for another *si*, which means death. One and four together suggest imminent or impending death, which is why no Chinese building has a fourteenth floor. In spite of the dramatic and unlucky number of my building, I had trouble remembering which one it was. My windows looked out on dozens of buildings just like mine.

The rent for the Fangzhuang apartment, although inexpensive as foreign prices went, became a subject of instant and tremendous interest in the office. My colleagues tittered and expressed gleeful horror after they saw my contract, which the landlord faxed me.

"Too expensive!" Xiao Li shouted. Even Gary got involved. Outside the office, his status as a foreigner was inconspicuous, so he was able to rent an inexpensive local place. "You should have had me negotiate for you," he said. "My friend has an apartment in Fangzhuang she would have rented to you for two thousand *yuan*," closer to $300. I wasn't convinced that Gary could have gotten me an apartment, but I was frustrated that everyone at work gossiped about the cheating. They discussed it incessantly, concluding each time that I didn't know how to operate in China, which was true. Plus, my rent was more than most local monthly salaries, which inspired everyone to go and peek at the human resource files in Charlotte's office to see what my housing allowance was. The question remained: how could I be making more money than anyone else when I was so young, knew nothing about China, and had no professional experience? I knew how to write in English. I could talk efficiently and confidently to Charlotte and to our giant, pale clients, who liked me. That was worth how much?

By my standards, the Fangzhuang apartment was frightening, but in Beijing it was luxurious to live alone. Many of my colleagues still lived with their parents. I clung to some sense of accomplishment at getting an apartment for a fraction of the prevailing foreigner's rent, but my sense of ineptitude was exacerbated by the apartment itself. It was filthy and bare when I moved in. It had a bedroom, bathroom, living room, and kitchen, separated by low-hanging carved doorframes, by which I imagined anyone over five-eight would be decapitated. The walls were covered in pink wallpaper with textured felt flowers that wound their way up and down in swirls. The lights, bare bulbs hanging from strings, made the flowers appear to shine and writhe. The floors were pink linoleum. The plumbing was connected to that of every other apartment in the enormous building, so every time a toilet flushed, I could hear it. Drafts of sewagey air wafted up from a drain in the floor.

My first night at the suburban farm apartment, I took out Rollerblades I had optimistically brought from the U.S., and skated from room to room. It seemed the only way to make use of the bareness.

Included in my rent was a priceless course in local Beijing life. The elevators were turned off every night at eleven P.M., which meant that almost five nights a week I climbed eighteen flights of stairs. The cement stairwells were unlit, so I carried a flashlight in my briefcase. This was a new building, and the elevators were automatic. But when running, each had an operator, because they were not only elevators but "iron rice bowls," stable jobs that citizens have forever. Everyone needed a job. At eleven P.M., the operators and the elevators went to bed. At five A.M., they woke. I had the same conversation every morning with one of them.

"Your hair is wet," she said each day. ("Yes.")

"Did you just wash your hair?" ("Yes.")

"You're going to work." ("Yes.")

Chinese small talk is not about weather; it relies on comfortable statements of obvious facts. When I got to the office, my colleagues shouted, "You've arrived," as a way to welcome me. It's nice when people acknowledge general, factual aspects of your presence; it confirms that you exist. I liked the elevator conversation; it kept us safe. But after a year of it, we moved on to other details, including the fact that all the *dianti xiaojie*, elevator ladies, lived in the building. Finally, I knew the elevator ladies well enough to ask if they might leave the elevator on. "Of course!" they said. "Or you can come and wake us!" It was that easy.

But my first night there, I was light-years from such understandings. My apartment, Building 4, Door 2, Floor 18, Apartment 1, had nothing in it, not a fridge, bed, phone jack, or cord. I was panicked that there was no phone, leaving me disconnected from the entire world. The landlord and her husband, a wealthy businessman, had promised me a phone when we negotiated, but landlines were hard to come by. For two months after I moved in, I asked my colleagues to call the landlord and demand a phone, while I called my mom and dad from the office to tell them I still didn't have one. Gary said I should take the landlord out to dinner and see if that helped. But I didn't want to have dinner with my landlord. She had even invited me out and I had declined. I spent my first half year in the apartment as a phone-less ingrate—unfriendly, not available, and quiet. Whenever my colleagues called the landlord to remind her about the phone, she complained that I never called her just to say hello, only when I wanted something.

I slept in a bed I made from a pile of suits, until Gary helped me get a mattress. My kitchen and bathroom had floor-to-ceiling mirrors. When I tried to remove them, I discovered that the walls underneath were covered with holes as big as extra closets. So I left the mirrors intact, greeting myself as I walked through the apartment, which I came to consider a kind of funhouse. The days were thematically consistent, all about watching and being watched.

In order to make my illegal apartment more livable, I hired Xiao Gao, an unregistered woman from Anhui province, to help me. I had sworn when I arrived in Beijing that I would not hire a maid, called affectionately *ayi's* or aunties, in Chinese, but then basic life proved unmanageable. All the other expatriates I met had *ayi's*. I attributed this to the spoiling of wealthy people who live in a poor country, but also came to understand that *ayis* were the only ones able to take on impossible administrative tasks, which had to be done dozens of times a week between nine A.M. and five P.M., when I was imprisoned at the office or the studio. These included paying the phone and water bills, changing the cooking gas tank, waiting for water deliveries, and *la'ing guanxi*, or "pulling a relationship" with the landlord. Someone had to be in the house when bill collectors, whom I could neither understand nor trust, pounded on the door to ask for cash. I never had any idea what they were charging for. Xiao Gao could tell the legitimate ones from the cheaters.

She and I were interested in each other. We were the same age, yet she was married and six months pregnant with her second baby, a problem for her, since she was supposed to have only one child. China instituted its "one-child policy" in 1979. The policy worked in the strictest sense; population growth slowed down enough to stabilize at 1.21 percent a year between 1991 and 1995.[5] Even economic growth did not cause an explosion in population growth, both because wealthy couples had fewer or no children and because there were fewer women of childbearing age than there had been in previous decades.[6]

And China made some progress in the 1990s toward implementing a somewhat more woman-centered approach to enforcing the one-child policy. There were a number of grassroots efforts to make family planning, education, and contraceptive choices a part of population control. But on the ground, the effects of such efforts had yet to filter down fully. China has received harsh criticism of its top-down enforcement of the policy, rumored to include forced sterilization. In the mid-1990s, when Sino-U.S. relations were at low points, the U.S. media published raging accounts of infanticide and selective-sex abortion in China. The Chinese media responded with stories analyzing America's human rights record, concentrating on the case of Rodney King.

Xiao Gao's first little girl, whom she referred to as a *xiao xi,* small happiness, was back in Anhui with her husband's parents. Xiao Gao said only boy babies were considered *da xi,* or big happiness. When she became visibly pregnant with her second child, I asked how the pregnancy was going.

"Okay," Xiao Gao said, "but I'm thinking of having an abortion."

She explained that her husband had wanted her to find out the sex of the baby in advance and abort it in the event that it was another girl. So she had bribed the doctor to perform an illegal gender test, and he confirmed that the baby was indeed a girl. I was in no position to give advice on the subject; I had no idea what I would do if allowed to have only one child. If Xiao Gao had been wealthy, she could have paid thousands of *yuan* in fines and tried again. Had she still been in her rural village in Anhui, her situation would have been somewhat easier. Disregard for the one-child policy was widespread by 1994; couples hid children with relatives, paid fines, or found loopholes in the rules. Some rural families were exempted from the rule, since they needed children to carry on family farms. But in major urban centers like Beijing and Shanghai, the law was enforced with regularity; failure to comply resulted in heavy fines or job loss. And as a member of the floating migrant population in Beijing, it would be difficult for Xiao Gao to send her child to school, get her health care, or hide her entirely.

When I asked how she felt about aborting her baby, she said it wasn't her decision, but one to be made collectively by her, her husband, and his family.

"Maybe you can talk your husband out of it," I suggested gingerly. "If you live in the city, even a girl will take care of you in your old age. Isn't the desire for boys based on a rural need?" Daughters were considered an economic burden, not only because they would eventually leave the house to marry into someone else's family, but also because of the cost of their weddings and dowries. Sons, on the other hand, carried on the family name, brought daughter-in-laws into the households, and made good on the investments involved in rearing.

"You talk of the practical side," Xiao Gao said, "I talk about tradition. It's not only about what I want. Boy babies are better; this is a fact of life."

She wasn't kidding about tradition. There are records of the Chinese preference for male offspring dating from as early as 1600 B.C., part of China's first written history, on "oracle bones." During the Shang Dynasty, bones were heated until they cracked, revealing truths about the future. Then the interpretations were engraved into the bones, which have lasted forever. One such cracked bone was interpreted to predict whether a woman named Lady Hao would have an auspicious birth. After a first crack at the due date, the bone summed up the results: "After thirty-one days, she gave birth. It was not good; it was a girl."[7]

"What about you?" Xiao Gao asked as I collected my briefcase. "Aren't your parents worried that they can't embrace a grandson?"

"I don't know," I said. "Maybe. But I'm only twenty-three." Xiao Gao was also twenty-three.

"Twenty-three isn't young. What if you're not married by the time you're twenty-eight?"

"I can't predict what will happen then," I said. "What if I get married and then in five years I'm not in love with my husband anymore?"

"Isn't it worse not to be married at all? To be alone and have your parents be unhappy and everyone around you feel it's wrong?"

She thought I was careless and selfish. Being married and having children was about joining the fabric of society, becoming a member of a community larger than oneself, even if that community was made up of one's in-laws. Being twenty-three and American was about the opposite: being carved out and individual, my small self at whatever cost. I wondered what my colleague Anna thought about daughters and marriage. She was my age, too.

"Anyway," Xiao Gao said, "maybe I won't do it. We can't be sure the baby is a girl."

"Because the tests aren't always accurate?"

"Because maybe they just want the money for the abortion, so the doctor lies about it." The same doctor who tested for gender was also the one who provided costly abortions.

Xiao Gao did not abort her baby and had a beautiful, healthy girl. On the occasions when she brought her daughter to work, her husband sometimes came along, snuggling the baby with unself-conscious abandon. Xiao Gao's family had decided it was worth the risk. They would keep one baby in the city and the other in the country and *manman lai,* take it slow. Her husband loved the girl, and Xiao Gao was beside herself with big happiness.

When *Foreign Babes in Beijing*'s Assistant Director Xu called me at the office, I did not know who she was and could not understand what she was saying. I heard my name. She was definitely calling for me. It was even harder to carry on a conversation in Chinese over the phone than it was in person. Phone etiquette was different in China. No "Hi, we met last week." No "How are you?" There was also a lot of grunting and acknowledging required. When someone spoke into the phone, if I did not make my presence known at least once a second with "enhs" and "unhs," the person shouted, *"Wei? Wei?"* to make sure I was still there.

"Wei? Wei?"

"Wei, nihao. Hello!" I said.

"Yang Niu Zai Beijing Assistant Director!" she shouted, but I had forgotten the word for "assistant." I said nothing.

"Wei? Wei?"

"I'm Du Ruiqiu," I said weakly, hiding Anna's Tang poetry book in my desk drawer and gesturing frantically to Anna to come to my cubicle. Assistant Director Xu was shouting a stream of Chinese into the phone. "I'm Du Ruiqiu," I tried again.

By the time I heard *"Wei? Wei?"* a third time, Anna had arrived. I thrust the phone at her, and she took it, talked fast, and then turned to me, covering the mouthpiece with her hand. "They want you to do this TV," she said. "Can you go to Beiying for decoration tonight?"

"Decoration?"

"You know," said Anna, "cloth-es."

I said no. I asked Anna to explain that I couldn't go to Beiying again. That I had enjoyed meeting everyone but was too busy. Assistant Director Xu told her to put me back on the phone. "You can act Louisa!" she told me. I had no idea what Louisa was.

"I'm sorry," I said. "I'm too busy with work." She hung up.

Anna was grinning. "Will you do this Beiying thing?" she asked.

I shook my head. "I don't even know what she's talking about," I told her.

I went back to work and worked the next three nights until midnight on banquet agendas and VIP seating charts. The fluorescent lights were turning my vision and thoughts gray; the rest of my corporate life snaked out hideously toward the horizon. I was desperate. I thought of the audition, the actors in white silk, the balcony set. I wanted to meet them, to explore further behind that set. I imagined wandering around behind the wall that separated the offices at Beiying from the sets, chatting with actors, learning to speak the language of kung fu movies rather than that of CEO speeches. I wanted to be an action hero, not an account executive. I was desperate to rush back to the studio and learn something, anything about Beijing. So at my Chinese lesson, I asked Teacher Kang to do me a favor.

"TV!" I said. We had just finished going over a poem about orchid leaves and cinnamon blossoms, so this was out of context. I tried to tell her about Beiying, but each time I said "Beiying," she corrected me by saying "Beijing."

"No, no," I said, waving my hands. "Beiying. It's where—" I mimed a TV camera.

"Oh, Beiying!" she said.

"Right, Beiying."

"No, not right. Beiying."

"Beiying."

She waited, either accepting my final stab at pronunciation or giving up. "So?"

"Uh," I said, "they request I act. I told them no, but am sad. I hate my job. I hate business. Can you call them?" I asked. It was an unorthodox request to make of a teacher, but she agreed. After the call, she said, "*Xing.*" Okay. That night, I went to Beiying for decoration.

When I arrived, I walked right back to the archway where He Jin and I had peeked at the fight scene. There were no actors on the set, so I detoured around behind it, and was intercepted by a man in a long army coat, who asked me what I was looking for.

"I'm here for *Foreign Babes in Beijing,*" I said, hoping to get by him. He pointed toward building sixteen. I nodded thanks and kept walking. Behind the fight-scene set was a whole world of sets; Beiying receded endlessly into the distance, one courtyard after the next. I walked into the first one I came upon, and there were hundreds of people filming a party scene, tables set up everywhere with white tablecloths and food being passed around. People were shouting crazily, actors were leaping up and sitting back down; a director was yelling orders into a megaphone. I slipped back out of the courtyard.

Out on Beiying's main path, I was directly across from building sixteen. As soon as I climbed to the second-floor office and knocked, Director Yao greeted me and said the costumers needed "to have a *kan yi kan.*" A look-*yi*-look. He sent a lackey to take me to the makeup studio, which was also constructed of light green cement. The hallways and stairwells were so dark I could barely see in front of me. The makeup room itself had mirrors propped up on desks, surrounded by big lightbulbs, only half of which worked. There were wigs lying around. I had the willies. The makeup artists sat me in front of a mirror with two working lights.

"Generally good to look at," they said, "but her style is quite chaotic." They pasted me together with hairspray and pancake makeup. "She wears jeans, like a cowboy," they said scornfully. Suddenly I had big hair and pink eyelids. They hung a fur coat over the green parka I had bought in the silk market. The parka had a picture of a duck and the label "Underduck Down." I liked it. It expressed something subtle about the way I felt in China.

Back in the *Yang Niu Zai Beijing* office, Director Yao looked me over and said, "We wanted you to play Louisa, the lead." I fluttered my shadowed lids. "But we've already given that role to the German girl since you said no." I wasn't sure what I was supposed to feel. Was I supposed to be disappointed? Relieved? Focused?

"Maybe you can play Jiexi, the other lead?"

"Maybe?" Did that mean they wanted me to and maybe I would say yes or that maybe they wanted me to? I stood there, tall and awkward.

"Do you like it?" Director Yao asked.

"Like what?"

"To play Jiexi?"

I wasn't sure.

"In the beginning, she has problems with love," he said, "she is a *disanzhe*. But her love is true, so she turns out to be a beautiful person. This show is the story of man's common search for truth and beauty." *Disanzhe* means "the third," the mistress, the lover. This should have been a warning to me, but I smiled and agreed.

I met my costar Wang Ling before we started filming. He waltzed into the *Babes* office while I was signing a contract Director Yao and Line Producer Cao had stamped with an official red seal. I could not read the content, but was in the habit in my early, illiterate Beijing days of signing things I could neither read nor understand. I would later show the contract to Anna and our company driver, who would tell me it was *biaozhun*, standard. I would stare blankly, since this was the word Teacher Kang used to describe good *laowai* Chinese. It took time to stretch context, to learn the endless potential places for each word in a new language.

Line Producer Cao gestured to the contract on the table. He had just told me that the studio had little money, and I had agreed to a salary of eight hundred *yuan* (a little over $80) per episode.

"Embarrassed," he said, handing me a pen. Embarrassed myself, I signed the papers quickly, scratching out characters for Du, Rui, and Qiu.

"Don't worry about the money," I said. "Good experience. Not for money." In my family, we had never talked about money; my parents did not tell my brothers or me how much of it they made or spent. They were "reasonable," and did not approve either of self-deprivation or of ostentatious displays. Their financial habits were midwestern. My family was well off but restrained, bought Japanese cars that lasted decades (which my father fixed himself in the driveway of our judgmental neighborhood, where other people did not work on cars), and spent money mainly on travel.

The producers, relieved that I wasn't going to pursue a negotiation with them, smiled and clucked around me, busy with paperwork. Then they lit high-octane cigarettes and offered me one, which I accepted and hacked down. Later I would find out that the show was a moneymaker and the investors and producers were wealthy men, even by my Western standards. By the time I knew all that, I had learned to love cigarettes and haggling, both of which I will forever associate with my contract-signing in the *Babes* office. I should have known from the joint-venture negotiations at the firm, renting the Fangzhuang apartment, and my basic daily interactions, that I was outclassed even in simple negotiations, but I felt superior. I thought of myself, guiltily, as a privileged Westerner, overpaid by my company and living in luxury at the expense of men like Producer Cao and Wu Jie. I even worried that Wang Ling might be making less money than I was, that he would find out and feel emasculated. Wang Ling told me later that they all found the foreign babes naive, and understood that we were willing to act for free because it was an honor to be on Chinese television, because we wanted to be pretty, and because we were deeply insecure. They were likely right.

Wang Ling came in and there was a flurry of introductions, during which I missed his name. Sophie, the red-haired German girl playing Louisa, came in, too, and shook my hand.

"I play Louisa," she said in English.

"Nice to meet you."

She gestured to Wang Ling. "He plays your boyfriend."

Wang Ling heard her, and I guess he knew the word "boyfriend," because he pointed at himself and said, "*Nan-*

pengyou." Right. He was going to be my *nanpengyou.* He was stunning, with angles all over his face. The fluorescent light shot off his cheekbones. Would we kiss in the show?

He turned to the directors after looking at me. *"Xing,"* he said. Okay. Did he mean I looked "okay"?

"What do you mean by *xing?*" I asked Wang Ling. I thought I was being cute, but everyone missed the cute part.

"It means 'good,' or 'okay,'" he said in a studious voice. Now he thought I was stupid.

I tried to correct it. "No, no," I said. "I know what it means. I was joking. It's a joke. I meant to say, 'What do you mean by that?'"

Everyone stared. "It means 'okay' or 'good.' Do you know this word, *'hao'*?" Wang Ling asked. *Hao,* which means "good," is half the Chinese word for "hello." It's the first word every *laowai* learns. I nodded, defeated.

We were to begin filming the following week, and I would need to prove that I had my work unit's permission to participate. So Beijing demanded that Charlotte sign my Chinese contract, since I belonged to her "work unit"; she was signing me over.

Charlotte was kind about the *Foreign Babes in Beijing* whim. I sat in her office and told her, deadpan, that I wanted to act in a Chinese nighttime soap opera. It was called *Foreign Babes in Beijing,* and we would film for four months and then be done, because it had to be reviewed by the censors. She nodded, called our Hong Kong office, and requested a part-time contract for me. I would work as many hours as possible while I filmed, and then come back full-time. She did not balk. Perhaps because of her understanding of American movie and TV culture, she understood the appeal of what might, to other executives, have seemed a frivolous pursuit.

Or maybe she just liked the story. She began to introduce me at company events as "China's Joan Collins." I barely knew who Joan Collins was, but guessed that to people of Charlotte's generation, this meant something specific about television. Such introductions were consistently met by Western executives with embarrassment, scorn, or lasciviousness, and by Chinese executives with blank stares. Unable to think of an antidote to chase the poison of these moments, I stayed quiet, pinned into my suit.

Nights, after filming, I sat in the office and wrote speeches for executives about the automotive industry being a "pillar industry." I filled out billing reports for our clients. Anna believed the work we were doing was valuable, that the American Chamber of Commerce and U.S. businesses were opening up China and providing opportunity for people like her. I wrote that our clients had long-term commitments to development and environment, and hoped that it was true, even though they were going to flood the Chinese market with exhaust, washing machines, sugar, and Western-style management.

Mornings, Teacher Kang and I studied the *Foreign Babes in Beijing* script. The firm job and the *Babes* job were similar; each role was just that, a role. I was playing dress-up, talking, writing, exploring, and posing. It was not until much later that I tried to sort out plots, nuances, and moral messages.

From *Foreign Babes in Beijing*
Episode Three

Louisa and Tianliang are standing in a pagoda at Jingshan Park.
Her hair is windblown. She wears endless layers of clothing.

LOUISA
It's your family, isn't it! They don't condone our love!
But I'm not marrying your parents.

She buries her face in her hands.

TIANLIANG
Loving my family is part of loving me. They'll be with me for my
whole life. Do you want to move into the courtyard? Help buy
and prepare food? Wash clothes?
(His voice is gruff with emotion)
Louisa, in a courtyard house there are no air conditioners,
hamburgers, or beef ribs.

列妞传
Lie Niu Zhuan

Biographies of Model Babes One: Anna

Anna told me her story in parts, hardest part first. In 1990, she had moved back from boarding school to Beijing for college and fallen in love with a Saudi Arabian student named Khalid. No one had approved. His embassy explicitly forbade its scholarship students to date Chinese women, and Anna's parents were furious and bewildered that she had a foreign boyfriend. But Anna and Khalid didn't care. They ignored the rules in honor of love, to hear her tell it, and were traveling in the southern Chinese city of Kunming when security guards broke into their hotel in the middle of the night.

"What were guards doing breaking into your room?" I asked.

"It was a standard check," she said. "Foreigners and Chinese were not allowed to travel together around that time, and it was a state-run hotel. We were certainly not allowed to stay in the hotel together, because we had no wedding license."

Anna admitted that she and Khalid were not married. The guards asked if she was a prostitute and demanded identification. Anna and Khalid produced student IDs, at which point the guards ordered Anna to pay a 500-*yuan* ($60) fine. The fine was corrupt but no surprise, since students were fined for offenses ranging from illicit affairs to failing or skipping school. But Anna and Khalid didn't have 500 *yuan*.

"The school officials were waiting when we got off the train in Beijing," she said. "To take me to the relevant bureau office and make me do self-criticisms." She smiled. "But I lied. I told them nothing about the feelings between us, only that Khalid needed a tour guide. They asked me again and again, and I refused to tell them; I think it's personal and that they're dirty. They asked me to write a report of what happened, and then they were silent for two months. They didn't ask me to do anything else, but I knew what they were thinking. They were waiting for me to come and beg for forgiveness and swear that this would never happen again. I never showed up or swore to anything."

In response to Anna's stubbornness, the university security department produced a poster detailing her identity and her story, which they hung all over campus. Her parents saw the poster, since they lived nearby. Anna's mother, who came from a wealthy land-owning family, was shocked and embarrassed. She advised Anna to end the affair immediately and said Anna's behavior was selfish, since it put the family and their good name at risk. Anna's father, an intellectual and music lover from a farming family, was quiet about his daughter's run-in with officials. He agreed that she should modify her behavior to mollify the school officials, but did not suggest that the love affair itself was immoral.

Her mother, Anna said, had been a "true revolutionary" during the Cultural Revolution, because as the daughter of a wealthy family, she was under particularly intense scrutiny. She overcompensated and became a low-level local leader, marrying Anna's father "for the cause," after "stealing him" from a girl with whom he was actually in love. He was a good catch, since his family was rural and poor, but he had been well educated. So he had the cachet of being both genuinely not bourgeois and also not an uneducated laborer. Her mother was concerned that she would be sent to the fields and either be forced to marry a peasant or find herself too old to marry upon returning to the city. As for why Anna's father had agreed to marry Anna's mother, Anna argued that her mother was strong-willed, and her father was afraid to stand up to her. He was "henpecked"; her mother was hard-core. Besides, she added, "no one married for love at that time. Marriage was a sacrifice for the state."

This was also Anna's explanation for why her father was more understanding of her predicament; he understood love and the loss of it. Encouraged by what she perceived as his empathy, and as if to punctuate her disregard for her mother's advice and face, Anna escaped the family by moving in with Khalid. No one would rent them a legal apartment, so they stayed in the second work unit apartment of a family who had two. Their landlords were a married couple, and both spouses had work unit living quarters. So Anna secretly rented their extra, tiny apartment for herself and Khalid.

It is difficult to exaggerate how daring a life choice this was for a twenty-year-old Chinese girl in 1992. Chinese women were in a startlingly new context. Anna's generation was the first in China to be independent financially and otherwise; Anna and her friends did not have to move directly from their parents' houses into the houses of husbands or work units. They had choices their mothers had never had, worked for foreign companies, traveled, and had genuine, often intimate contact with the outside world. Family stability and service to the state took back-burner positions to selfhood. Feminism was tearing through Beijing in the years I spent there; young women were making money, renting apartments, learning English, traveling, going punk, having premarital sex, and speaking out. Even the government appeared to be encouraging women's rights; its mixed messages were understandable, given how new the manifestations of the youth movement were.

In 1989, China's first all-woman rock band, Cobra, began to whip audiences and critics into a frenzy of delight and rage. The girl band created a spiked-hair, screaming brand of feminine models, a challenge to China's quiet, nonconfrontational ones. Girls were busting out of the seams of a role Cobra's drummer described as limited to "giving birth to children and cooking."[8] One young woman talked about her 1992 experience at a Cobra concert: "It is as if my feelings were burning and I could even hear the wonderful sound of blood flow as it went gurgling on."[9] Her blood moving through her to the music sounded suspiciously to me like the "burning feeling" of teenage revolt anywhere. But in China, while tough heroines weren't entirely unfamiliar, such personal expressions of their emotions, especially as the result of raw rock music, were new. Chinese heroines have had rebellious streaks for thousands of years; in China's Song Dynasty opera *Peony Pavilion*, the heroine defies her father's wishes, falls in love, and ends up not only dying for the love she was forbidden to have, but also coming back to life and marrying him without her father's consent. In the end, though, she is forgiven and will be a model wife. She does not throw her body into a mosh pit, bear her midriff for a Western press photo, or marry a foreigner.

Cobra and open-minded women like Anna were a threat. And the government responded with the form the masses favor most: TV. The hit television series *Expectations* aired in 1991, promoting a chaste and self-sacrificing anti-Anna heroine named Liu Huifang, who marries for pity, raises an orphaned baby girl on her own, and then is forced to divorce her husband because he is selfish and unloving. She pledges grin-and-bear-it loyalty, and remains good-hearted and uncomplaining throughout her trials. Heroine Liu was hailed by critics as a moral example, and loathed and rejected by the young urban women I met. They were tired of role models who took abuse willingly.

In 1992, the *New China News Agency* admitted in a stark report that women were holding up more than their half share of sky, echoing with surprising irony the Cultural Revolution slogan "women hold up half the sky." The *New China News Agency* attributed women's problem to "diehard feudal ideas of women being inferior to men," and confessed that in China, "women are still being discriminated against to varying degrees."[10] That same year, while Anna was moving in with her Middle Eastern boyfriend, only 61 percent of rural women had a choice in whom they married, a statistic Anna called "inexcusably feudal."

In April 1992, after winning its bid to host the 1995 International Women's Conference, China's National People's Congress passed the country's first law declaring men and women equal.[11] The law focused primarily on unfair practices in the workplace, and committed China to ensuring equal protection to women as well as training and appointing women to high-level positions as cadres. China also approved the first-ever Chinese women's hotline, a phone line devoted to advising women on sexual harassment, cheating husbands, and discrimination. But there was only one line for millions of women, open five days a week for four hours each day.[12]

Anna loved Cobra and hated *Expectations*. By the time we were twenty-four, she made more money than her parents and rented her own apartments. In between apartments and jobs, she stayed with me. Her English belonged to her; her parents could not understand her phone conversations or the content of her work for an American company. Her nights belonged to her; she had dates, sex, and foreign friends and boyfriends, all unapologetically. We were best friends, and once I was on TV, I became, in Anna's parents' eyes, *the* symbol of everything Western and incomprehensible in their daughter's life. She was like Tianming, and I was like Jiexi, taking her from China. But even before my personal influence fanned the fire, Anna was at the forefront of a movement that had yet to be understood as exemplary or even acceptable, and thus incurred the disapproval of every adult in her world.

All Anna would ever say of the scorn, of the humiliation, of the poster detailing her affair with Khalid, was that she was sorry Khalid had to endure it. As a Chinese, she said, she was innately trained to absorb and expect such treatment, but the authorities should not dare embarrass or insult a foreign student. Yet, to my mind, the cost to Khalid was slight, whereas the one to Anna was severe.

When Anna finally tore down a poster and took it to the Foreign Students' Office to complain, Khalid's embassy demanded the posters be removed. "All the students saw the poster, and then they saw it disappear," Anna told me, triumphant. But the university police lost face, blamed Anna, and picked up the pace of her daily interrogations. They grilled and humiliated her every morning until the day she graduated, seven months later. Anna never spoke unless absolutely forced, and then responded only with monosyllabic grunts. She and Khalid kept living together for a year, until he returned to the Middle East.

Every day for two years, Anna wrote a letter to Khalid. He never wrote her back; he was a diplomat and wasn't allowed to write to Chinese girls. When I asked Anna why she wrote, she said that she wanted to marry him.

The press stayed hard at work discouraging such plans. In a 1997 article from China's *Liberation Daily*, a reporter wrote: "As China is getting rich, foreign girls have married Chinese boys and lived in China." There was no mention of other combinations, even though most intercultural marriages were between Chinese women and foreign men. Anna laughed at the article's statement that "the overall quality of present marriages between Chinese citizens and foreigners is not high, for the marriages of some couples did not mean love. This resulted in a high rate of divorce."[13]

But even the government mouthpiece papers could not deny that, like American marriage, which was failing at a rate of over 50 percent, Chinese unions were besieged by the problems of modern love. The overall divorce rate in China surged in the 1990s; by 1996 there was one divorce for every nine marriages, quadruple what the ratio had been ten years before.[14] The *People's Daily* published startling figures: in 1980, there were 10.403 million marriages and 389,000 divorces in China. By 1996, marriages had decreased to 9.389 million and divorces increased to 1.132 million.[15] The government implied absurdly that the rising rate of divorce was connected to interracial marriages, even going so far as to publish management regulations for marriages between Chinese and foreigners. Ostensibly for the sake of avoiding " 'quickie' or duplicitous marriages," the rules made marrying a foreigner an endless red-tape battle. Marital problems are global, not cultural. But Anna insisted upon a simple, cultural solution, one that predictably set her in direct opposition to the government's and her parents' desires.

"I can't marry someone who is Chinese," she said.

"That's crazy," I told her. "Doesn't your Khalid story mean you can't marry a foreigner without having life here be impossible? Why not marry a Chinese?"

"No, because if I marry a Chinese, then I become part of this cynical system," she said. "What if I want to be free of all this? Have more than one child? Travel? China doesn't understand me. As Chinese girls we are told to lose our characters, our personalities. We all even have the same brand of bicycle! Flying Pigeon. Do you know this Chinese expression, *'Chujia congqin, zaijia youshen*: the first time a woman marries, she follows her parents' wishes, the second time, she follows her own'? I plan to skip the first time. I will follow only my own wishes."

Of course, no country understands its individual citizens. Anna's rebellion was against a general villain: What Was Expected. There were times when she could not tell what that was, and struggled to go both with and against whatever she felt was the flow. Anna was fierce. She told me that she was certain her parents had lovers, and although she never acknowledged to her parents that she was aware of their arrangements, her understanding of the ways in which their marriage was "failing" fueled her confidence in her own cause. She could approach her own career and love life without bending to the whims or opinions of those who had not perfected their own situations. When she moved in with Khalid, she was just shy of twenty; no adult was likely to approve. But there was no one whose moral or behavioral advice she sought, and it was the sway of Khalid's career ambitions and the Saudi Arabian embassy that ended their romance, not the pressure exerted upon Anna by the Chinese authorities or her parents. When she finally got her own place during our friendship, she was overjoyed with the freedom it gave her. Everything, for Anna, was about being free of constraints.

Anna's love for Khalid expressed itself in part as a desire to be free of the one-child policy. That desire, like the policy, was as complicated for Anna as it was for my *ayi*, Xiao Gao. Anna acknowledged in our conversations that the government's number-one priority was stability, and that it had to control the population, on behalf not only of its own interests, but also those of the world. And yet what that meant to Anna personally was that she was not allowed to travel freely or decide for herself how many children she would have. This fact, coupled with my particular freedoms, defined the framework of our conversations.

"Can't you have more than one child if you pay a fine?" I asked.

"Yes, but fines are thousands of *yuan*, and that's exactly my point. It's unfair that the only people who have to follow the rules here are the ones who can't pay to break them."

"But that's true everywhere," I argued. "And maybe China thinks that what you want for yourself is a threat for China. If what I wanted were a threat to America, I'd never be allowed to do whatever it was."

"Yeah, but Americans love individuals," she said. "You think the rights belong to each person for herself, so no matter what you want to do, it doesn't matter what happens to everyone else as a result. In China, it's the opposite. The rights belong to a group of people, so if I do the thing I want to do, it will hurt the group. If I have 'freedom of speech,' maybe I will use it to say something that breaks the group down into chaos. And if I have ten kids, someone else can't have any. And the population is a real problem, just like *wending.*" Stability. There was pride in her voice.

"So you can't actually blame the government for its policies," I said.

"No, the Chinese government does an amazing job. It feeds billions of people, and keeps the country calm. But our interests are different—not just mine and the government's, but also mine as a Chinese person and mine as just a person. As part of China, I support the notion that there have to be limits to certain freedoms, in the interest of everybody. But as an individual, I can't stand to have these old men decide for me how many times I get pregnant or where I live or if I love Khalid. Of course, if I had had that five hundred *yuan* when the security guards asked for it, maybe they wouldn't have told the school. As it is, I can't think anything other than what I do is no one else's business. China and my parents say I am selfish."

I thought about how unlikely it was that I would conflate America with my own parents the way Anna did her parents and China. My life was at least as selfish as Anna's: I did not live in the same city as my parents or siblings, did not send them money, and did not take into account their feelings about my romances or lifestyle choices. I did not know whether my parents had lovers, but I suspected they did not. They had been married thirty years and seemed quite happy. They also, like most Americans, did not see my move to China, or my failure to send money home, as evidence of my selfishness. They thought I was young and adventurous, "unique" and independent. Those are not considered good qualities worldwide.

I did not associate Anna with the Chinese government. What was less obvious and more interesting was that until 1999, when NATO bombed the Chinese embassy in Belgrade, the Chinese I met did not associate me with the American government. Nor did they hold me responsible for my government's actions, views, or policies, even when I was most closely associated with America, through pop culture. My Chinese friends recognized that America is a chorus of conflicting voices, not represented by a unified party line. The distinction between Americans and our government came up in conversation constantly in China. It was less common for Americans to acknowledge this complexity in the Chinese, whose presentation tended to be less directly confrontational, since open protest and criticism were not condoned. We often assume a likeness between citizens and their nations; Anna consistently reminded me that it's worth being careful in assumptions about what people present and what they actually believe.

"Do you think you are selfish?" I asked Anna.

"No," she said. "The people I love, I care deeply about them."

"Do you think selfishness is a Western quality?"

"Westerners are allowed to be selfish. It's their right."

I shaved it down to the real question: "Do you think I'm selfish?"

She smiled. "I think you are independent."

"Like you," I proposed.

"More like me than I am," she said.

———

Anna and I were in the office planning a media briefing about constant velocity shafts for an automotive components client when she told me that she wanted to introduce Khalid and me.

"Has he written you back?" I asked, surprised.

"He's in town," she said.

Khalid had appeared back in Beijing to polish his Chinese again, after two years at home in Saudi Arabia, during which time he had apparently married a Saudi Arabian woman in an arranged marriage. He called Anna right away to tell her he was back in Beijing and wanted to see her. He also told Anna on the phone that he did not love his wife. When Anna reported this to me, I was nervous.

"Whether he loves her isn't really the point," I said. "He's married. And be practical. You can't move to Saudi Arabia and be his diplomatic bride. You're not at all diplomatic, first of all."

Anna was worried, and said I might not like Khalid, because now he was "a successful career and a failed personality." I would remember that sentence for years, as she moved restlessly from public relations to real estate, automotive sales to a technology company, computer company to a nonprofit group. Perhaps precisely because of her global brand of career-jumping, Anna kept her personality, which I came to love and admire, intact.

She was quiet as we walked from the company office over to Uncle Sam's Fast Food, a terrible hamburger joint, because Anna said she wanted to have Western food when Khalid and I met. We were unwrapping fast-food packages when he walked in. He was handsome and grown-up-looking, with groomed dark hair and dress pants. We shook hands. I noticed how well manicured his hands were. Anna fluttered around, talking.

"Khalid's Chinese is excellent," she said. She was using Chinese herself.

113

"It's nice to meet you," I said in English. I thought it would be more polite to use English. I didn't want to be patronizing and there's something show-offy about using your nonnative language in a conversation in which you have a choice. But it turned out that Khalid didn't speak English, so I came off as an ugly American for the assumption. We had only Chinese in common. His Chinese was better than mine, and we had few other topics either of us could imagine bringing up.

"Your Chinese is impressive," I said.

"So is yours," he responded.

We all looked around the restaurant. I tried to picture them knowing each other, and remembered a photo album Anna had brought to work one day. It was full of cheesecake photos of her, posing on bridges and under pagodas. Khalid had taken all of them, and they spanned seasons: Anna on ice skates on Houhai Lake, under trees with orange leaves, in a bathing suit at the Beidaihe seashore.

"What's it like being married?" I asked suddenly.

"Good," he said, no beat missed.

We were at a disadvantage with each other, since we were both speaking second languages. We talked across Anna, who was watching us closely. He took my line of questioning as nonhostile, which was half how I intended it. I wondered how Anna understood it. I wanted to like him and to understand what Anna had loved about him, but I was also wary of his reinvolving her after years of not responding to a single letter and marrying someone else.

The three-way dynamic was uncomfortable; I felt more acutely than usual the fact that we outsiders were in Beijing by choice while Anna was there by circumstance. I felt the power Khalid held over Anna not as one I also held in China, but instead as a kind of control he had over me, too. Feeling defensive, I figured he and I would never see each other again and cut to the conversation underneath.

"What's married life like for your wife?" I smiled.

He smiled back. "My wife's life is better than the lives of women in other countries," he said.

"How do you figure that?"

"If you're a woman in Saudi Arabia," he said, "no one disrespects you on the streets. If you're in trouble and men stop to help you, you know they will help you."

"Whereas in other countries . . . ?" I asked.

"You must know the answer to that," he said. "In America if you stop on the street and need help from a man, he's likely to attack you, rape you, even."

"That's ludicrous," I said. "No one who stops to help you in the U.S. is likely to attack you. And besides, why does 'on the street' matter so much? What about in your own house? Or in schools? Professional circles?"

"In Saudi Arabia," he said, "there's no chance of violence against women. Men there respect our women and would never dare hurt them. They're untouchable."

Anna had to translate the last word, "untouchable," but there was no doubt that it belonged to Khalid. We did not touch the subject of women in China, even though I wanted to. I wanted to fight. But Anna stood up suddenly. "We have to get back to the office," she said.

Khalid and I shook hands again and told each other that it was nice to have met.

After work that day, Anna and I trekked to her sister Li Na's house on the western side of town. We took a Chinese bus, squeezed in between office workers leaving work. There was a constant stream of people pouring onto the bus; few seemed to disembark. People were pressed into each other and exhaust blew in from the streets and stuck to us.

We finally shoved our way off the bus into a packed meat market, where I was pushed by the crowd until I was suddenly face to face with a skinned dog, his eyes bulging from between bone and muscle that reminded me of a plastic seventh-grade science model. Anna had stopped to buy groceries for her sister Li Na. The skinned-dog vendor saw me staring at her dog and told me it cost sixty *yuan* per pound. I shook my head, to signal that I wasn't interested in buying, and she muttered, "Yeah, someone told me you *laowai* don't like dogs." I squeezed by her table with my eyes closed.

Li Na's apartment was only a block away. We went through iron gates into the compound, where there were several trees lining the back of the building and a single bush at either side of the entrance. Hers was a nondescript cement building, but someone had carefully planted flowers around its edges, in so little ground that they seemed to straggle out from under the brick walls. The garden gave the impression that if the building could be lifted, underneath might be fertile soil, lush with plants. There was so little grass in Beijing. I could smell garlic frying and hear the sounds of cooking and shouting coming from the windows in Li Na's building. We walked up three cement flights, the air thick with the sweet smell of garbage. Li Na's apartment turned out to be one room on a long hallway. She and her husband shared a bathroom and gas stove with nine other units in the same hall, which was crowded with boxes, furniture, cooking utensils, books, bicycles, and magazines. One bare bulb hung halfway down the hallway, barely illuminating the piles of belongings. There was a laundry wire with faded baby outfits hanging in a tidy row.

Li Na was freshly married to her longtime boyfriend. She was two years older than Anna and worked for a state-owned carpet factory. Anna described her as a "typical Chinese girl." When we arrived, she was scrambling eggs with tomatoes and scallions. Anna introduced us, and Li Na turned shyly from the stove to shake my hand. She had a round face, wider and blander than Anna's, with a short forehead and circular hairline. She gestured to her room and told us to make ourselves comfortable on the bed, that she would serve the food in five minutes. The room had only enough space for the bed itself, one wardrobe, a metal chair, and fifteen boxes stacked from the floor to the ceiling. There were fashion magazines on the bed and chair, and pictures on the room's only visible wall, right above the bed. One was a Chinese New Year poster, featuring fat, pale babies surrounded by floating money and flowers. The other was of Julia Roberts, circa *Pretty Woman*. The door to Li Na's room was open, and neighbors stopped by to chat and snack. It was *renao,* festive of the hot and noisy variety; some people were discussing America and *laowai*, which I did not acknowledge, since I suspected it embarrassed Anna. One woman said that Americans were rich, the other that I must be skinny because I ate Chinese food. All other Americans were fat.

Anna shut the door. "My sister's place has no privacy," she said. "I'm sorry these stupid people are talking about you."

"Please don't apologize," I said. "I like your sister's place. It feels like living with your family, like other people care what's going on with you. If something happened and you didn't come home for a few days, everyone would miss you immediately."

I was overcompensating, but I couldn't help it. Poverty isn't quaint, but I couldn't bear to agree with Anna that the apartment was a nightmare.

Li Na was "more Chinese" than Anna, as Anna put it, and therefore had a job in a state-owned enterprise and lived in her work-unit apartment. She did not speak English, had no money, married a patriotic husband, and was beloved by her and Anna's mother. Their mother could talk to Li Na, not only in a way she could not talk to Anna, but also about Anna. Li Na told Anna everything their mother said; this was how Anna knew her mother thought she was selfish and foreign. All of Anna's information about their father came from Li Na as well. "Li Na is on the inside of my family," Anna said in Chinese. "My father loves me, but that doesn't keep me from being on the outside. My mother can't stand or understand me."

Li Na had opened the door and was holding a plate of gleaming yellow eggs and tomatoes cut into cubes, which she set down on a fold-out table. She handed us chopsticks. She had been listening to our conversation.

"I think it's uncaring," she said, "the way American parents kick their kids out when the kids turn eighteen." This stereotype was a favorite among the *Foreign Babes in Beijing* crew; in the script, Old Man Li tries to convince Louisa's wealthy expatriate father, Jack, to help Louisa buy an apartment, but Jack refuses. "She's grown up," he explains. "I never help her."

This filtered down from the script to our conversations on the set. By way of explaining the relationship between Tianming and his parents, Director Yao and Wu Jie told me that families in China were "not like your Western family." They meant that the Li family would be sad to see Tianming go, and that leaving his parents and his country would feel to him like a sacrifice. Unlike my parents, the Lis would not be relieved to see their child leave as soon as he was eighteen. I defended my parents earnestly, explaining the truth: they still took care of me, even from afar, and would have been delighted if I had stayed with them until I was old and infirm. I insisted that my parents paid not only for my college education, but also for dinner when we went out to eat. We did not split the check, as the producers suggested; my parents were still and would likely always be my parents. Director Yao and Wu Jie found this filial and charming, but were not persuaded. The evidence spoke for itself; my parents had let me fly to China unchaperoned. Would Director Yao and Wu Jie have let their children study or live in the U.S.? Yes. Would they have been relieved to see the kids go? Of course not. No parent likes to see his or her child leave for a land far away.

Li Na amended her statement, perhaps because Anna shot her a look. In case I was offended, she added, "All the same, I'd love to have curly hair, like an American." She pointed to Julia Roberts, smiling above the bed with huge, square teeth.

"That's a perm," I said. "You can get one at the Palace Hotel in Beijing."

Li Na smiled disbelievingly and went out into the hallway to get a thermos of tea. Anna was seated on her sister's bed with a plate of food on the mattress in front of her. She was organizing her food around the sides of the plate. "It was awkward with you and Khalid today," she said in English. "You were unsuitable for each other. Maybe because your cultures are so different."

"Maybe," I agreed. "Maybe we just don't know each other so well. I mean, aren't your cultures different, too?"

She sighed. "I guess so," she said, and as evidence, she told me that Khalid's new wife had to sit in the back of the house with a "cloth" over her face whenever men came over to play cards, five nights a week. I was surprised he wasn't busier with matters of the state. Anna glanced at Julia Roberts.

"Khalid's and my dream of love is over," she said. Then she paused before asking, "Do you think his wife is pretty?"

"I don't know," I said. I had an urge to tear Julia Roberts off the wall.

"God," she said, "now he's married to this arranged girl. It's such a waste."

"What do you mean, a waste?"

"If she has to wear a cloth over her face anyway, then why couldn't she have been Chinese?"

From *Foreign Babes in Beijing*
Episode Nineteen

Jiexi and Louisa sit in Jiexi's dorm room.

JIEXI
(Putting her head in her hands)
My father won't condone my marriage to Tianming.
He says Chinese people are lazy and uncultured.

LOUISA
(Gasping)
But that's prejudiced!

FOUR

Reqing

Passion

W e filmed *Foreign Babes in Beijing* backward, starting with the last scene on the first day. It was apt, since my sense of time and life in Beijing was upside down. In the final scene, Tianming and Jiexi say good-bye to Tianming's family and leave for America. Because I had not read the script, I had no idea what events had led up to this decision. I knew only that Jiexi was a foreign exchange student and that she and Tianming were lovers.

I was distracted from asking questions by the reality of how brutally cold it was on the set that day. No one gave direction. Assuming we were happy to be going home, I grinned and shivered, covered from head to foot in the fur coat with which the costumers had originally decorated me. Fashioned from two short coats sewn together, the fur monster dragged on the ground. I was careful not to trip. Underneath the coat I had on a minidress of my own. The crew had chosen all of Jiexi's outfits from my own wardrobe, save the fur coats and rhinestone earrings. From the piles of clothing they asked me to bring, they preferred the few with bright colors in them, including one red business suit, a strange choice for a foreign exchange student. They were disappointed that I wore mostly earth tones, black and white. "But foreigners wear loud and colorful garments," they protested.

The day she and Tianming left for America, Jiexi had been embellished by the makeup team, and had frosted lips and tall hair. I looked like a *Dallas* rerun from the 1980s. I told the costumers that no foreign girl living in Beijing would ever dress so fancily. "We wear jeans and boots," I said.

"It's not what you want, *Ruiqiu*," they said. "It's what the audience wants to see."

On the set, the props manager handed me two empty suitcases, which I carried around until he took them away again. Sophie, the German girl they had cast to play the good girl, Louisa, was posing in the "living room" of our set with people I guessed must be playing Tianming's parents and brother. Sophie was a good girl even in real life, studying Chinese acupuncture and trying to lead a local life. She was a China-hand of the I-have-better-Chinese-than-you-do variety, and her life there had yielded a long list of local accomplishments. She lived in a work-unit-like dorm, said almost exclusively polite things in Chinese, and carried needles to the set every day, begging for arms and ears on which to practice. I did not offer limbs up, but Wu Jie did. He encouraged me to let Sophie stab my arms, telling me how good she was. "Relaxing!" he said.

Sophie was a good ambassador, and calmed people down on the set. She pulled me aside when I first arrived and spoke English so crisp and fluent that I was hugely relieved. "We're all sad, you see," she said, "because Jiexi and Tianming are leaving."

"Okay." I did not ask questions. Instead I savored the first tiny bite of information I had understood all day.

"You're Jiexi," she added, diluting my pleasure with this already-easy, redundant knowledge. I needed more useful straws to grasp.

We stood in the doorway, then stood on the landing. Director Yao wanted a close-up of my face. He said something I didn't understand.

"Look unhappy," said Sophie. I looked unhappy.

"She can act!" said Director Yao. "Now," he directed, "walk up to Tianming's father and gaze at him and cry out 'Baba!'"

This was before I learned to ask questions. I walked up to an old man on the set, said "Baba!" and tried to gaze at him. It was awkward.

"Can you be more *reqing*?" Director Yao asked. Passionate. Sophie raised her eyebrows encouragingly.

I walked up to the old man again, and hotly yelled, "Baba!"

"Good!" said Director Yao. It was a take. Then he wanted a second close-up on my face, and I took a compact out of my coat pocket. I had a smudge of lipstick on the side of my face, which I wiped at. The crew waited.

Director Yao said to the cameraman, "She's *ziai*." *Zi* is "self," and *ai* is "love."

I told Director Yao I had understood the word, and he said, "It's a good quality. It means you are concerned with taking care of yourself." They thought I was vain, which made sense. Jiexi was vain, too. Director Yao looked me over. "You need to wear warmer clothes from now on, Jiexi," he said.

I did not mention that I was worried that stacking clothing might prevent me from looking glamorous. No one else seemed worried about that, but I had always thought television was a fantasy to be lived through; actors were beautiful and had bright white teeth and halos over their hair and skin. I had always understood that to be part of the reason people watch TV shows; glamour is aspirational. But in China, foreigners are cast fairly regularly, often at random, so those on TV look (at best) like regular people. It wasn't important to the *Babes* team that I look like anything other than an American girl, yet looking harried and sloppy seemed to me to be a failure at the medium.

Tianming was on his knees shouting, "Father!" and holding his arms out to the old man, who half fell and half bent down to pull up his bowing son. Jiexi was supposed to be standing still at Tianming's side, holding on to her suitcase. Director Yao took the shot several times. Each time, Tianming cried louder, and Director Yao demanded he be more *reqing*.

I had watched so little Chinese television that I didn't realize yet that acting means a different thing to Chinese audience members than it does to Americans. Even before "reality TV" came along, American shows always tried to suspend their audience's disbelief. We watched a plastic but gorgeous depiction of reality, not a complete abandonment of it. Even soap operas, which flaunt eyebrow acting and histrionics, are subtle compared to *Babes*.

TV in China highlights the acting, not just the actor. There is no pretense in China that art should be reflective of reality. Television acting there is the love child of the studied, exaggerated movements and vocals of Peking Opera, and the melodrama of socialist theater. If art is to be revolutionary, a vehicle for political and moral messages, its audience must be distanced, watching, listening, and learning. And if the acting style in China seemed odd to me in the context of the restraint I observed there in daily interactions, Chinese may have perceived my desire for understatement as a departure from real life as a loud foreigner.

The crew was delighted with Jiexi's "sadness," and I was too relieved not to have disappointed them to consider how my performance would look later. But that same week, when I opened the *China Daily* to do press clippings for Charlotte, there was a picture of me gazing at Wang Ling with uncharacteristically hot emotion. Some kind of panic fanned out in my chest. The *China Daily* was China's only national English-language publication. Its circulation was three hundred thousand, mainly expatriates, Chinese businessmen, and economists. The headline read: "Series Shows Foreign View of Beijing."

Xiao Li asked me to sign her *China Daily*. She tacked the picture to her bulletin board, but the rest of my colleagues crept around, avoiding me. I was bewildered, but it made perfect sense. I had been in the office for only four months, was about to be on TV, and paraded with a fur coat and a tower of hair in the Communist Party's English-language paper. Everyone's suspicions had been confirmed; I led a weirdly different life and was not to be befriended casually.

Feeling protective, Wang Ling stayed nearby all the time, translating Chinese into other Chinese he thought I'd be more likely to comprehend. I was becoming more like Jiexi every minute. I understood nothing, not even the scenes we were shooting the next day. Wang Ling worked to figure out what time I had to be at the studio, and tried to warn me in advance. The fourth day, he told me I had to be at the studio at five A.M. I expressed shock, and Assistant Director Xu, eavesdropping, couldn't resist breaking in with, "We told you! It's more convenient to live at the studio, like the other actors!"

The crew had lost face because I refused to live at the studio with Sophie, who was *ting hua*, obedient, just like her character Louisa. I told them that I could not live at the studio and continue my part-time work for the American firm, which was helping build bridges between China and the U.S. I said I loved my new Chinese apartment and had signed a year-long contract. They offered to call my landlord, but I declined. My real reason, which of course they understood, was that there was no actors' union in Beijing. I worried they would wake us during the night to film, and I was unwilling to be available day and night either to the crew or to my office. Plus, I had just bought a couch, a stove, a new gas tank, and some spatulas for the Fangzhuang place. I had a fabulous sense of accomplishment, and did not want to give up my housewares to move to a double dorm room with Sophie.

Director Yao, annoyed that they might want to find me and be unable to, presented me with a pager. "It's a gift," he said, signifying that I was to show gratitude.

"Thank you!" I said.

"Now we can find you all the time, Jiexi!" he said.

I pinned the pager to the belt loop of my jeans. "Looks good, too!" I joked.

I arrived at Beiying at five A.M. the following day. There was no one to be seen. The air was so cold and dry that it burned down my throat and into my lungs. I closed my eyes and imagined it was airplane air. I walked back out to the gates, hoping to see Sophie or Wang Ling arrive. When a street vendor appeared, I bought a *mantou*, steamed bun, and breathed the heat in to thaw myself. No one arrived until eight, by which time I thought my face might have to be amputated. We did not begin filming until eleven, and I asked Assistant Director Xu repeatedly when they would need me. Each time, she responded, "*Mashang.*" *Mashang* is my least favorite Chinese word. It means literally "on horseback," or "on the way/immediately." The Chinese idea of immediately was so far away from my idea of it, that I came to think *mashang* meant, "First I'll ride horses for several hours, and then I'll tend to whatever your request is."

At three, I struggled not to cry when Assistant Director Xu told me it had "turned out" that they didn't need Jiexi that day or the next. I stalked out of the studio, holding my breath, and went directly to the office, where I turned my attention to press clippings for Charlotte. My Taiwanese colleague Gary had given me responsibility for all the newspaper reading, and I often wondered through what eyes he had read the articles I now read. Sino-U.S. relations were at the lowest point they had reached in sixteen years, because America had welcomed a visit from Taiwan's leader Lee Teng-hui in May 1995. Gary never revealed whether he cared in any way other than "for the benefit of our clients," as he often put it. The Chinese press was full of scathing reviews of America for "recognizing Taiwan," and he became increasingly withdrawn and hostile in the office. I wondered whether Sino-U.S. relations could filter down into my moods in the same way.

In October, President Clinton and Chinese President Jiang Zemin had met at a United Nations summit, so by December reconciliation seemed a happy possibility. I read the *New China News Agency*, which featured articles about brides preferring cattle to money as dowries in rural China, butter statues made in honor of the Panchen Lama in Tibet, and human rights abuses in the U.S. The Western press was filled with Beijing's threats to Taiwan, infanticide in rural China, and human-interest stories about pandas mating.

Beiying paged me that night at one A.M., but I had no phone and could not call the studio. The pager's ID screen flashed Beiying's number angrily. I looked around my apartment: mattress, black vinyl couch with some jeans thrown over its arm, blond wood table, fridge. I had bought two shadow puppets, one an intellectual with a cap and glasses and the other a Red Guard with an armband and uniform. They were flat on my table, posed with their little limbs attached to marionette sticks. They looked like Jiexi and Louisa to me, grotesque and exaggerated. Unable to sleep anyway, I ventured down the eighteen flights of stairs with my flashlight.

By the time I got downstairs, it was 1:10 A.M., and the compound was jet-black and smelled like fresh-poured pavement. I wondered whether people had been at work on the parking lots that day. There were no phone booths open, since the blocky public phones were manned by *ayis*, aunties who collected payment for calls. Everyone was asleep. I should have known; I had come back late at night often enough to know that this far out on Second Ring Road, stalls closed early. A tiny dog yapped from someone's apartment nearby. Most of the compound's inhabitants were members of China's new middle class; they were well off enough to have yipping lapdogs, which cost 1,000 *yuan* each to register, per Beijing's 1995 dog laws. Instead of diminishing in numbers, dogs became hairy status symbols, name brands on leather leashes, barking out, "I cost at least one thousand *yuan*, not including food and shelter." Charlotte had six Maltese puppies, which she once brought to the office. One of them had thrown up on the others in the car, so they all reeked, but the staff crowded around, diligently chirping about how cute they were, and quietly thinking about the 6,000 *yuan* they cost to register.

A construction zone flickered in the distance; its workers looked like moths fluttering by the lights. I walked in circles for a while, thinking that daytime and nighttime smelled different in Beijing. I couldn't remember whether that was true of the West. Did America even have a smell? Did it differ at night? Had I never paid attention in my own world, and if not, why not?

At 1:15 A.M. in Beijing, it was 1:15 P.M. in Michigan. I took a cab to CITIC, watching the nighttime go by. Every sign flashed at me, neon Hyundai, Coca-Cola, Motorola, traffic lights. By the time I got to the office, I couldn't bring myself to call Beiying. I didn't want to be Rui Qiu, who couldn't understand or respond properly even to the simplest gestures and words. I didn't call Beiying because I didn't want to hear my Chinese name. Instead, I called my parents, and told them that my life was so weird I wasn't sure I was a person they had met.

"Of course we've met you, *Yang Niu* [Foreign Babe]!" my father joked. "Keep in mind, this is the kind of experience most people never get to enjoy. Live it up a bit. Call Beiying back in the morning; whatever they need can wait."

"The work itself is impossible," I said. "They never even tell me in advance what we're doing or why or when or where."

"I think that's true of most productions," he said. "Try not to hold it against the studio."

"But I'm gangrenous from waiting outside," I fussed. "This never happens to Screen Actors Guild actors."

"How long did you have to wait?"

"From five until three, and then they didn't have any of my scenes anyway."

130

"China is a patient place," my dad said, kidding me. "When in Beijing, do as the Beijing *ren* do; give it five thousand years." He put my mom on, and she comforted me and offered to airmail soup.

I rode back to my apartment and climbed the thousands of stairs to sleep. Three hours later, at five A.M., Beiying was paging me every twenty seconds. I ran downstairs and called the studio from a reopened public phone.

"Where are you?" Assistant Director Xu shouted into the phone.

"Home," I said.

"You're late!" she said.

"Today none of my scenes," I said.

"Changed! Today has!" she reported.

"No one told me."

"We paged you."

"I have no phone."

"Come to Beiying, *ba.*"

"I have to work at my office today."

"Today has—you fall in love with Tianming scenes."

I did not know how to say no to them. China made me passive in strange ways; the pressure to do things people asked of me was intense and confusing. It was easier to do them than to argue or avoid doing them. This was part of being a guest, of feeling like I did not own my place or time in China and was not fluent enough to explain with empathy or finesse why I wanted or did not want to do things. So I rushed to the studio, where everyone was in a fury that I was late, and I was in a fury that I'd had to cancel my company hours. The cast was on the cast bus. We were going to *Bing Deng*. I took out my tiny dictionary and sat down next to Wang Ling. "*Bing Deng?*" I asked. He

131

flipped through the dictionary. *"Bingqiling de bing."* Ice-cream ice. Okay. So *bing* was ice? How did that explain where we were going?

"How far is it?"

"Don't know," he said. "Maybe five hours."

"Maybe five hours?"

"Maybe two hours," he said.

"Is it five hours or two hours?"

"Bu qingchu." Unclear.

"Where is it?"

"Beijing *bei bianr.*" North.

"Is it outside Beijing?"

"Beijing *bei bianr.*"

I contemplated walking down the aisle to ask the bus driver how far it was, but the aisle was filled with people: makeup women, consistency staff, lighting guys, grips, styrofoam boards. I couldn't move. I sat back, determined not to be restless, even though I couldn't be informed. Why not just sit and enjoy the ride? I had slept two hours the night before. Who cared if I had no idea what we were doing or where we were going?

But I was wide awake, wired. The buildings became sparse and trees multiplied. Two hours out of the city, hills sloped up either side of the highway. I could see mountains in the distance, thin wisps of cloud just above them. The landscape was blotchy, its colors fanning out into thinner sky, blue now that we were out of range of Beijing pollution. I cracked the window and inhaled deeply; the air was freezing and lovely. Migrant workers in padded clothing walked along the highway, carrying baskets, children, and tools. I watched a grandmother hold her grandchild up so that he could pee out of baby pants with a fully open seam. Most babies in

China wear buttless pants and seem quite happy to be free of wet diapers; I was surprised only that the baby would wear such pants once it was cold. Wang Ling napped, inclining slightly toward me on the seat. I wondered whether he had a baby.

Seven hours later, after the bus broke down and was repaired by a team of mechanics whose own bus broke down immediately after they fixed ours, we finally came upon *Bing Deng*, which had an English sign: "Ice Lantern Festival." It was a tourist site for Chinese tourists, an ice palace the size of a small city. The palace featured intricate infrastructure, including a gigantic arched ice roof and essential public works: ice bridges, pagodas, corniced roofs, and city walls. It was an enormous, overbearing, poetic igloo of a choice for the place where Jiexi and Tianming should court, full of sparkly renditions of real creatures: purple birds with icicle beaks, snow-maned lions, and life-sized model-worker Popsicles. The crew chattered about the beauty of the place, with sincerity so enthusiastic that I mistook it for obligation. I was bemused that anyone would undertake the effort to build such an ice city; the crew talked as if they had stepped into our script.

We walked under the roof. Everyone froze. Colorful neon lights projected onto the statues, glowed out from behind ice walls, poured down ice mountains, and made deceptively warm the structures in which Director Yao told us to *wan*, or play. The word "play" in Chinese has less of an age limit than its English equivalent, and all the same suggestive appeal. It's also half the Chinese word for "fun," which is *hao wan*, "good" and "play." I thought of the Chinese syllables I used as Legos. They were bright and snapped together to create compound shapes. I memorized new ones by color, setting up toy language structures in my mind.

When people spoke to me, the sounds of their words were Tetris shapes, falling. All I had to do was put each one in its bright, satisfying place.

"*Ni pa leng ma?*" Wang Ling asked me. I took the sounds apart. You, fear, cold, question. Do you fear cold? I thought not only of the syllables, but also the stroke marks of each character, coming together to form its word. My teeth chattered.

"I'm freezing," I said.

"Wear long underwear, *ba.*" When he used the imperative *ba*, it sounded manly.

"I'm trying to look *haokan* for the show." *Haokan*, "good" and "look." Good-looking.

"What does long underwear have to do with that?"

Director Yao pointed us to a wavy ice wall filled with holes and directed us in Chinese. Wang Ling mimed for me, running prettily along the wall and poking his hands through the holes. I joined him. "Yes!" he said in English. Then he went to the other side of the wall and I followed. "No!" he said. Okay. I was supposed to be on one side and he was on the other. We peeked through at each other. "Now *pao bu!*" said Director Yao. We ran.

Jiexi and Tianming's prancing ended at an ice sculpture of a large bird with pink light projected up and off its wings. "Beautiful!" Wang Ling said, looking up at the bird.

"Here you will have dialogue," Director Yao told us. "Rui Qiu, button your coat! It's freezing! Do you know your dialogue?"

Jiexi was supposed to say to Tianming, "*Nandao ni kanbuchulai wo xi huan ni.*" Don't tell me you can't tell I like you.

Tianming would respond, "*Wo bu ben, Jiexi, danshi wo shi jielehun de nanren.*" I'm not stupid, Jiexi, but I'm a married man.

Reqing, Passion

We stood facing each other. Ice crystals crowned Wang Ling's hair. The props handler took my People's Liberation Army coat, on loan from the studio, ready to throw it back on me as soon as Director Yao said, "Take." Underneath, Jiexi wore a flashy pink felt coat with big buttons. She peered out at Tianming from under a suede cap.

"Action!" said Director Yao.

"Don't tell me you can't tell I like you," Jiexi said through her chattering teeth. I was still attracted to the possibility of balancing out the unsubtle dialogue with some facial understatement. So Jiexi smiled up at Tianming with half her mouth, perhaps imperceptibly.

He looked at her. "I'm not stupid," he said, "but I am married. I have responsibilities to my wife and family."

Jiexi nodded, attentive. Was this supposed to be news to her? Wang Ling looked at me. I had neither met nor heard anything about Wang Ling's wife, except monosyllabic responses to the few questions I had asked about her. How is she, what does she do. She was fine and worked for a French company. I wasn't sure whether the responses were curt because he wanted to avoid a discussion or because he wanted to improve my chances of understanding them. It occurred to me that he didn't want me to know he was married.

"I don't want to break up your marriage," Jiexi told Tianming. "I just want to be your lover, okay?"

"That's not okay in China. This is a traditional place," Tianming said.

"As far as I can tell," Jiexi responded, "there are lots of lovers in China. This situation is standard."

They stared at each other. Tianming grinned, whether at me or Jiexi, I wasn't sure.

"Cut," said Director Yao. He walked over to us.

"Do it again," he said. "More *reqing*, Jiexi." More passionate, exuberant.

I looked at Director Yao as if I couldn't understand. I didn't want to play this moment with "hot feeling." He moved his face into a rubber mask of some hugely exaggerated emotion I couldn't identify and shouted at Wang Ling, "I love you! Be my lover!"

I stood there for a minute, contemplating the effort it would require to argue.

"Okay," I said in English. I redid the scene, à la Muppet.

Director Yao gave me a thumbs-up with both hands. "Yes! Take!"

We waited while the crew organized the lights for the next shot. My feet began to pulsate and then went numb, as if power to them had been shut off. Wang Ling taught me how to say, "I can't feel them," in Chinese. "Yes," I parroted happily, *"ganjue bu dao."* Then, inspired, I added an expression I had learned in Chinese class at college. "They're frozen to death!"

"How do you know how to say this?" Wang Ling asked. The props and makeup people were gathered around, as was an increasingly large crowd of random rubberneckers, who had gathered to watch us film. "I learned at college," I said.

Someone in the crowd shouted, "She can talk!" meaning I could speak Chinese, but holding on to the basic principle that no foreigner can ever actually learn Chinese and therefore keeping the declaration nonspecific.

Encouraged, I continued. "I took Chinese class for two years. It was difficult. The teachers liked to be strict." There was an audible inhalation from the crowd. People looked embarrassed and then dispersed. Wang Ling stayed.

"What happened?" I asked him.

"Nothing," he said. We boarded the bus.

Two days later, while we were filming Jiexi and Tianming's trip to the wax museum, Wang Ling told me what my mistake had been. We were standing in front of a diorama of wax statues, waiting to talk about sex. The lights crew was setting up spotlights on our pores.

"*Yange,*" he said, looking directly at me, "strict."

"Uh-huh," I said. "Strict. *Ni shenme yisi?*" You have what meaning?

"Do you remember?" he asked in newly learned English.

"Remember *shenme?*" I asked in Chinglish.

"Uh. You say—" he began.

"Use Chinese," I suggested.

"The other day, when you said that the Chinese teachers at Columbia were strict?"

"Eh?" I asked, fidgeting.

"*Yange* should be third tone, third tone. But your *yange* was first tone, first tone."

I blanched. "*Na?*" So?

"Well," he said, "this kind means . . ." he stopped. He glanced around and then down. He took his fingers and moved them below his waist in a scissors motion, snipping away.

We looked at each other. Circumcised?

"Get it?" he asked.

I was eager to have this conversation over. "Got it *le,*" I said, closing off the phrase with a *le,* indicating that the action of "getting it" was complete.

But he sensed it wasn't true and flipped through his dictionary. "Like the eunuchs," he said, pointing to the word "castration."

We turned toward the cameras. The wax scene behind us was set in a bedroom; its stars were plasticky renditions of an emperor and his concubine. "Who are they?" Jiexi asked, gesturing toward the sticky dolls.

"The emperor and his concubine," said Tianming. I could hear the cameras.

"What about you?" Jiexi asked.

"What about me?" Tianming echoed.

"So it's not true that you Chinese men can't love anybody other than your wives?"

Wang Ling and I watched each other carefully, acting.

"Look away from her, Wang Ling!" Director Yao shouted. We took the shot again.

"Who's that?" Jiexi asked.

"The emperor and his concubine," Tianming said. He looked away. Then he turned back to look at me. We smiled at each other. One of his eyebrows raised.

He rubbed my socked and frozen feet for the second time on the way home. Electricity traveled from my feet to my knees. I wondered what the boundaries were for flirtation in Chinese. In fact, they were stricter than my own experience had prepared me for, and this gesture was more suggestive than I understood.

The next day was Saturday, and I had agreed to put in hours at the office by participating in a donut meeting. Until May 1995, China had a six-day work week, so the office was lively all weekend. Our client and their Chinese joint venture partner were holding a press briefing and banquet to announce and celebrate their new donut partnership. Several days before the meeting, I had written a press release about how donuts would improve the quality of life in Beijing, and how vast were the benefits of new technology for refrigerating donuts during morning rides to retail outlets. After I faxed a copy to our American contact at the donut company, she called me to talk about the translation into Chinese and asked, with no irony, whether "the Chinese have a word for 'prowess.' "

"I assume so," I said, marveling over the fact that she could think English speakers had a monopoly on 'prowess,' or that the concept was an American invention.

First thing Saturday morning, people gathered in the conference room, and Charlotte incited controversy over whether Chinese people like to eat sweets. Xiao Li and Anna were both present. "Chinese people don't like sugar, right? They hate chocolate!" Charlotte told them. "We need to advise the client of this problem. Perhaps 'sweet rings' is not a good name for donuts in Chinese." My colleagues couldn't agree, primarily because some people like to eat sweets and others don't, but also because no one wanted to contradict Charlotte.

But the question of whether Chinese people like donuts never came up at the client meeting itself, because the nine hours we spent with the joint venture partner, Mr. Sun, were devoted entirely to fighting over minutiae. Charlotte struggled to follow; Anna was doing her best to translate everything, but the conversation was heated and redundant. We were unable to make progress on any of the agenda items, since each one, as we approached it, became tangled and elevated to an unmanageable level. Gary and Mr. Sun argued bitterly over the wording of a banner. No Chinese event happens without at least one banner, usually a red background with white lettering. The arguing started with background and lettering colors (forty-five minutes), moved into where the banners would be hung (forty-five minutes), and ended with whether the English version needed to be drafted or approved by our company (an hour).

Charlotte misinterpreted the pace as evidence that Mr. Sun was stupid, which she seethed about when we took a bathroom break. These men, she said, were disorganized, and with a little bit of Western management training, China's state-owned sector would not be failing. This idea, that the West should come into China and convert the system to one like ours, through public relations or any kind of training, was ludicrous. Edward Hume, a twenty-nine-year-old Yale graduate who went to China in 1905 to help start a medical school and hospital in Changsha, put it this way: "Unless a foreign institution or a foreign individual can become absorbed into a living tree, the thing dies. We have got to bend our energies now with renewed strength to the grafting of ourselves into the living tree of China." What were needed, he argued, were "foreigners who *love* the Chinese."[16]

Charlotte and Gary were not foreigners who loved China. They lost their tempers in meetings, scolded employees, cabdrivers, and waiters; they made *ayis* execute their most basic daily tasks. Later, I knew that foreigners who did love China were plentiful. I met dozens who had spent decades in and out of the country, who spoke and studied Chinese, loved Chinese food, and had profound friendships with Chinese people. But it took me time to find them.

"There are no English speakers at your company," Gary said to Mr. Sun, the pitch of his voice shooting up and the underlying accusation, that the company was not global or sophisticated, louder than the sentence itself.

"We will write both banners," Mr. Sun said. "The content is our responsibility."

"So, what will the English one say?" asked Gary.

"It will be a translation of the Chinese. We have translators at our company, too." Implying that Gary was a translator, when he had Gary's name card and knew that he was a senior consultant, was deeply insulting. Gary balked.

"We suggest the Chinese banner be a translation of the English, since our client is funding the whole event and their senior executives are coming from America."

Mr. Sun held his hand flat out and waved it at Gary, cutting him off before he had a chance to add that the American partner owned 51 percent of the joint venture.

In American negotiations, any gain for one party is a loss for the other. There is back-and-forth movement associated with negotiating in the U.S., whereas in China the movement is a sideways one. A great example of sideways negotiating is the 1972 Shanghai Communiqué, during which America and China reached an agreement that there was "one China." With diplomatic relations yet to be established, the U.S. could not agree to recognize Beijing as the one China. Beijing would not abide the U.S. mentioning Taiwan. So both sides agreed that there was "one China," but they did not agree on which China was the "one." It was conflict-avoidance ambiguity; by not making an argument explicit, everyone could move on from it or *wang kai san mian,* leave three sides of the net open.

Charlotte had no patience for leaving the net open. "There are native English speakers at our company!" she said, not realizing that Gary and Mr. Sun had already had that conversation dozens of times. "We can't have broken English on the signage." I watched

141

Anna, the only PRC national sitting on our side of the table. She was staring down.

No one dared bring up any strategic question, not even the one about whether to call donuts "sweet rings"; such a conversation might have lasted months. We finally agreed that the joint venture partner would draft the sign and we would be allowed to proofread it, precisely what Mr. Sun had originally suggested. But by the time we reached "consensus," we were so wilted from the haggling that we felt we had won a small victory. And that, of course, was Mr. Sun's strategy. It was a common tactic in China; even the missionaries who traveled to China in the late Ming and early Qing Dynasties had had the same experience as Charlotte. They were so swamped with entertaining, meeting, and negotiating with the emperors that their lifetimes swept by without them converting anyone but themselves.[17] In PR, we were not good at learning from China's history. Instead, we reinvented wheels and sacrificed our colleagues', clients', and partners' faces. Often, while repeating history, we lost face ourselves.

As for Charlotte, she was one small player in a long tradition of Westerners harboring the happy illusion that they both could and should change China. While we Westerners have come and gone, China has changed at its own pace, gradually at times, quickly at others, within plan at times, but most often outside it. What may be more predictable is how China changes us.

I was in the unenviable position of responsibility for a "contact report," which meant that I had to record every moment of the meeting. I was grinding my teeth and thought they might be turning into sand. Anna suddenly passed me a note. Her face was turned sharply down now, angrily, I thought. I myself was so annoyed that I assumed she was embarrassed by the behavior of the JV partner or Charlotte's shouting about broken English. But Anna's note read: "Gary does not consider himself Chinese."

Perhaps she chose me as the audience for this remark since there was no question or expectation of my considering myself Chinese. But I wondered why that would make me a less offensive presence. I nodded vaguely in response, a worse ambassador than Gary and yet taking part in an exchange at his expense. I was tempted to record Anna's note in the contact report; it was the meeting's only moment of truth. Gary did not, in fact, consider himself Chinese. He was proud to be distinguished from Mr. Sun and the local staff, and proud of his democratic homeland of Taiwan. And Anna, like anyone faced with a patriot from elsewhere, became patriotic herself.

O n Sunday, we were supposed to film, but crisis erupted on the set. I brought Chinese Lotte-brand cakes, as soft-soundings research into whether Chinese people would like to eat our client's "sweet rings." But as we were digging in, Assistant Director Xu told Sophie that Sophie had gotten "too fat." Hence, her face looked *mei name piaoliang,* not so pretty, on camera. Sophie, exhausted by twenty-hour days (they woke her to film at night), boxed lunches three meals a day, and no privacy, had a meltdown. She cried, and I comforted her on the stairs of the courtyard house and told her the truth, which was that she wasn't fat. I reminded her that the producers were interested in expediency and were willing to sacrifice her well-being. Assistant Director Xu was just being defensive because Sophie looked tired. Nothing worked. "But you're beautiful," I said, over and over. "Who cares what Assistant Director Xu says? You're lovely—everyone agrees. Assistant Director Xu must have some other reason for having said this. Has she lost face in some way? Why did she say it?"

"Because I'm fat!" Sophie said, and then she went to lie down. We couldn't film all morning. There had to be some kind of resolution, so we had it out on the set.

"I only care about her," Assistant Director Xu told me, "that's why I said her face is too fat. She has to be careful about her health."

Everyone directed comments at me. In this single instance, I became the expert on foreign women, since they believed I could convince Sophie to come back and hurry up with filming. Wu Jie, in his adorable and miscalibrated way, bought her a box of chocolates. He walked into the office, where Assistant Director Xu, Director Yao, Line Producer Cao, Wang Ling, and I were meeting. He handed me the chocolates. "So I can be too fat, too?" I asked, grinning. No one laughed.

"Deliver to Sophie," he said. "A gift from me."

I stared at him to see if he was joking. He wasn't.

"Thank you," I said. "Good choice."

"Now," said Line Producer Cao. "We have to film right now. You Americans are so selfish. There's a whole cast of actors waiting for Sophie."

"She's German," I said.

"Selfish," he said again, under his breath. Was he not admitting that she wasn't American? Were all Westerners selfish? I thought about it. Maybe. There is a certain selfishness about shutting down a production just because your feelings are hurt, and I would have done it, too.

"Her feelings are hurt," I said. I knew what had to happen, but by now I had a weak grasp on the rules, which included never saying what you wanted to happen right out. This was not something I was good at, and in this instance I didn't really care when we started filming again. Having been at the mercy of this group many times, I rather enjoyed watching them wriggle under Sophie's control. She never broke rules. I was always the one in trouble. Only several nights before, I had caught Line Producer Cao reimbursing the Russian babe for cab fare, and burst into humiliated tears, because my own negotiation tactics were so pathetic that I was paying my own cab fares every day. They were chagrined that I cried; it was a loss of face for the whole studio every time one of us was unhappy enough to cry. We worked out an appalling deal: they paid 10 *yuan* for every one of my 100-*yuan* cab rides.

Sophie's wound was harder to remedy. No one likes to be told she's fat, especially while memorizing Chinese dialogue and delivering it in romantic scenes. It's not rude in China to suggest that someone is *pang* or has *pangqilai le*, gotten a little fatter. *Pang* is a cute word, one that suggests a chubby prosperity. But "too" pang is rude. I knew that Assistant Director Xu had, in fact, been rude to Sophie and had meant to hurt her feelings, but a productive solution would involve spinning the story so that Assistant Director Xu had been thoughtful and caring when she suggested Sophie lose weight. She had meant Sophie's face would look more healthy (we revised from pretty to healthy). Sophie, who was sensitive (but not oversensitive), was hurt.

"It's a cultural problem," I suggested, since everyone on the set liked to talk about cultural problems.

"Ah!" said Director Yao. "This is just what the show is about."

"Maybe you should just say 'sorry' so that we can continue filming," I suggested gingerly to Assistant Director Xu. "You meant well, but Sophie is used to her Western customs and so she feels bad." When I said this, I had an out-of-body experience. Some other Rachel floated up and asked me whether Bumper Harvest Du was actually sitting in building 16, explaining that Sophie was "used to her Western customs." I had heard such sentences and felt scornful; people who spoke them were living after-school specials. There was suddenly a small, American version of me, sitting on my shoulder, whispering into my ear: "There's no escaping it. This is actually your life. You will begin to say things like this more and more often." Indeed, within several months I found myself justifying things I did (including not being friends with the landlord, not going on our company retreat to an amusement park, not wanting to guzzle endless amounts of fire liquor at client banquets, and not singing karaoke) by explaining that I was "used to my Western customs." It was, of course, something the script would have had Jiexi say, not to mention a confession that all Westerners had "ways" in common, something I was in the habit of denying.

When Assistant Director Xu apologized to Sophie for the fat comment, she justified herself repeatedly. "I meant to say that I want you to be healthy and that you look prosperous, but I regret that it made you feel sad," she said. We all gritted our teeth and agreed to believe our own separate truths. Sophie began a melancholy hunger strike.

Fat was a hot topic that year. The government, worried that its newly wealthy population were becoming McDonald's-scarfing couch potatoes, launched an anti-fat campaign in 1994.[18] Information on 365 kinds of fat-preventing sports, including table tennis and stretching, was to be disseminated to the public. But as with any nation on the fast-food track to wealth, China failed to thin out through exercise. Between 1988 and 1998, the percentage of obese children, or *xiao pangzi*, little fatties, ballooned from 2.7 percent to more than 8.65 percent of the population.[19] The number of overweight teenagers in China tripled in the nineties, and the country's fattest child, Deng Xuejian, was a celebrity by 1998. The young son of a farmer, Xuejian weighed over three hundred pounds by the time he was eleven. The government paid for him to live full-time at the Love All People Fat Reduction Center.[20]

China was conscious of and self-conscious about fat. Everyone talked about it, even Anna, commenting daily on whether I was fatter or less fat than the day before. And after *Foreign Babes in Beijing* ran, people talked incessantly about whether we foreign babes were as fat in real life as we were on TV, or whether we just "filmed fat." We were yet another juicy symbol of contemporary concern; China, more prosperous and flash-fried than ever, was fattening itself up to join the first world. As the *China Daily*, China's English-language government mouthpiece, euphemized, China had "long emphasized morality and education, while neglecting health."[21] It's a lovely spin that Chinese were becoming obese because they were too busy with their morality and studies to exercise. Actually, people were smoking and overeating because they could afford it. And just like in the West, as wealth and girth increased, so did the desire to be thin. Early in the *pang* boom, people wanted to be plump enough to suggest prosperity, but then ideals became increasingly emaciated. As China beefed up, its billboards and magazines sported razor-thin models of beauty. Diet products, herbal remedies, and fat-reduction farms spread across the country.

The ever-diminishing Sophie initiated a robust fight about morality and education, right after losing the one about her health. The fight she picked was over a scene Director Yao had written, in which several characters have a conversation about hand-me-down clothing from a Western organization. The Chinese characters in the scene burn the clothing, because it "might be infected with AIDS." Sophie was concerned about the misrepresentation of how AIDS is contracted, and the implication that AIDS is an import from the West. At the same time, perhaps the only way to mention such critical issues at all on television was to couch them in government-friendly plot lines or terms. Director Yao believed he was doing viewers a service by mentioning an unmentionable topic. Before 2000, China did not admit that it had an AIDS epidemic. Since the millennium, and partly in response to media coverage, the Chinese government has shifted its policy on AIDS to one of slightly more direct discussion and education.

Sophie recruited me for the fight, since, as passive as I felt, I had a reputation for argument. Director Yao listened to Sophie, and then told us that the implication of the scene was not that AIDS was a foreign disease, but that people should be careful about contracting AIDS. Right, we said, but you can't get AIDS from clothing, and why does the clothing in question have to come from the West?

"This is the mistaken impression of the character, though," he said, "not of the script itself, or of us." There are two ways to say "us" in Chinese, the exclusive *women*, and an inclusive *zamen*. He used the inclusive "us," inviting Sophie and me into his grammatical inner circle.

"It has to be cut or changed," Sophie said.

"Usually actors don't get to decide on the script," he said.

"We know," I agreed, "but in the special case of this important show, we are representing our cultures, and we don't want to spread bad words or feelings about our own countries."

"Wo mingbai nimen de yisi," he said. I understand what you two

mean. "At the same time, it is late in the production schedule to change the script. I'm afraid we will not be able to do anything about it."

"We're afraid we may not be able to continue with the filming process if the feelings of our home countries are hurt," we said.

"Enh. I will talk about it with the production team and we will *tongzhi* [notify] you of our decision." I liked his choice of the bureaucratic term *tongzhi.*

The relevant bureau, Director Yao himself, agreed to cut the scene. It was a small concession, really, since when we watched the show there was a scene mysteriously close to the one they had promised to cut. Yet neither Sophie nor I was in it, and the actors who were burning "used" clothes did not mention the origin or infection of the clothes.

After they sleep together, Tianming tells Jiexi, "I want your opinion on something." His face is a map of worry.

"My opinion? Is it important to you?"

"Yes, of course it's important. If I get divorced, will you marry me?"

She stares at him, unable to answer. Offended and disillusioned by her lack of commitment, he stands and leaves the room. It is only as Tianming is leaving the dorm downstairs that Jiexi realizes her love is true and that she must commit. She opens the dorm window and shouts out for the world to hear, "Tianming! Wait! *Wo jia gei ni!* I'll marry you!"

Life in China has taught a flighty foreign babe the weight of her own actions. Director Yao mimed the climax for me, running slowly and leaping into Wang Ling's arms. I did it over and over, incorrectly. Finally, I realized what Director Yao wanted: slow motion. I had always thought that slow motion was a magical editing device, not that actresses had to run slowly and try to leap joint by joint and ligament by ligament. In the final take, after Director Yao was too annoyed to watch me do it ever again, Jiexi is laughing uncontrollably. It's meant to be a serious moment, in which Jiexi and Tianming have made an irreversible commitment to each other. The camera was supposed to freeze on her plaintive face as the lovers embraced, but I was laughing so much that it froze on Wang Ling's instead. If the crew had used simultaneous sound, I would have laughed out the closing song: "Take my hand, this real feeling, I'll give you my life, my everything."

That night, Wang Ling asked me out to dinner. It was the first time he and I had ever gone out alone. He took me to a Korean barbecue with sizzling iron plates of meat. Onion smoke filled the air. There was a collective inhalation when we walked in. A group of men, smoking and playing drinking games, gawked at me. Wang Ling glared at them. Even though we were not recognizable yet, a handsome Chinese man with a Western girl at his side still attracted gleeful attention in 1995. In big cities it no longer does; China has grown accustomed to the *Babes* scenario. And the West, thanks in large part to imported basketball star Yao Ming, is beginning to accept that Chinese men are actually macho, confident, and hip.

Wang Ling was furious that the men were staring. "What are you looking at?" he asked, "*Tamade* TV?" They turned away, only to whip their heads back a moment later and continue staring and chattering. My take-away from this was that *tamade*, which translates as "belonging to his mother," meant "mother fucking."

Wang Ling turned his attention to the table and served me

many-legged sea monsters from the barbecue. We drank two huge Yanjing beers and I dizzily gathered my nerve.

"Do you have a mistress?"

The stark question sat on the table between us. There had been no chance of ramping up to it, since I still didn't know the right words to fill in the edges around rude questions. And although I realized the implications of the question, i.e., that I wanted to audition for the role, I thought I'd be able to avoid them. I wasn't willing, perhaps more because of pride than morality, to be anyone's *disanzhe,* third, or *xiaomi,* a word that comes from *mishu,* secretary, and means "concubine."

"A *disanzhe?*" he asked. "Do you mean the French girl?"

"I guess I do."

We sat there for a minute. I felt a surge of unjustifiable jealousy.

"You have a French mistress? What about your wife?"

"What about her?"

"Is she upset?"

"*Buzhidao,*" he said. Don't know. He neglected to include a pronoun, common in Chinese when saying "I don't know," but confusing for me in this instance.

"*She* doesn't know about your mistress or *you* don't know if she's upset?"

"We haven't talked about this kind of business."

"What kind of business?"

"Each other's personal business."

"Sex with other people is your own business?"

"Of course," he said.

"Do you care if she has sex with other men?"

He blanched a bit at this, but shook his head. "I don't mind her business."

"Why stay married?"

"*Wei le fangbian,*" he said. For convenience. "Our families are happy. We go home together and we have nice dinners with our parents. They want us to be married. The government is happy, and we are happy. And we can do whatever we like."

In Shenzhen, the city Deng Xiaoping touted as a model for all developing Chinese cities, an *ernaicun* or "second wife village," had blossomed. These neighborhoods, also called "concubine villages," flourished in the suburbs of Guangzhou and Shanghai as well. Their streets were lined with apartments in which the women kept by their married lovers primped, played mahjong, and occasionally started businesses in real estate, interior decorating, or beauty. Shenzhen's *ernaicun* featured wall-to-wall karaokes and salons. Since Shenzhen is directly across from the Hong Kong border, businessmen who traveled frequently could keep their second wives close by and yet distant enough to help prevent chaotic discoveries or encounters.

So Wang Ling had a *disanzhe,* too. I shouldn't have been surprised. Most of the married production and crew members brought girlfriends out to our dinner and karaoke nights. No married women brought boyfriends, not because they didn't also cheat, but because it wasn't socially acceptable to flaunt male *disanzhe* publicly. Wang Xingjuan, who was the founder of China's Women's Institute in 1988 and ran China's only nationwide hotline for women in the 1990s, was quoted once as saying that of the ten thousand calls she had received, half were about extramarital affairs, "China's top women's issue."[22]

Wang Ling rescued us by talking about his new Jeep, which he had named *Kelindun,* the Chinese transliteration for President Clinton's name. The Jeep was produced by a Sino-U.S. joint venture and Wang Ling was proud of its American heritage. Additionally, he loved President Clinton, who was a champion of most-favored-nation status for China without humiliating and time-consuming annual renewal negotiations. Wang Ling had parked "Clinton" directly outside the window of the restaurant, so we could gaze fondly at it during our meal.

When Wang Ling drove me home, I noticed that he had left the plastic covers on Clinton's seats. He stopped at my apartment and turned the conversation backward. "We've kissed several times," he said. We had in fact kissed nine times that day alone. And the week before we had kissed seventeen times, while the crew tried for good lighting next to a dark lake. I inhaled and peeled my legs off the rubbery seats of Clinton the Jeep.

"We've never kissed without everyone around," Wang Ling continued. I liked this logic.

There was a little stuffed toy glued to the dashboard. It had just stopped moving. The car engine was still hot through the hood.

"That's true," I said, swallowing.

"Maybe we should try it," he suggested.

I could feel the heat rise to my face and was grateful for the dark. I liked Wang Ling and would have liked to invite him up to my apartment, but Jiexi kept me from doing it. If the *Babes* crew had not made Jiexi so immoral and quick to bed Tianming, I might have slept with Wang Ling in spite of my own better judgment. But my desire to resist Jiexi overwhelmed my desire for Wang Ling. I was sitting still when he boomed out in a soap-opera voice, "*Wo ai ni.*"

The words crystallized. "You what?"

He switched to English. "I love you!" he said. Maybe this was a friendly outburst. Maybe it meant something other than what it did to American teenagers, who in my experience waited months before breaking out "I love you" like a fine, aged thing.

"But we've only known each other for a short time," I said stupidly.

"So? Time and love have nothing to do with each other."

"Uh, and you're married, and—"

"I know," said Wang Ling. "But it's possible to love more than one person." He was Jiexi, and I was Tianming.

"Yeah, good point," I said.

We kissed for real for the first and only time. And I ruined it by thinking about Director Yao, expecting to hear, "Take." I have no idea what Wang Ling was thinking about, but the horrible awkwardness did not further inflame any kind of love. Instead, it ruined our friendship, just as illicit kisses ruin friendships everywhere. This is a global fact, although at the time I attributed it to cultural misunderstanding.

From *Foreign Babes in Beijing*
Episode Three

Robert, the only Western guy in Foreign Babes, *and Tianliang, Louisa's love, face each other at a small table covered with food.*

ROBERT
Do you love Louisa?

TIANLIANG
That's my private business. Are Americans interested
in everyone's business?

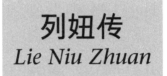

列妞传
Lie Niu Zhuan

Biographies of Model Babes Two:
Kate

On my way to a party in the suburb of Dragon Villas, a taxi driver named Mr. Gao asked where I was from.

"Guess," I said. "Guess a little—where I'm from."

"Russia?"

"No," I said, "I'm American."

"Oh!" he said gleefully. "Americans are friendly and rich."

"Thank you," I said. I was watching through the iron grid that separated the front and back seats and sliced the driver into vertical rows. The driver caught my eye in the rearview mirror and smiled, politely, I thought. He was in the know about Americans because he was training in basic English, part of the city's extensive preparations for the United Nations' International Women's Conference, scheduled to be held in Beijing in the fall of 1995. China had worked hard to win the position as host; the leadership competed vigorously for such high-profile events to reclaim the international prestige lost in the global TV glare of Tiananmen.

Outside on the street, workers were pruning bushes into voluptuous muses in honor of the event. But the international press was mercilessly covering what was going on underneath the decorated and decorous surface: China's attempts to screen out activists from Taiwan and Tibet, lesbians, and human rights groups. According to Western press reports, the chair of the Women's Conference committee was a man, and only two women served on the committee of five. On International Women's Day in 1993, the *Beijing Youth Daily* held a survey in which 60 percent of Chinese women said they wanted to be men;[23] this story was picked up by dozens of Western publications.

The controversy flared, and it was in this context that China set up what it called a nongovernmental organization, the Human Rights Society of China. The organization's ties to the government included its president Zhu Minzu, a former government spokesperson, and its suspicious "undisclosed" funding.[24] In its first report, issued in 1994, the Human Rights Society rebutted the U.S. State Department's report on human rights in China. The report pointed out that it took the United States 144 years to give women the right to vote, whereas in China the government stipulated "gender equality" immediately after forming in 1949. Of course, the report did not mention that the gender equality referred to in the slogan "women hold up half the sky" was of a cloudy, unspecified variety. It did point out that America had spurned the 1979 United Nations convention on ending discrimination against women. The report concluded with the resounding fact that 130 people froze to death in Washington, D.C., in January 1994,[25] whereas in Harbin, China, not a single person froze. The temperature in Harbin had dropped to minus 34.5 degrees Fahrenheit (minus 94.1 degrees Celsius), but since Chinese citizens actually had rights such as warmth and food, its government had not let them freeze.

The women's conference, in addition to inspiring reports and controversies, reinvigorated old slogans and conversations in China. The government set about surveying progress on women's issues. In June 1994, China's State Council issued a new white paper called "The Situation of Chinese Women,"[26] in which it celebrated the progress made by women over the last fifty years, but admitted that the "condition of Chinese women is still not satisfactory."[27] The Western press published reports on the high suicide rates among rural Chinese women, kidnapping, wage discrepancies, female infanticide, and "old, feudal ideas" holding women back. In Canada, a Chinese woman was granted political refugee status after arguing that if she returned to China, she would be forced to undergo sterilization for having had two children.[28]

Every taxi driver I met that year wanted to discuss the conference, if not the issues themselves. Chinese wanted to know how foreign women perceived Chinese women and women's rights in China. And they wanted to share their views on foreign women and foreign women's views. Nobody was without a strong opinion. Driver Gao had been trained not only in English, but also in what to do if a foreign woman took her clothes off in his cab.

"Why would she do that?" I asked.

"Foreign women are *kaifang*, open-minded," he said. "You know how they are."

I turned my attention to his ID photo, attached to the dashboard; in it, he was wearing a white collar under a dark suit jacket and looking so young and serious that the picture might have been from a high school yearbook. I suddenly thought I understood what it meant to him that I was American and *kaifang*: I was a drop in the sudden flood of foreign girls into his city and backseat, where we might take our clothes off at any moment.

I met Kate that night, an American girl who posed a genuine risk to Beijing's taxi drivers. Kate was a feminist Jiexi, as *kaifang* as we come. She was the Western girl Beijing wished for, and, at the same time, complicated, brave, and bizarre in ways the *Foreign Babes* scriptwriters could not have portrayed. When we met at Dragon Villas, she was drinking Great Wall wine and eating *dofu-gan*, smoked tofu squares stacked on toothpicks. She approached me, smiling, her puddle-colored hair rippling against her face. Kate was tall and chopstick-thin, most of her height in long skinny legs. She introduced herself, grinned widely, and blinked with baby-doll eyelashes and blue eyes I thought might click open and shut.

Kate was restless, a journalist who said she had been "addicted to China" since she had first visited as a twenty-year-old junior on her college year abroad. China was a charged escape from her sheltered childhood in a small-town suburb, where her parents had moved when she was two years old. They had been living in Istanbul, Turkey, when Kate was born, and she loved to think of their adventurous, presuburban life. Although her father worked as a computer administrator and her mother as a school principal, Kate talked about them only in terms of the years they had spent traveling the world, serving as Peace Corps volunteers and living on a boat. The first time I met Kate, she told me their story, and in the many years of our friendship, she would tell it often, always coming to the same bewildered end: they had left their adventure to settle down in suburbia.

"I don't have any memories that don't take place in that stupid town," she said. "As soon as I read *The Good Earth* in ninth grade,

I knew I was out of there. I spent my whole childhood wanting to leave. When I got here, it was exactly what I wanted."

Later, she would return to the U.S. for graduate school, and even toy with all the tender appeal of settling somewhere mellow and starting a family. But Kate had determined early on that her story would start and end on journeys; she would not succumb to the temptations of a *shufu*, comfortable life. If she married, she would marry an "international" guy, preferably Chinese, and live a global life, visiting America with her children on Thanksgiving and Christmas.

For Kate, returning to the U.S. for a year to finish college after her year abroad in China had been unbearable. Her agony at being back in the U.S. was ameliorated by her college friends, who were all international students. They had a community that interested Kate, as well as cultural stories, bonds, and traditions that to her mind Americans did not have. Sometimes it is impossible to see your own community from the inside, or your own traditions. Kate boasted of her lack of interest in American men. She was, in this regard, a model babe, in China for the adventure and romance with Chinese men, "daring to hate and love," just like Jiexi.

Kate's first love was a Chinese journalist named Peter Pan. Their love affair culminated in their visit to his family's house in the countryside for Chinese New Year. She told me, with pride and embarrassment, that his parents had given her her own room, in spite of the fact that their courtyard only had three bedrooms and there were eight people staying there. Peter Pan had sneaked into Kate's room in the middle of the night, trashing all propriety and tradition for her, a sacrifice that made her swoon. Chinese men were repressed by nature, she said, and there was nothing more fun than breaking them out of their patterns and social shells. It was

Chinese men who had broken Kate out of her own social awkwardness. She had been "unpopular" in the West, she told me, and had never gotten more attention than when she came to China. But Chinese men loved Kate; in China, she was exotic. She loved the feeling that gave her. But while Peter Pan dated Kate, his fiancée was working in Italy and planning to come home and marry him. When his fiancée returned, she and Peter Pan got married as planned. Kate was crushed.

She was nursing her heartbreak in the southern city of Kunming when she discovered she needed a pregnancy test. Over-the-counter tests weren't available. On the way to the hospital, she became disoriented and asked an old man for directions.

"What's wrong with you?" he asked.

"Uh, nothing."

"Do you have *laduzi*, pulled stomach [diarrhea]? You *laowai* aren't used to Chinese food," he said.

"Uh, yes, must be."

The curious old man insisted on accompanying Kate to the Kunming Military Hospital, a cramped cement building with long hallways, dim lights, and rows of offices with blond desks. He helped Kate register; the test cost three *kuai* fifty, equivalent to twenty-seven cents. Then the old man discussed Kate's pulled stomach with two orderlies in the hallway. When she was admitted into the examination room, there were four women gathered around. One was wearing a lab coat and three were wearing street clothes. One of the ones in street clothes had a camera.

"I need a pregnancy test," Kate said.

The woman with the camera took her picture.

"Congratulations!" the doctor said.

"No, no," Kate told her, "I don't want to be pregnant."

The woman with the camera asked, "You're not married?"

Kate flushed. "No," she said, "I'm not." The woman wrote this down.

"Why are you writing that down?" Kate asked.

"I'm a reporter," she said, "I'm doing a story on the hospital. It will be interesting for our local readers to know that foreigners get treated here, too! It's so lucky that you came in today for your pregnancy test!"

"No," Kate said. "I don't want to be in the paper. No more pictures and no more of my story. Please."

The reporter wrote this down, too. The doctor handed Kate a plastic cup for a urine sample and sent Kate out back to the bathroom, which was in a courtyard outside. Kate was walking back with her steaming cup when a young Chinese guy approached her in the courtyard. The nurse was waiting for her in the doorway of the hospital, accompanied by the journalist. Kate tucked the cup behind her.

"Do you speak English?" the young guy asked. "Maybe we can practice English together. I am a student," he continued.

"No," Kate said, and continued toward the hospital back door.

"So unfriendly!" the nurse said when she returned. "He just wanted to find a friend." The journalist took notes.

"But I was inconvenienced, carrying my pee!" Kate defended herself. The journalist nodded and continued writing.

Back in the exam room, the doctor looked at Kate's results. "Congratulations!" she said.

"Oh, my god!" Kate said. "Am I pregnant?"

"No! I thought you didn't want to be pregnant, that's why I said congratulations."

Kate went back to the hotel and slept the rest of the day. She left

Kunming the next day, before the morning papers came out. She never told Peter Pan the story.

When she told me this story in the Beijing suburbs, I was mainly stunned that her first love's name could have been Peter Pan. It turned out that Kate had given him the name because he was, as she put it, "youthful and optimistic." The name Peter Pan characterized Kate as well. She approached life, men, and Beijing with equivalent portions of enthusiasm and optimism. She was neither sarcastic nor jaded. I brooded, was an insomniac, and either mistook my interactions at face value or overanalyzed them. Kate was a social organizer and spokesperson for Western women in China, a hybrid. She said inappropriate things only in English, and knew how and when to keep quiet in a Chinese conversation. She was not a showy expatriate, did not ask of others "How long have you been here?" or "How is your Chinese?" and did not flaunt her own *biaozhun*, standard Beijing-speak. She was beautifully fluent in Chinese, especially slang, a talent she attributed to "pillow-talking" Chinese guys.

When Kate and I talked about other Westerners, it was in a language full of China and Chinese. We identified people by saying either, "He knows a ton about China" or, "He knows nothing about China." No hard-core China hand was willing to pay more than twenty cents for a beer or meal, whereas no self-respecting expatriate would set foot in too "local" a restaurant. Each lived in his own private Beijing, and got to be his dream self, whether in self-imposed exile from a land famous for frivolities and excess, or in a wealthy and full-serviced haven, richer than he could have hoped to be even in America. A typical expat rotation in China is three years. An old hand might stay five or six or seven; she becomes a "lifer" beyond that. Beijing has a Casablanca quality to it; it's a place to and from which *laowai* escape. Our framework for thinking was all about China; we needed to know about each expatriate whether he was escaping from China or to China, whether he slept exclusively with Chinese women, spoke brilliant or pitiful Chinese, acknowledged other foreigners, only liked other foreigners, shouted at cabdrivers, played rugby, or participated in plays at the British embassy (where Chinese were not allowed to attend the shows).

An Australian friend who worked in Beijing once told me she found offensive the way in which Americans ask each other where we went to college. But as an American, you can gauge a lot about another American by asking what college he went to: class, disposition, intellectual style, and social leanings. In Beijing, a person's China attitude, address, and articulacy were as revealing.

Kate found her first Beijing job at NBC, where she helped cover the women's conference. Then she was able to cobble together a living from odd jobs scouring Chinese newspapers for the *Washington Post,* NBC, and various other news organizations. When NBC offered her a long-term part-time gig, she went home to America for three weeks, packed two more suitcases to add to the one she had been living out of for two years, and moved back to China for nine years. During those years, Kate worked her way up in the media until she was a producer for a British network, where she worked primarily, she said, on stories about panda mating rituals, Chinese weddings, and Sino-U.S. tensions. She hated the job, but it allowed her to travel all over East Asia, meet the Dalai Lama in a private interview, and attend Chinese ministry briefings.

In 1998, Kate had just finished a story about mating songs sung in a Chinese village when she ranted to me about broadcast journalism. "Every time we send the tapes in," she said, "our editors in the UK are like, where are the people in Mao suits? Can you get a shot of that guy on a bicycle? And every time we say we want to do a real story, a modern story, they're like, how about one on pandas mating? Or Chinese wedding rituals? What's the point? So the West can keep its idiotic ideas about China?" Her work in media gave Kate a dizzying sensation. Little of the coverage she herself produced looked like life in Beijing.

The whole nine years she was there, Kate lived a "local" life, moving from illegal apartment to illegal apartment, uncomplaining each time she was kicked out by overzealous neighbors or nervous landlords (six times). She rode her bike eight miles every day to the office. She dated exclusively Chinese men, and knew all the lyrics to every song by China's first and most popular rock star, Cui Jian. He was considered the "Father of Chinese Rock," and was Kate's biggest crush. In May 1986, in a televised pop music competition, Cui Jian had performed what would turn out to be the biggest hit in Chinese history: "Nothing to My Name." At the otherwise pastel, romantic ballad-fest, he wore army fatigues and a green Communist Party of China T-shirt, sang in a gravel voice and ground his hips. The appearance had an Elvis Presley effect; Cui's rock sent shock waves across the country. By the following day, Chinese youth all over China were singing "Nothing to My Name"; by 1989 in Tiananmen Square, it had become their anthem. Standing in the square, Cui Jian tied a red bandanna over his eyes and sang to millions of Chinese who felt like they had nothing to their names; with his words, he implied that the Chinese nation itself had nothing. No one had ever dared put it the way he did: "I keep asking endlessly / When will you go with me? / But you just laugh at me / I've nothing to my name. / I'll give you my dreams, / and give you my freedom. / But you just laugh at me

/ I've nothing to my name." His music was both the most commercially popular and politically contentious in China.

After being banned in 1989, Cui Jian resurfaced in the mid-1990s on the underground circuit. Kate secured tickets to his shows for the next seven years, and thrashed her hair in the front row of every concert he gave.

Kate would later realize an early China ambition and date Cui Jian's saxophonist. And as with most anyone who dates her fantasy, Kate would be disappointed that he turned out to be way less dreamlike than the dream of dating him had been. They broke up fast. But she never stopped turning the radio up when the saxophone backup was featured in a Cui Jian song.

If I had never met Kate, I would not have believed that *Foreign Babes in Beijing* could be like anything but itself. But the first time she saw the show, Kate declared that the script was the story of her life. Reality, I thought, took place in Michigan and New York, where I had parents, brothers, cats, routines, and a complete vocabulary. In English, I was at home; in Chinese, a tenant on the brink of eviction. Every time I heard the name *Du Ruiqiu*, I clenched my jaw, knowing that whatever followed it would be at least partially incomprehensible to me. My role as an account executive was as surreal and unfamiliar as that of Jiexi. I went to parties at Dragon Villas and East Gate, drank Great Wall and Dragon Seal wine, danced at the Nightman Disco and NASA, lived in a project called Suburban Farm, ate at the Neon Seafood Restaurant, and bought Chinese appliances at the Blue Island Department Store.

Meeting Kate gave me an injection of hope and energy. If Kate resembled Jiexi, then perhaps there was an underlying logic to Beijing, and she could introduce me to my own life, Bumper Harvest's life. Plus, she knew a ton about China, seemed well adjusted, and had offered the international, worldwide bonding contract of girls: instant disclosure.

"Let's be friends," I said, thinking that it was a comfortable Beijing remark, but something I hadn't said to an American since third grade. I didn't know whether to consider Kate an American or not. In fact, I no longer knew whether to consider myself one. It was Kate who taught me that once you lived in Beijing, you could no longer belong entirely to either world or identity. Kate called the process "becoming more Chinese," and embraced it in a way similar to the way in which Anna enjoyed and flaunted her "Westernness."

Few cities in the world could boast more vivid cultural hybrids than Beijing. The gamut ran from those of us softly turning into slightly more Chinese selves, to blond Chinese boy bands performing Beatles, Tears for Fears, and Wham! covers. My favorite translator at our office, a Chinese guy named Charles, knew the release date and lyrics to every American rock song ever written. It was his "hobby," he said, to memorize such things.

Everywhere in China, youth cultivated a growing national obsession with Michael Jordan and Allen Iverson. No matter how remote the Chinese city, its children wore NBA jerseys, *Titanic* T-shirts, and carefully imitated brand-name shoes and clothing. Some Chinese Nikes boasted both a swipe and a Puma logo, more brand name for your *renminbi,* people's money. The Gucci purses had Fendi clasps, and there were treasures even the NBA store couldn't provide: Michael Jordan 76ers pajamas, an Osama Bin Laden jersey, and the best gift I ever bought Kate, a "Chicago Balls" uniform.

From *Foreign Babes in Beijing*
Episode Nineteen

Old Man Li and Grandpa Lu are feeding the birds in the courtyard,
sipping tea directly from the spouts of teapots, and chatting.

OLD MAN LI

Foreign Babes are so flighty! Today they love one guy,
tomorrow they love another!

FIVE

爱情的事
Aiqing di Shi

Love Business

He Jin had been telling the truth when he said he was going to open a bar and call it Peking Chalet. I introduced Anna and Kate there, in a broken alley off of North Sanlitun Road. In the mid-1990s, cabdrivers had never heard of Sanlitun Road; now the lane is called *jiuba jie*, or bar street, and is as well known to Beijingers as the Forbidden City. Anna and Kate and I walked from the intersection of Dongzhimenwai and Sanlitun Road. There were no streetlights, and the road in front of Peking Chalet was torn to shreds. Piles of broken glass littered the lane; the neighbors were so angry about the noise coming from the bar that they had thrown bottles. Nighttime noise was not considered *renao* yet. Now Beijing's nightlife competes with Hong Kong's or New York's.

Inside, the bar was close and filled with people. The expatriate girl crowd was all there, the blonde from the metals company, a wild-girl freelance reporter, and a Swiss woman who had a baby with a Chinese drummer named Tiger. The walls were covered with batik from the south of China. The tables were mismatched, some antique and low to the floor, others new and mod. The bar had two levels, and a knotty wood banister along the staircase. It served Thai food: meat wrapped in leaves, lemongrass soups, and fried rice.

Kate and Anna and I sat at a small table and Kate told Anna that her parents had been Peace Corps volunteers in Turkey when she was conceived, and that she had wanderlust in her blood, "especially the lust." She also told Anna that she loved Chinese men. I kept quiet until Anna asked me directly about my "impression of Chinese men." I told her about the ill-fated kiss with Wang Ling. She was not impressed.

"First of all," she advised me, "he does not love you."

"Right," I said. "I guessed that much."

"Second, he only says this thing about his wife so that he can seduce you. They do not have this arrangement he says they have. Probably if she knew, she would be furious."

"It's a nonissue, Anna," I said, "I didn't pursue it." I admitted that I dated mostly Western men; they were easier for me to talk to, and I needed a break from speaking Chinese at the end of my culture-shocked days.

Anna said, "I like Western men, too, because they are liberated and global."

"Liberated and global?" Kate asked. "What can that possibly mean? Chinese men are way more cultured and interesting. Americans are fratty."

Anna asked what "fratty" was, and it took Kate half an hour to explain American fraternity culture. The explanation of "hazing" was particularly complex. "So these guys let their friends punish and strip and torture them, so they can be in a group together?" Anna asked. When Kate nodded, I pointed out that a very small percentage of American men haze each other, but Anna shrugged.

"Aside from your American 'hazing,' I prefer men who have traveled and know about more of the world than just China," she said. "It's not the fault of people here, but China has been so closed that it's hard to know about other places. Better to bring the out-side world in and *ban yi ban,* mix things up."

Anna, Kate, and I had numerous boyfriends while we were friends. But Kate and I were under no real pressure to revise or apologize for our liberated standard of living. We were more sure of ourselves for being in China than we would have been in Amer-ica; China expected wildness from its barbarian guests, and most of the foreigners I met rose to the occasion like naughty kids.

Anna's situation was tougher. Even though she had the benefit of China's doubt and could have earned for herself a reputation as upstanding and demure, she was a maverick to her core. Anna could no sooner have kept to herself or followed rules she believed "feudal" than she could have followed the Tang Dynasty analects for womanly behavior: "Don't turn your head while walking. Don't show your teeth while speaking. Don't move your knees while sitting. Don't sway your dress while standing. Don't laugh out loud when happy. Don't shout when angry."[29]

Anna analyzed life, both the events of China's history and her own days, with energy, usually preferring forthright truthfulness to tact. She was interested in why Western girls would choose to live in China. It wasn't a paradise like other Asian countries; Beijing had no Balinese beaches, Tokyo neon nightlife, or Singaporian urban cleanliness. Daily tasks were impossible in Beijing, but it was hard to explain to Anna that that was precisely what kept most of its expatriates there: the feeling that Beijing was, in fact, a paradise one could enjoy only by earning that enjoyment. The process by which we learned to love life in Beijing became an in-joke, a success shared by few enough to feel like an elite club.

Kate answered Anna simply, in Chinese. "Everything in China is new and cool," she said, her pronunciation and slang beautifully crisp. "I'd move eight times a month to stay here, live in a closet, and bike a hundred miles a day."

When Anna asked me why I liked Beijing, I said I couldn't resist the newness and weirdness. But I also admitted that, for me, loving the city and loving my life there weren't necessarily the same. I spent the days trying to manage life as a manager, and my nights in cold sweats over a soap opera. On the weekends, I went to Chinese department stores, which were so people-packed they felt like elevators. The stores sold polyester dresses, spices, pork, turtles, and washing machines. I was forever looking for esoteric electronic components such as "plug heads" for which I had to learn new vocabulary (*cha* is "plug" and *tou* is "head"). Each time I was able to plug something in, my stereo, fridge, or lamps, I felt like an astronaut who had succeeded in landing on an unchartered planet. I wanted to raise a flag. When I wasn't working on PR, or shopping for *chatou*, I was prancing around on the set of *Foreign Babes in Beijing*, a "carefree" *laowai*, giving her heart and soul to Beijing.

Beijing gave its Western guests easy options for the stories of who we were. It's the only place I've ever had roles, jobs, and identities offered to me without much effort on my part. I watched everyone I met, trying to figure out what kept us in Beijing. The city not only made us our most Western and foreign selves, but also changed us into more Chinese versions of those selves. My minerals and metals friend was a corporate manager during the day, but at night and on weekends became a Taoist, meditating and going on retreats, hanging ancient scrolls in her meditation room, and consulting *fengshui* specialists about where to place her furniture. She took taiji martial arts classes and Chinese medicine; she had her pulse taken weekly by a Chinese doctor, who prescribed roots to improve the functioning of her spleen.

The wild freelance reporter sneaked all over China. During a flood in the south, she interviewed soldiers as she floated by, holding on to the roof of an uprooted house. She hid her journalist passport in her underwear before being questioned by authorities. The night I introduced Anna and Kate, the freelancer stood on the bar, lifted her miniskirt, and thong-flashed everyone. She became a legend among Chinese guys, who called her *guang pigu nu*, naked booty girl.

The raucousness inspired Anna, who called her own love of movies, men, and dirty jokes "American" by nature. She pointed us in the direction of the Chinese rock bands Cobra and Black Panther, even once she herself began to prefer Wham! and Mark Knopfler. She took us to Chinese clubs, including one called NASA, where dry-ice mist poured up from the dance floor and lights spun the room. The club's balconies were stacked with frantic dancers. International journalists, busy covering the new China, snapped pictures of the crowd: Western businessmen in suits, students with backpacks, club kids, and policemen with batons. The first night Anna took us there, the music broke off suddenly at midnight, and a stiletto-thin Chinese emcee appeared. She was dressed in a bright yellow suit and heels, weirdly miscalibrated, yet festive and suggestive. I had never seen vaudeville in a disco.

"Welcome to tonight's show!" she shrieked in emcee's official falsetto, poking her right hipbone out toward us. She said some-

173

thing else I couldn't follow and the spotlights flared, lighting up two cages on either side of her. Smoke gushed from both. When it cleared, the audience roared; in each cage was a dancer dressed in a sports bra and underwear. As the lights roamed over the cages, the girls grabbed the bars and danced. They were enthusiastic. The lights brightened slightly and I suddenly realized that one was a blonde. I turned to Anna and asked, "Who are those girls?"

"Don't worry," she shouted over the music at Kate and me. "They're Russian."

She meant we shouldn't worry that they were American, because if they had been, we might have been directly implicated by their dancing. But I wasn't worried, just surprised. Wasn't China the middle kingdom of its own beauty? Why not have Chinese women starring in the disco show?

"Chinese are good at importing foreign things and adapting them to Chinese conditions," Anna joked.

Suddenly a fight broke out in the back of the club. The crowd rushed frenetically in both directions, and Anna pulled us to the front door, fast. Outside, the air stood still with winter. Mutton kebab vendors were shouting out prices, spicy heat funneling from their carts. Skyscrapers sparkled over short buildings with slanted roofs. The highway overpasses were lit up with year-round Christmas lights. In the shadows, we could see our breathing. Everyone was chattering about the fight. A Western student had danced too close to a Chinese girl, in view of her Chinese boyfriend, who had broken a bottle over the student's head. The student was carried out by his friends, blood pouring from his hairline. We saw no sign of an ambulance, but dispersed as dancers overflowed the steps.

"What did you think of the show?" Anna asked. She had

bought a mutton kebab and was picking meat off the skewer with her teeth.

"I thought it was weird," I said.

"What is this word, weird?"

"*Qiguai,*" Kate said, translating.

"You mean 'unfamiliar.' "

I smiled, thinking everything was so unfamiliar that I could never explain myself.

"I just mean 'weird.' "

"But you must have this kind of show in the U.S."

"Yeah, but I'm never at this kind of place in the U.S."

"You never go to discos?"

"No, I do, we just don't have cage dancers at the kinds of disco I go to. Or at least the dancers aren't foreign girls in the same way."

The night got colder. Bits of trash blew around the sidewalks near our ankles. We stood watching the nightlife disperse in various directions.

We finished filming *Foreign Babes* four months after we had begun. Spring had arrived, and dust from the Gobi desert blew in, covering the sunny city in a blanket. I felt happy and free, gaining fluency and friends.

The last day on the set, Jiexi ate a vacuum-packed duck. I have never seen those ducks outside of China. They are widely available in Beijing's supermarkets; they look like giant rubber toys until the plastic wrappers pop and then the birds reveal themselves as real, naked, saucy ducks, glistening with Jell-O.

"You want me to eat this?" I asked when Director Yao set down the duck. Wang Ling was laughing, standing over an iron stove in our "living room" set, which was still negative five degrees. I had told him I was a vegetarian.

"Tear the wrapping off and begin eating hungrily," Director Yao instructed me.

"The whole duck?"

"Tear the leg off."

"I don't really like to eat meat," I said, "especially duck. Can I fake it?"

He looked at me for a minute and asked, "Well, does Jiexi?"

"Does Jiexi what?"

"Like duck."

I had become unpopular for making the point that Jiexi and I were not the same person.

"She loves duck," I said, licking the aspic off my fingers, and we were even for the trou dropping.

We filmed the first scene last. It was the show opener, shot in Jingshan Park, where we "play among the pigeons," as Director Yao put it. Pigeons were everywhere, cooing, fluffing, and flapping their ratty wings. We skipped along with our hairdos flying higher than the pigeons.

Sophie, still on her hunger strike, had become a toothpick. I mentioned that I thought she had lost too much weight, thinking even as I said it that it was strange that Americans think it's okay to tell people when they're too thin, but not when they're fat. It's as random as any Chinese custom. Sophie shrugged when I told her she should make sure to take care of herself. I was just like Assistant Director Xu, commenting on something sensitive and private.

To celebrate the end of filming, we went to China's Lantern Festival. Tiananmen and the Forbidden City were lit up with elaborate lanterns, some decorated to look like animals. Wang Ling told Sophie and me that the lanterns were intended to scare spirits away, lest those spirits pluck the living from the streets. Young women, dressed in their best dresses, posed for boyfriends in suits with brand-name labels still attached to their sleeves. Old couples ballroom-danced. Children wove through their parents' legs, carrying candied crabapple sticks and eating moon cakes. Each street off of the main square shone; the usually stern expanse of concrete was suddenly a bright, beautiful disco featuring singers and dancing dragons. In one moonlit corner of the square, a few lucky vendors were selling moon cakes, toys, and plastic neon jewelry. Just off the Avenue of Eternal Peace, Beijing winter life went on; construction workers, all sinew and shout, labored across the skyline. Diners crowded tables in local restaurants. The air was dark with coal heat and cold. The lights of millions of television sets flashed CCTV's Lantern Festival special. CCTV has a special gala show for every Chinese holiday, and even in China's most remote villages, television penetration had reached 98 percent.

Each year after *Foreign Babes in Beijing*, I went to the Lantern Festival to look at the lanterns, which became increasingly thematic. They were built to look like the Great Wall, pandas, and rockets. After Beijing finally won its Olympic bid in 2001, the lanterns represented linked Olympic circles, torches, athletes. Chinese, just like Americans, love superlatives; every lantern in Beijing's Chaoyang Park competed to be the biggest or best at something. My all-time favorite was the "Temple of Heaven" lantern, claimed to be one-third the size of the real Temple of Heaven, where dynastic rulers worshipped heaven. That's an impressive claim, since the actual temple, with its surrounding buildings and gardens, covers an area five times the size of the Forbidden City.

I was buying a candied crabapple stick when Sophie invited me to ballroom dance, to the amusement of the old dancing couples. Once we were twirling, Sophie whispered, "Everyone thinks you and Tianming are having an affair."

I laughed. "Everyone thinks you and I are having an affair, since we're dancing."

"I'm serious."

"Everyone thinks Wang Ling and I are having an affair? Who cares? It's not true."

"Maybe you should act a little less *suibian*," she suggested.

"Can someone please explain to me what *suibian* actually means?"

"Casual. It seems like you and Wang Ling are really comfortable together."

"We're not. In fact, our *guanxi* [relationship] is incredibly awkward."

"But it seems like you are."

"Might that be because we have to make out five times a day and film naked scenes?"

"I just hear that your *guanxi* is close. For the Chinese," she said, "it's better to be private about this kind of thing."

"You speak for the Chinese? And what kind of thing?"

"Love business. For the Chinese, it's not polite to display romantic things publicly."

"But we don't have any love business."

"Tianming is married!" she said.

"There is no Tianming," I pointed out. "He's a character."

"Well, Wang Ling is married."

"Yes, I know. And there's nothing going on. What about you

and Gao Ming?" I asked about her on-screen love, making a point of using the actor's name.

She giggled.

"Are you sleeping with him?" I asked.

She shrugged. We stopped dancing.

"Well," she said, "I'm not saying anything about it except *he's* not married." Then she laughed again. "Except to Louisa, I mean."

Wang Ling wandered over and cut in, cutting off our conversation. I was stewing, and danced especially close to him. While we were dancing, he confided in me that Tianming and Jiexi's love scenes were intercut with scenes of Tianming's wife doing virtuous chores.

"How do you know anything about the scenes?" I asked Wang Ling. I was pretty sure that this information was not available in the script, since Teacher Kang and I had made our way through it just in time to finish filming.

"I've seen the *something something,*" Wang Ling said.

"The what?"

"The *yangpian,*" he said, slowly. The *yangpian*?

"*Meitian kan de pian,*" Wang Ling said. The every day watch films.

Every day watch films. Every day. Films. "Dailies! There are dailies?"

We stopped dancing. Wu Jie came to get us for dinner. He piled us into the cast bus. Once we were roaring toward his favorite duck restaurant, I cornered Wu Jie.

"Wu Jie," I said, "there were dailies for *Foreign Babes in Beijing*?"

"Of course there are *yangpian,*" said Wu Jie.

"Why didn't I get to watch them?"

"You were busy with your work for the American company. For example, you were too busy to act the part of Louisa or live at the studio. We respect your American work unit, and did not want to trouble you for extra time," said Line Producer Cao.

"Did everyone else watch them?"

"Some actors like to watch dailies to improve their performances." Sophie was grinning. "Did Sophie watch them?" I asked.

"Sophie loves to watch *yangpian*."

So everyone had been studying up and improving their performances, while I'd been writing speeches about pillar industries and sourcing scissors suppliers. I had shirked my work-unit duty and was not a model worker. In order to deflect criticism, I accused them of planning to intercut virtuous Saozi into our naked love scenes.

"So," I said, trying to decide how much and what to ask. "Trouble you guys to ask this: why put scenes of Saozi in between Jiexi and Tianming's love scenes?"

Wu Jie smiled and Line Producer Cao looked blank. Line Producer Cao was surprised and annoyed that I should have brought up anything under their jurisdiction. Wu Jie found it cute. But neither of them said anything.

Wang Ling tried to rescue everyone by saying, "It's just *aiqing di shi*," love business.

"Love business? Then why not give Saozi a lover, too?" I suggested.

"Chinese women are conservative. And she's married. It is Jiexi who is the *disanzhe*," said Line Producer Cao. The mistress.

"Right. But do you actually believe that all Chinese women are conservative?" I asked. "What about all the mistresses people bring to our dinners and karaoke nights?"

There was an awkward pause.

"*Buqingqu*," Wu Jie said with a smile. Unclear.

"Okay, then do you think that all foreign girls act like this?"

"Like what?" asked Wang Ling.

I used their phrase, "open-minded."

"Don't they?" said Line Producer Cao.

I thought about it, wishing I had come to the conversation armed with a "key message," of the sort the firm prepared for all our clients. The stereotype was that foreign girls, Americans in particular, did what we wanted, when we wanted to, and were unapologetic. I couldn't really bear to deny that. On the other hand, I didn't want to suggest that we were morally degraded.

"Maybe before marriage," I suggested.

Wang Ling cocked an eyebrow at me. "Maybe what?"

"Maybe before we get married, we can be a little open-minded, but afterwards, if you're too open-minded, you get divorced." None of them responded. I settled on, "Well, we're not all adulterers."

Still no response. "We're not all *disanzhe*," I said again, drawing out the words. I thought of American TV, wondering whether China was making any more dangerous a statement about Americans in love than America was itself prepared to make. Everyone on TV cheats.

After a drawn-out pause, Wang Ling said, "*Foreign Babes* is just TV, Ruiqiu. It's what people want to see."

"What people?"

"Chinese people."

"You mean *laobaixing*?" I asked. *Laobaixing* is the Chinese word for "commoners," which means "a hundred surnames." Originally, only the aristocracy had surnames, since a surname meant one could own property and pass it down a lineage. Because social organization was based on the family unit, the earliest cultural patriarchs extended their surnames to the masses, who shared. It's understood in China that Huangs are descendants of the Yellow Emperor (Huang Di) and Kongs are descendants of Confucius (Kongfuzi). Surnames played a vital, if largely fictitious, role in family teachings, codes of conduct, ideologies, and legacies generally. Ultimately, whole villages were run by generations of Lis or Wangs, all *laobaixing*. Now the word is used to mean common folk.

"Of course *laobaixing*," Wang Ling said. "Who else?"

"Government officials? Reporters? Censors?"

"I mean everyone," he said.

"The show has already passed the censors," Wu Jie said happily. "Soon you will be famous! Everybody loves *Foreign Babes*."

Wang Ling put it simply: "Everyone likes to know more about foreigners. It's interesting to Chinese people. And foreign girls are open-minded, right?" He grinned at me and added in English, "I like to know!"

Line Producer Cao tapped on a pack of cigarettes. "Wang Ling's English has gotten quite easy on the ears," he said suggestively. I rolled my eyes.

We arrived at the banquet hall. Ducks hung by their necks in an oven visible from the entrance, lively and inviting. Their skin, which had been inflated away from their bodies, usually by inserting a straw and blowing air between the duck and its skin, crackled in the heat and darkened into the crispy strips we would wrap in pancakes with scallions and sweet sauce. My father once accidentally blew a Peking duck up in the basement of our house; he was using a bike pump to separate the duck from its skin, and blasted duck all over the rafters. On more successful occasions, he hung the partially inflated ducks in the shower to dry before roasting.

Aiqing di Shi, Love Business

It was at the final *Foreign Babes in Beijing* banquet that we said good-bye to our daily work and characters. All the tensions that developed during the filming, about logistics, sex, acting, and content, were magically set aside, translated into a comic mode, turned into self-deprecating vignettes, or melted down from irritations into experiences.

Comings and goings are as frequent in modern China as they were in imperial China. In ancient times, China's educated, ministerial elite had careers that obliged them to move. Poems of parting form a large part of China's lyrical Tang poetry. The world of expats is also marked and celebrated by partings. Every momentous occasion is marked by a mountain of complicated food.

Sophie and I were given seats of honor next to Director Yao and Wu Jie. Wu Jie rushed about, making sure that everyone had enough *baijiu,* grain alcohol, for the infinite number of required toasts. After the first fiery shots, I no longer found the thimblefuls hard to take. Every time my glass was empty, a waiter hastily refilled it and I drained it.

"A toast to Director Yao!" someone shouted. "*Ganbei!* Dry your glasses, cheers!" We threw our heads back and poured hot liquor down our throats. Sophie looked blurry to me, like a well-lit movie star. "You look beautiful!" I shouted. "A toast to Sophie! *Ganbei!*"

There were endless courses of food, each more ornate and lovely than the last. First came the small white bowls of glistening shark's fin soup, then iron-grilled beef strips with onions wilting delicately over them, green plates of pea shoots with shredded ginger and garlic, dried, spicy green beans, numbing tofu, and a beautiful whole steamed fish with scallions and soy sauce. The duck came last. Each person got a small plate of sauce and scallions. There were pancakes stacked neatly on the lazy Susan, and a duck spinning in the middle. For dessert, the waiters brought out watermelons carved into dragons and phoenixes. The food was a tourist site, a tribute to manual labor: dumplings wrapped into duck, basket, and fish shapes, and walnut shells carved into cities and civilizations.

"Look at that carving!" I told Sophie, while fondling the outside of a dragon watermelon. "It's like the terra-cotta warriors! Or the Wall! So much work and detail!"

Wang Ling came over and put his hand on my shoulder. "Sometimes you can add water to your *baijiu*," he whispered, emptying my shot glass onto the tablecloth and replacing it with mineral water. "Then you can pretend to drink and not lose face for refusing."

I drank the water in my liquor thimble, but it was late for damage control, and as soon as karaoke began, I performed *"Mingming Baibai Wode Xin,"* or "Understand My Heart" with brutal pronunciation and intonation. After I sang, Wang Ling escorted me back to my seat and remarked that I reminded him of a "Chinese guy." I thanked him, imagining that this meant I was charming. In fact, it meant I drank *baijiu*, did not want to lose face, and sang alto, all shamelessly. I was starved for drunken karaoke opportunities, since whenever we went karaoke'ing for company events, no one dared upstage Charlotte.

A "Chinese guy" was the furthest one could be from a foreign babe, and also the closest to one. According to the *Biographies of Model Women*, for a woman to be "like a man" was no small sin. In the dramatic chapter "Biographies of Pernicious and Depraved Women," Mo-Shi, a concubine, "had the heart of a man" and wore a sword and cap. Her machismo caused the fall of a kingdom.

As soon as I was drunk enough, I stood up and proposed a toast. This task, until I took it upon myself, had been left to the men. I thanked the *Foreign Babes* crew for including me in their project, community, and portrait of Beijing. They had taken a topically touchy situation and kept it complicated, I said. Director Yao was right: the show, like our lives, was a search for truth and beauty. What each of us found, I left unsaid.

After the banquet, Wu Jie left town to drill oil, Wang Ling went back to his married life and acting career, and I went back to work at the company. Magazines began to appear with Sophie's and my huge white faces grinning ludicrously out of shiny pages. Radio stations and reporters called in advance of the show, to "talk about the Western view of Beijing."

No one at work talked to me, save Anna and Charlotte. Gary had seen the *China Daily* article and told the secretaries, who told Anna, who told me, that I was going to get too big for my casual Friday britches. Gary was having an affair with a client and trying to save Microsoft's reputation in China. Microsoft had crisis after crisis, not only because Bill Gates was considered by the Chinese to be arrogant and greedy, but also because the company had chosen its Chinese name by translating "micro" and "soft" directly into *weiruan*, "flaccid and little." The failure of that to build a strapping corporate image speaks for itself.

Before *Foreign Babes in Beijing* was scheduled to air on Beijing Television One, Anna and I went to the Blue Island Department Store so I could buy a multi-system VCR. Since *Foreign Babes in Beijing* was going to be on TV, I thought I might want a record of it.

From *Foreign Babes in Beijing*
Episode One

Jiexi and Louisa sit in the dorm, gossiping. They are
supposed to be studying ancient poetry.

LOUISA
I've met a wonderful Chinese guy!

JIEXI
Is he a prince on a white horse? Was it love at first sight?

LOUISA
(In a dreamy voice)
No, he's plain. There's nothing extraordinary about him.

列妞传
Lie Niu Zhuan

Biographies of Model Babes Three: Zhao Jun

Zhao Jun was a model citizen of the new China. We met in a bar. He was wearing faded Levi's, Timberland work boots, and a black T-shirt. He looked like a Chinese movie star playing a working-class American. Zhao Jun had deep dimples when he smiled, and teeth as white as street lamps. They lit up the bar. His arms were heavily worked out, and he sat in a way that suggested he knew it, straight-backed, arms on the table, flexed. Zhao Jun looked more American than any American I had ever met, and more like a People's Liberation Army poster boy than even Wang Ling. I described him to Anna and Kate as Westernized, a hybrid, Chinese, traditional, macho, and global. Zhao Jun was bilingual and Beijing-based, fresh back from a decade in L.A. He and I started dating mere moments after my declaration to Anna and Kate about liking to speak to American guys at the ends of my days. It was as if China had written the script. Kate was delighted.

"See, Chinese guys are great," she said. "I told you."

"Don't get your hopes up," I said. "I'm not a fetishist. I just like him personally."

Kate looked at Anna knowingly. But Anna shrugged. "I guess it will be nice to have a Chinese boyfriend in Beijing," she said. "He can teach you lessons about China."

"Like Tianming, you mean?" I asked, horrified.

Zhao Jun was both Westernized and aggressively traditional. He had grown up in Kaifeng, home to most of China's Jewish population. Ten thousand Jews lived in central China during the Sung Dynasty. The Kaifeng synagogue has since been turned into a hospital, which Zhao Jun and I wandered around one day, hoping to find relics.

The first night we met, Zhao Jun offered to "be Jewish with me," if I liked, even though he wasn't "technically" a Kaifeng Jew. There were still descendants of Chinese Jews in Kaifeng, and Zhao Jun said if you studied them, you could see that they were Jewish because they had taller noses than most Chinese. Identities in Beijing were liquid enough that I matched Zhao Jun's offer with my own, to be Chinese with him, which he did not take me up on. Zhao Jun liked only Western women.

He had been raised by his maternal grandmother, who, when she discovered her husband had a mistress, drove him out and never allowed his name to pass the lips of anyone in the family again. She was a ball-busting matriarch who gave Zhao Jun her surname and a violent temper. As a ten-year-old he fought with two teenage boys who yanked his hair out, and his grandmother shaved his head to rid future bullies of any advantage. She chain-smoked cigars, weighed 250 pounds, and died of a stroke at sixty. Zhao Jun's earliest memories were of running to the neighborhood

kiosk to buy her tobacco while his mother and father were participating in the Cultural Revolution. When his parents arrived
home, his grandmother continued to run the family iron-fisted.

Zhao Jun's father, whom Zhao Jun called the "most open-
minded person in China," was on his way to Taiwan in 1949 as
part of the Nationalist Party's effort to attract Chinese students. He
and his two sisters, Zhao Jun's aunts, were in Hangzhou, waiting
for a Taiwan-bound boat, when one of Zhao Jun's aunts met and
fell in love with an army doctor. The doctor invited the three of
them to visit the hospital where he worked; while there, they
missed the boat to Taiwan, and waited three days for the next boat.
The Communist Party took over mainland China during those
three days. So, instead of going to Taiwan to join the Nationalists,
Zhao Jun's father joined the People's Liberation Army (PLA), where
he taught rural soldiers to read. Then he was hired by the army acting troupe and starred in operas. It was an unconventional path
during the revolution, and Zhao Jun took pride in his father's
story. His dad was an intellectual who had made a sacrifice in order
to survive, not a credulous revolutionary who took either the propaganda or his own role in the revolution at face value.

Zhao Jun himself was a Peking Opera actor, trained since he was
four years old in martial arts, acrobatics, and vocals. I asked him
about the acting connection to his father, a question he shut down
fast with a response about how the two lives and styles and careers
were unrelated. The kind of acting his father had been made to do
for the PLA was nothing like the Hollywood career Zhao Jun had
sought and found. His voice was sharp.

He responded with greater warmth to my second question,
which was whether Zhao Jun's life was just like Director Chen
Kaige's movie *Farewell my Concubine*. As soon as the words were out

ORGANIZATION

of my mouth, I could hear them stupidly coming back: might he ask whether my life was just like *Foreign Babes in Beijing*? More and more, it was, and yet he spared me.

"My life was a lot like that movie," Zhao Jun said. "Peking opera school was a violent environment." In the film *Farewell my Concubine*, children at the opera academy are beaten and made to perform acrobatics under such intense pressure that one of them kills himself.

Encouraged, I asked, "Did they beat you?"

"Of course. If you want a four-year-old to do a handstand on the table, you have to beat him."

Zhao Jun knew more than I did about beating people. He had knifed an eighteen-year old when he was fifteen, in a gang fight. Zhao Jun and a Peking opera school buddy were attacked by four older kids from the school, and Zhao Jun, in what he called self-defense, pushed a knife into the stomach of one of his attackers. When I expressed surprise at how young he had been, he said fifteen wasn't young in China, that Chinese emperors often took the throne at thirteen. Zhao Jun embodied some of the qualities of China's young rulers: his anger was not of the generation X variety, that is, free-floating or vague. It was directed, specific, and historical. He watched historical documentaries by the dozens and used them to support his often wildly offensive claims about ethnic groups. He believed that cultures are responsible for the atrocities they wreak, and that the Japanese, for example, were not to be forgiven for 1930. Since he was so loyal to America, I argued that slavery should be counted among the unforgivable sins of the past, but Zhao Jun's rage was specific to invasions of China by outside forces.

Zhao Jun's framework and philosophies were Chinese, even

when his presentation, lifestyle, and accent seemed almost entirely American. He described growing up as a series of dualities, echoing Chinese grammar and the Chinese propensity for dividing things into two. People in his hometown were either global or feudal, Chinese were patriotic innocents or cynical sophisticates, Americans were yokels or artists. Elders in Kaifeng, most of whom had been sent to labor reform camps in the countryside during the 1960s Cultural Revolution, had believed there were two ways to protect their children from ending up in the countryside. So Zhao Jun and his contemporaries were sculpted to be either elite athletes or performers. Desperate to keep their children safe if not close by, parents broke their spines to make their kids into stars. By the time Zhao Jun's generation graduated, the Cultural Revolution era had ended, and there was no longer any chance of anyone being sent to the countryside. But their lives had been determined and shaped by their parents' fears of a repeated history. Zhao Jun took eight entrance exams to get into Peking Opera School and then learned to do straight hours of handstands. The teachers beat him, both to motivate and punish. Competition among children was bitter and fierce. Zhao Jun said simply, "Everyone had to be the best at everything. There was no room for weakness; we all fought to be better, meaner, stronger. It was military school with makeup."

He paid for the knife fight. At sixteen, he went to prison, where he spent two years in a cell with an eighteen-year-old boy who had killed someone. The eighteen-year-old was to be executed, and Zhao Jun's job was to watch over him. They were close friends for a year, and Zhao Jun could do nothing but watch when guards came and took the boy to be executed outside in the yard. Zhao Jun sat in the cell alone, terrified. His own prison sentence would last indefinitely, until the fate of his victim became clear. Since the victim recovered fully, Zhao Jun was released from prison when he turned eighteen. Disgrace prevented him from returning home to Kaifeng, so he joined an acting troupe at an oil field, where he drilled during the day and performed at night. When the Beijing Film Academy held an open audition in the late 1980s, Zhao Jun won a spot in the class and graduated four years later, after which he moved to L.A. and acted in martial arts movies, usually playing, as he put it, "Japanese mobsters and bad guys."

When I asked how a person could move in a socialist society from Peking Opera to prison to oil fields to B movies, Zhao Jun responded, "I married an American woman."

Jiexi's line, "Can't you Chinese men love anyone other than your wives?" flitted across my mind, but neither she nor I said anything. There was a long lull.

"We're divorced now," Zhao Jun said. I was unsure of whether to believe him, but I invited him to my illegal Chinese apartment, where he stayed for a year.

Zhao Jun did not approve of my participation in *Foreign Babes in Beijing*, which he called "artless, patriotic cheese." We barely discussed *Foreign Babes*. I knew he found the show degrading and I suspect he also did not like me parading on Chinese TV seducing other Chinese men. I hated his criticism. It was strange that we were able to have a romance in which we never discussed that I was a foreign babe in Beijing, or that hundreds of people on the street would eventually stop to discuss it every time we stepped outside. Sometimes Zhao Jun threatened people; other times he stayed quiet. Once, he hit someone.

Lie Niu Zhuan, Zhao Jun

"Patriotism is unthinking bullshit," he was fond of saying. Eventually, he said this every time I made a Chinese friend. Everyone was too patriotic for Zhao Jun. He wasn't wrong about patriotism; it's jingoistic and tired, no matter where you find it. And yet, in his secret heart, he, too, had doggedly patriotic moments and goals. His dream was to direct movies that showed the China he believed was real: a gritty, dark, and genuinely modern place. Zhao Jun admitted that he had felt more attached to China when he wasn't there, precisely how I felt about America. I was much less likely to criticize the U.S. while in China, since I had many friends to do that for me, and since I was homesick. Zhao Jun said he had never let anyone in the U.S. criticize China. His movies would be straightforward depictions, he promised, never propaganda. In them, characters would speak Beijing *tuhua*, slang, and never make self-conscious points about culture gaps. Given the chance, he would make the opposite of *Babes*.

Movies were Zhao Jun's primary frame of reference. His understanding of the West's best assets came from Martin Scorcese and Quentin Tarantino, and his ambivalence about China was spelled out in Chinese movies, most of which were rooted in a history of propaganda. Zhao Jun was forever criticizing and editing everyone's scripts. He hated the work of world-famous Chinese director Zhang Yimou, because Zhang's movies "pandered to Westerners" and showed a rural, poor, and exotic China. I liked Zhang's movies, especially *The Story of Qiu Ju*, about a peasant who works her way through China's complicated and unfriendly legal system after her husband gets kicked in the crotch by the village chief. When I told Zhao Jun that I liked Zhang's movies, he said, "Of course you do."

Zhao Jun acted to support his dream of directing, but the acting jobs included projects he found undignified and cheesy, such as the romantic comedy *Love in Banna,* and several Hong Kong action movies. The fact that he was often cast as a Japanese infuriated him.

He showed me dozens of Chinese movies, my favorite of which remains Wu Tianming's *King of Masks,* about transformation, role-playing, and identity. Zhu Xu, the man who plays the mask king, is a beautiful actor, papery in his old age. In the movie, he replaces his face over and over with elaborately painted masks. This is his art, transforming his old face into youth, beauty, and femininity. He adopts a boy to be his heir, but the child turns out to be a girl in disguise, and Zhu Xu's character must learn to love her anyway.

Zhao Jun was fascinated by movies about transformation. He had transformed from a Peking Opera star to an inmate, a laborer, an actor, and an American. In spite of the fact that he often flashed his U.S. passport, even at our friends over dinner, he was coming back to China to transform again. He had come home from L.A. with only a suitcase, halfheartedly imagining he would return to the U.S., but ultimately settling in Beijing. Like the rest of us, he wanted to be near his roots, even if emotionally removed from them. Zhao Jun's Beijing life was a rough-edged work in progress. I once asked him where he actually felt at home, and he said in Chinese, without melodrama or much inflection, "Nowhere, and you?"

"In the U.S., I think. Tell me what the U.S. was like for you," I said. "How did you go from here to there? Who were you?"

"The first thing I did when I got to America was clean my teeth surgically. I had the gums fixed." He rapped on his teeth. "I had never been to a dentist. I think it was the dentist's first time to see someone who had never been to a dentist before. Americans care more than any other people about their teeth—and their accents.

You can't have a Chinese accent in America, or people think you're delivering food or doing their dry cleaning. I wanted to get acting parts other than fucking Long Duk Dong—so I hired a speech coach."

"What did she teach you?"

"He taught me sounds. Open sounds. And *th* sounds, *s* sounds, 1 and *r* sounds."

"Say Rachel."

"Rachel."

Zhao Jun had perfect teeth and almost perfect English. It was hard to say exactly what accent stayed behind his sentences. There was a disjointed quality to his English that made it unmistakably nonnative, but he sounded more like a hoody teenager than a foreigner. He attributed this effect to the nontranslatability of certain thoughts. Only hoodlum slang, he said, could work in English.

"Ironically, Beijing slang has a perfect equivalent in English, more than any other kind of Chinese does."

"What do you mean, any other kind of Chinese?"

"Beijing slang is the Chinese that's most like English. Unlike scholarly Chinese, or even lyrical Chinese." I had had this thought, too, that Chinese was closer to English slang than to academic or lyrical English. But this was not about the language itself, of course; it was simply about my inability to speak it.

"Are you sure that's not because you're more comfortable speaking and thinking and writing in a kind of modern slang? Or because you don't know scholarly English, just like I don't know scholarly Chinese?"

"I'm pretty sure. Because in Chinese, I'm scholarly, and in English, I'm harsh. I can use elevated Chinese language, but there's no English equivalent, at least not a precise one. So if I want my scripts to be 'real,' in terms of their language, then they have to be in *Beijing hua,* which is totally interchangeable with English. Sometimes, when I write in *Beijing hua,* I am thinking first in English."

Zhao Jun's own movie, which he finished and released in 2003, was about transformation and was articulated in Beijing slang. He planned to call it *The Perfect Woman,* but the censors did not allow that title, less for political reasons, they said, than because they thought the title was "unrelated" to the story of the movie. They insisted he call it *Jinggan,* or *Manhole,* named for a manhole cover stolen by peasants in the opening shot. The story was of a woman who used to be innocent but had become, in the new China, modern and sullied. The protagonist, after being released from jail after ten years, goes to find the schoolgirl virgin he believes awaits him. But like China, she has become a promiscuous, heavily made-up nightclub hostess, flattering and entertaining wealthy clients. When the recently paroled hero can't afford the diamond ring his girlfriend wants more than anything, he must rob someone to win her back. In the new China, he cannot succeed unless he turns back to a life of crime.

Zhao Jun's movie was both cynical about patriotism and nostalgically patriotic, a combination I no longer find contradictory. Zhao Jun's task, to carve out a figure of invincibility for himself in both worlds and modes—was too difficult not to involve the fission and fusion of apparent opposites.

One weekend early in our romance, I returned to Beijing from a business trip to Shanghai, and Zhao Jun picked me up at the Beijing airport. The arrival room was sardine packed with people waving and climbing up onto security railings to get a better glimpse at arriving passengers. I spotted Zhao Jun in a sea of people near the exit doors. Just as I saw him, I heard someone shout, "Hello, pretty girl! *Laowai!* Taxi? Taxi?" to me from the front of the crowd. In a flash, Zhao Jun was muscling his way to the front, the veins in his neck popping. He was shouting at the man who had called out to me, as I rushed down the ramp with my suitcase. I tried for restraint when I asked Zhao Jun to leave it alone. It was his world, and I didn't want to be the cause of face loss. I told him that cabdrivers in New York shout at tourists, that he should let me mind my own business, and that I was perfectly capable of handling comments directed at me. He said he wasn't sure I knew what people were saying or implying.

"Your point is that people are insulting and I'm not picking up on it?" I asked.

"Not always," he said, "but sometimes the things you say are inappropriate."

"The things *I* say?"

"Responding at all. You shouldn't respond when people talk to you, especially men."

"This guy wanted me to take his taxi! Don't be crazy. And even if he was talking to me, how could that possibly be your business?

"I'm just trying to protect you."

"From what, taxi drivers?"

"People staring and commenting."

"I'm not interested in being protected."

He took my bags and led me to his blue Beijing Jeep, a gift from an old friend of his who worked in advertising. Zhao Jun had many friends and received many gifts; one such friend, Shi Wei, was waiting in the front seat of the Jeep when we arrived. Shi Wei had a goatee and a large scar slicing down his left jaw. It was the pirate kind, with obvious stitch marks up its side. He was wearing faded jeans and a silver Harley-Davidson belt. He worked buying B movies in L.A. and then selling them to CCTV, and he invited me to his office at Beiying to screen movies.

Shi Wei knew everyone on the *Foreign Babes in Beijing* production crew. He grinned at me when I mentioned the show, and his scar slid up the side of his face in a parallel smile. He told me that Producer Cao was an asshole and Wu Jie was a millionaire. "What do you think of Wu Jie's purple suit?" he asked, adding, "He drills oil to make his fortune." The muscles in Zhao Jun's jaw flexed.

"You must work hard hours," I said, changing the subject.

"Why do you say that?" he asked.

"Beiying is hard to work for," I said. "I know from experience."

"No, no," he said, turning to face me in the backseat. "You don't understand. Beiying is just my work unit. My business is my own business." He glanced sideways at Zhao Jun, who kept his eyes on the road. "I do whatever I want." Beiying was a flexible work unit, serving essentially as a tax agent. Shi Wei did a nominal amount of work there, and had a private company through which he made money. Such moonlighting was both legal and typical; as long as workers fulfilled their tax obligations and put in vague amounts of time, their work units turned a blind eye to outside *shi*, or business.

Zhao Jun had an American passport and no work unit. He cobbled together so many jobs and meetings that his life in Beijing was an eclectic collage, hard to follow. Every new lead suggested the possibility of wealth; he was excited about each one, but they tended not to pan out. Zhao Jun's friends had become wealthy in the new China since he left for the U.S. Shi Wei had a big silver sedan and two apartments: he had bought one for himself and the other for his parents. Zhao Jun had some money made from various movie roles in Hong Kong and the U.S., but he had no steady income, or stable "iron rice bowl," and was agitated by the success of his friends. Their babies, movies, and other achievements were a kind of torture for him, and his struggle to create a niche for himself in Beijing included countless meetings with and favors from old friends. There was some possibility that Zhao Jun would do project work for the friend who housed him or the one who bought the Jeep, but the work didn't materialize. In the off-hours, he and Shi Wei both worked on screenplays.

Advertisements flashed by: Nokia, Hyundai, Delphi. Lines of rain streaked the sky, and the signs stood out like comic strips. New, nonindigenous grass implanted along the roadside underneath them depleted the water supply and died each season. Every time an international event took place, the dead grass was replaced with new, imported grass. Out of these lawns a few scraggly bushes and trees wrangled their way toward the billboards; the signs themselves seemed to be the only plants that grew naturally from the pavement in Beijing. I wondered again why Beijing felt so exciting, and what forces keep us from leaving the spaces we make.

Zhao Jun was telling Shi Wei he would leave the following day for Hong Kong, to meet with an investor about "potential cooperations." He had not mentioned this to me.

I asked if they were entertainment industry projects, and Zhao Jun said no, "probably real estate."

"Probably?"

"It's not confirmed."

"What do you know about real estate?"

"We're talking about a bunch of things. Maybe we'll open a bar."

"A bar? I thought we were talking about real estate."

"Anyway, I want to meet someone to talk about my screenplay, too, so it's useful."

When we arrived at my apartment from the airport, I invited him and Shi Wei in for a drink. They refused, saying they had "some business" to which they needed to attend. I did not ask what it was.

At Spring Festival I accepted Zhao Jun's invitation to go home to Kaifeng, and tried to shed the feeling that the visit would be reminiscent of *Foreign Babes*. I wanted to make a joke about this possibility, to tell Zhao Jun that if I felt alienated, I would take him up on his offer to be a Jew with me. But such jokes had become uncomfortably resonant with the matters we didn't discuss. We would not talk much in Kaifeng, but instead would visit the historical synagogue turned hospital and hang out with his parents. When we arrived at Zhao Jun's parents' house, his mother and father both shook hands with me warmly. No one hugged or called out, "Baba!"

Their apartment was a small two-bedroom on the ground floor of a low-rise building. Like all apartments south of the Yangtze River, it had no heat. China has to heat the bitterly cold north, and frugality and population make heating a luxury. Those who live south of the river use small coal-burning stoves. A soft curtain of coal smoke hung over Kaifeng. The apartment was cold enough to make my eyes and skin burn. I was surprised Zhao Jun had not warned me, but for him such realities were so obvious that they didn't cross his mind. I was mortified not to have brought appropriate clothing, especially since I didn't want to draw any attention to either the cold or my discomfort. I felt big and Western in the modest apartment, overdrawn like a caricature. When I finally told Zhao Jun I was freezing but didn't want to embarrass or insult his mother, he told her right away. His mother, delighted to attend to a need, clucked around me, dressing me in warm layers of her clothing. I never took any of it off during the five days we stayed.

Once I was padded, the four of us ventured outside into a small fenced-in yard and took a picture. It appears to have been taken in some other century. We look old and faded, smiling seriously and wearing padded clothing. Behind us is a small garden.

Zhao Jun's parents offered Zhao Jun and me their room, since it was the most comfortable in the house and had a double bed. It reminded me of the Old Lis giving Louisa and Tianliang their bed. Zhao Jun's mother cooked six meals a day and moved about the house in a fit of energy and spoiling and worrying. She reminded me of my own mom, reinforcing the basic truth that all mothers are identical. This sense of familiarity collided with my ever-present one of foreignness. In addition, I was reconvinced that we were all becoming our parents. As far away as my friends seemed to me to be from the people who had raised them, what comes around goes around everywhere, even in Kaifeng. Zhao Jun's parents' life was so distinct from the one he and I led that it took me work to believe his parents could be responsible for who Zhao Jun was. Zhao Jun's mother was a revolutionary, and his father a non-conformist. He had not believed fully in the revolution, had hidden books and photographs, and had been an actor and a teacher. I had come to accept that Zhao Jun broke the mold Americans expected Chinese men to come in, so it should have come as less of a surprise that his parents would break from roles I expected they'd play.

But there were aspects of our visit that kept me feeling like I could never be at home: the cement apartment, long silences, glutinous moon dumplings filled with sesame paste that lingered rough against the backs of my teeth, and shrines to Zhao Jun's ancestors in our bedroom. There were late-night Mahjong games with Zhao Jun's buddies from Peking Opera School. I hardly followed their conversation, which was fast, heavily accented, and full of references to places and people I did not know. They had been in gangs, operas, and prisons, drilled oil and grown up in a language and framework I still struggled to understand. I felt both welcome and the loneliest I have ever been. I went to bed early, watching the photographs of Zhao Jun's dead relatives with candles and fruit placed before them, feeling as though they were watching me. They had lived in a China absent of foreign women; what would they think of a pajama'ed one in their great-grandson's bedroom? During the Cultural Revolution, ancestral shrines and rituals had been banished, but people had hidden photos and left out food nonetheless. Zhao Jun's parents had felt safe enough to put the photographs back on display only in the 1980s.

Early in the morning, Zhao Jun's father took us on a bike tour of Kaifeng, which was wider and quieter than Beijing. The streets were less developed and felt spacious. Billboards were sparse. In spite of the cold, some kids were flying frozen kites, eager for spring. I was incredulous that Zhao Jun's father, over sixty years old, was able to bike so many miles in the brutal weather. When he had headed home, I told Zhao Jun I was impressed, and he said, "What do you mean? He bikes every day. How do you think everyone here gets around?"

His anger was in response to an accusation I had not made, but could guess at: he hadn't bought his parents a car. We were standing on a bridge. Underneath us, children skated across a frozen pond. At its edges sat sad swan boats, still retired until warmer weather. I had just bought a stick of candy-covered crabapples, which I was trying to eat while keeping my scarf over most of my face. I wanted to ask what the material differences between Zhao Jun's and his parents' lives meant to Zhao Jun, but set about it in a clunky way. There was no way to ask this question without implying criticism: that they were poor and he was unfilial.

"What do your parents think of your life?" I finally asked, in English. When he didn't respond, I gilded the lily, badgering him into a corner: "Are they surprised by us? By the fact that you lived in L.A.? That you're divorced?"

They were, at least in part. Yet he heard only the oversimplification of these questions. Zhao Jun saw, as if on a giant screen rolling across the sky, credits for the reference points on which I relied: the parents in *Foreign Babes*. He glanced over at me furiously. "You look like a fucking foreign babe, eating that thing," he said. The candy apple stick gravitated toward my side. The wind seared across us; he did not respond to my question, nor I to his comment. Somewhere in that moment, we both gave up. I was too cold to outlast him in a stare-down or a fight, so amazingly, we let it go. I dropped the candy and climbed back on my bicycle, watching the blank streets open as I rode through them. There were some chickens walking along the side of the road. I swerved to avoid them, attracting frantic clucking.

From *Foreign Babes in Beijing*
Episode Sixteen

Jiexi and Louisa face off on a sunny campus path.

JIEXI

Tianming and I are in love. What we do is our business.

LOUISA

How can you say that?!

JIEXI

Obviously you're Chinese. Because you're obsessed with
other people's business.

SIX

拥抱洋妞
Yongbao Yang Niu

Embracing Foreign Babes

Whoen *Foreign Babes in Beijing* ran on Beijing Television
One, the press reported that six hundred million people were watching. I was one of them, perhaps the only
one in a cold sweat. I had some idea that the script was an unsophisticated depiction of foreign life in China, but I wasn't sure
what to expect, and I was panicked. Late at night, I stayed bolt
awake with Jiexi and the number: 600 million people? It was too
huge a number to think about. If we all held hands, would we
cover the planet? TVs were flashing in apartments everywhere in
China, Jiexi's hotel sheets in everyone's living room, her slurping
kisses and freckles 3-D in their houses.

The first night the show was on, I bought a Chinese TV guide,
which reported that *Babes* would be on Beijing TV One at 9:06 P.M.
Every night the show began at a different time. I went to the
Fangzhuang carpet store and bought a rug so I could sit on the

205

floor to watch TV, closer than a chair would allow. I wanted to see every shot, to look for the reflections of Director Yao's directions, to make sure Tianming and Jiexi's love both seemed and didn't seem real.

Anna and Kate came over to offer moral support. Together, we watched the commercials that led up to each episode, for washing machines and electronics. *Babes* began with the montage we had filmed in Jingshan Park: individual, grotesque close-up shots of our faces as we squinted horribly into the sun. Those frames opened up to a shot of all of us, holding hands and skipping through a patio in the park. Then a small square window in the left corner of the TV introduced each of us and expanded to take up the entire screen, zooming in on our faces, with the gritty, shot-on-a-hand-held-camera style of pornography. There were subtitles only for the theme song, and no one had spell-checked them; they read "Forigen girls, forigen girls in Beijing, Beijing." Then the Chinese: "They give their hearts and their lives, everything to Beijing. Because they're all *laowai*, but they all speak Chinese, they can understand by listening. I love Beijing!"

Anna took personally the fact that the production team hadn't spell-checked their subtitles. "This stupid, lazy work!" she said, "Why can't they ask you how to spell it?"

While the song played, Kate laughed uproariously, memorized the song, and began to sing along each night. The small square in the TV's left corner filled with images of the babes giving Chinese people clocks, green hats, English lessons, and thumbs-ups.

The first episode begins with the same scene Director Yao had used for Bill's and my audition. Bill played the Western loser, Robert, or "Lobote," an unpleasant homonym for" radish." When Robert wants to take a cab, "like a real foreigner," Louisa convinces him to take the bus. He is of course overwhelmed by the number of people, gets crushed, and has his coat shredded by the bus door. The throngs inspire in him a public transportation rage, and Robert punches a stranger, the baby-faced but macho Li Tianliang. Naturally, the white guy gets his ass kicked. China's hostility against Western men, the barbarians and invaders of its past and present, is played out in every one of Robert's scenes: he gets rejected by both Jiexi and Louisa in favor of Chinese men, and then gets cancer. When Western medicine fails to cure him, he must move back to China for Chinese herbal remedies.

During that first clash-of-cultures fistfight, Louisa is a traitor to her own countryman; she falls for Li Tianliang as soon as she sees his glowering dark eyes and right hook.

Anna watched me watching, and my jaw must have been hanging open, because she said not to worry, it was just *suibian*, casual TV. Kate was shouting for me to introduce her to the actor who played Li Tianliang, and I told her he was dating "Louisa."

"Great!" she said. "he likes *yang niu*!"

After deciding it's love at first sight with Tianliang, Louisa runs back to the dorm to tell Jiexi, who is drinking beer while she does her homework. I was wearing the white sweater I had worn to the audition and looked like the Michelin Man. Jiexi asks whether Li Tianliang is like the hero of a romance. "He's plain," Louisa says, showing that she can appreciate a simple model citizen. Standing out in China, unless you're a conspicuous babe or *laowai*, is not the point.

In their paltry introductory scenes, the Japanese girl, Zhizi, plays chess like a genius (she is a war strategist in disguise, perhaps), and the Russian girl, Nadja, rides her bike and gets a traffic ticket after shiftily pretending not to speak Chinese when a cop pulls her over. No cop has ever pulled over a foreign girl on a bike in Beijing, but this is an idea the producers thought would be cute. The Russian girl later works in Beijing's clothing business, since that's what Russians are thought to do in Beijing. And as a finale to the first episode, Louisa goes to Peking Opera with Li Tianliang's father. (Unlike his modern sons, he is an expert in ancient Chinese culture.) Louisa, unable to appreciate the rich history of the opera, falls asleep and snores, only to wake and scream and cheer when the performance is over. She leaps from her chair and knocks it over; Mr. Li buries his face in his hands, perhaps trying to prevent a full loss of face.

Even though Jiexi was barely in the first episode, I went to bed stunned that the show had been on TV at all, and amazed that it had looked as bad as it had. I wondered what the sex and *disanzhe* episodes could possibly look like. Maybe no one had watched it, I reasoned. Anna and Kate left, laughing and chattering about Louisa's love for Tianliang.

In the office the following morning, my colleagues were in hysterics. Everyone had watched the show, and they put a fine point on it: "*Ni paide ting pang.*" You film quite fat. I made a mental note to get rid of the white sweater.

In the next episode, Louisa and Jiexi go swimming, a fast if unconvincing way in which to have a bathing suit scene. Sophie and I look so uncomfortable it's comical, both of us hunched over our half-naked selves, and then forced by the director to run to the edge of the pool and dive in. After the swim, Li Tianliang comes over to the dorm to study English, is harassed by the guard for trying to get into the foreign dorm, threatened by Robert at the entrance, rescued by Louisa, and plied with beer by Jiexi. Louisa says, "This is a pencil," but Li Tianliang is too drunk to continue the lesson. Louisa's English is dubbed by an actor who does not speak English. "Pencil" is almost unrecognizable.

I gaped at Jiexi's most horrible moments: she is doing laundry when she meets Tianming. She wears the scandalously tight sweater I bought with Anna in Wangfujing. I felt like the mother of a teenager when I saw myself wearing it on TV. How had I let myself out of the house in that? As soon as she sees Tianming, Jiexi gives her girlfriends a lusty thumbs-up. The producers loved the shot and it was featured in the show opener night after night, rerun after rerun. Watching myself, I saw a puppet, my own double. The thumbs-up became a symbol for *Foreign Babes*, and for years, policeman and strangers gave me double thumbs-up on the streets. The first few nights, while my own hysteria began to set in, and long before the media's did, I foolishly hoped there was no obvious connection between me and the Muppet I played on TV.

I watched Jiexi and Tianming dance with Louisa's entire family at the Great Wall Sheraton disco to Lisa Loeb's "Stay." Louisa's blond mother asks Tianming and Tianliang's father, Old Man Li, to dance, but he says he cannot do the modern dances, and leads the whole disco in a martial arts lesson. Ancient Chinese music magically replaces Lisa Loeb.

Tianming and Jiexi motion to each other from across the room. They hold hands and go silently upstairs to a hotel room. As soon as the door shuts, they begin wildly making out. Then Tianming picks Jiexi up from the floor with horrible awkwardness, her head dangling over his arm, and carries her to the bed. They are halfway there when they run into a hotel maid, who has been innocently folding towels in their room. There is no privacy in China. In the world of *Foreign Babes in Beijing*, people are forever spying, telling on each other, and writing anonymous notes to reveal each other's secrets. These are both conventional plot clichés and direct reflections of the fear in China of other people's proximity. The maid gasps and runs from the room. Within one day, the maid has told the whole city about Tianming's indiscretion, and Tianming gets fired from his job. It's laughable that his TV boss would care about Tianming's *disanzhe*, since in Beijing, mistresses are as common as lapdogs.

"I love you," Jiexi says, after the maid scampers out. "I don't care who sees. It's got nothing to do with anyone else. It's our business. The business of two people." She gazes up at him longingly, and then the camera cuts to his wife, Saozi, working overtime in a factory, lining up bottles. The walls of the factory are gray. She wears a cafeteria-style hat. Her eyes look tired and her face is tofu-toned. When the camera returns, Tianming and Jiexi are taking off their shirts, rolling on the bed, and giving odd, less-than-passionate backrubs.

Kate was screaming with laughter. Anna was rolling her eyes. And then, in my favorite *Foreign Babes* moment ever, the scene cut to a Kentucky Fried Chicken commercial, full of close-up shots of big, raw, veiny legs and breasts being dropped into a vat of frying oil. Chinese fetishization of food is different from the West's. In China, most food has neither been processed nor wrapped neatly. Instead of the unrecognizable, plastic-wrapped breasts sold in American supermarkets, everyone buys whole, fat, feathery chickens. They want to see the fresh animal they're about to eat. Raw shrimp with their antennae twitching decorate packages of flavored potato chips. Pork barbecue chips feature pig cartoons, and chicken-flavored chips flaunt feathery, hairy birds on their bags. When the commercial break ended, the show opened with a shot of our naked legs and feet. We looked like edible chickens.

Yongbao Yang Niu, Embracing Foreign Babes

Each *Foreign Babes in Beijing* episode ends frozen on the face of a plaintive or delighted character, credits rolling and a slow song worthy of *Friends* or any American primetime drama: *"Qian Zhe wode shou, zhen shide gan shou, gei ni wo yishengde suo you."* Take my hand, this real feeling, I'll give you my life, my everything. In spite of my desire to keep an ironic distance, I loved the ending song. It soared with 1980s slow-song magic, and made me fall for a moment into suspension of disbelief.

Right before *Foreign Babes*, China had semi-privatized its television and film, but still employed a powerful and active censor. The show was censored numerous times; the script had to be approved before filming began, and then each episode was screened and censored. The final cuts were then screened one more time before the show aired. I was not privy to what the censors determined should be cut, even though I asked. The fact that the show was approved was a source of pride for the producers; questions about what edits had been made were understood as criticisms. The Beijing leadership supported the deployment of television, since they were smitten with the potential of TV to convey messages to the masses. But actual programming was directed by more powerful forces: commercial advertising and the public's taste for the exotic (Western girls, for example). Wu Jie's *Foreign Babes* had to make both money and some kind of moral statement. The producers' tasks were to hook audience members, sell advertising, and convince the state that *Foreign Babes in Beijing* was a moral drama, all at once.

And it was nothing new in this regard. From Confucian analects to Mao's talks in Yan'an, from Communist manifestos to China's current "open-minded" economic slogans and nighttime soap operas, there has been a subtle balance at play: the merger of entertainment and education, a "tempt and teach" strategy. Confucius sums it up smoothly: "Guide them by edicts, keep them in line with punishments, and the common people will stay out of trouble but will have no sense of shame. Guide them by virtue, keep them in line with the rites, and they will, besides having a sense of shame, reform themselves."

Chairman Mao did not differ from Confucius on this point. During Mao's talks at Yan'an, where the Communists prepared in the 1940s for the revolution, his primary points were that literature must speak to the masses by addressing their lives and struggles to survive, and that writers first and foremost must serve the political agenda.

In the early 1990s, Comrade Li Ruihuan, a member of the politburo and "overseer of national ideology,"[30] parroted Mao by suggesting that the government "appeal to the masses in order to educate them,"[31] by entertaining first, and using forms that masses favor. Soap operas. But his comments require a grain of irony. When the government decided to make the entertainment industry pay for itself, bureaucrats like Li Ruihuan faced the same difficult task as the *Foreign Babes* producers: make money, but convince China that it is good, socialist money. Bureaucrats justified profitable artistic products by claiming additional educational purposes for crowd-pleasing antics. The censors could call *Foreign Babes in Beijing* anything they wanted to call it; the show was certainly "favourable to the masses," and was also a moneymaker. Just a spoonful of exoticism helps the messages go down. Sweet to audience members and censors alike were the fresh, risqué depictions of modern China and true love. If pressed, officials could claim to approve only of the seemingly socialist messages—those about the cost of inviting flies through open doors.

The way I saw it, there were three versions of *Foreign Babes in Beijing.* There was the show the censors saw, a light drama. Then there was the show the censors said they saw, an educational model with strong moral implications. The third was the show the Chinese audience saw, a hot depiction of sex, wealth, and success.

As such, and in keeping with the history of Chinese literature and politic, it braved the danger of all "tempt and teach" literature: that audiences will be absorbed by the sexuality of a nighttime soap—or the lurid exploration of lascivious acts in Buddhist morality tales (Ming stories of courtesans)—and lose sight of the moral message. *Foreign Babes in Beijing* spoke an old, risky language in a new, risky way. But if the girls embodied a fresh kind of seduction, then only the brand name was new. China had always used sex to describe its relationship to the outside world, and as a metaphor for moral encounter. The addiction of millions of Chinese men to opium was a "draining of Chinese men's virility." Japan's invasion of China in the 1930s is the infamous "rape of Nanjing."

In the 1990s, an era of reform and reaching out, or, as Director Yao put it, "man's common search for truth and beauty," producers of "modern" shows had to translate such past symbols into the modern languages of technology, world communication, and entertainment. In contrast to the "rape of Nanjing," the modern intruder was female, not male, and the process was seduction, not rape.

Louisa, good girl or not, was like Jiexi in that she was also the aggressor throughout her courtship and marriage to Bambi-like Tianliang. When Louisa has gone on two dates, Jiexi asks, "So, have you slept with him yet?"

"We haven't even kissed!" Louisa says.

"You have to be more aggressive," Jiexi advises.

So Louisa makes her own pitiful pass at Tianliang, saying, "Time waits for no man," and puckering her lips. On their wedding night, Louisa has just taken off her jewelry and hair ornaments with long sticks and bobbing rocks sticking off of them. She slinks into bed with her hair down, wearing an old lady's padded silk nightgown, giggling and sighing. Tianliang tells her to be quiet.

"Be quiet? Why?" she asks.

"We don't want my old folks to hear us."

"Don't tell me your parents don't have sex."

"In China, sex is private and secret."

"Tell them to plug their ears."

But she crawls discreetly across the bed, trying not to make a single squeak, until Old Man Li shouts in from the next room, "Don't be so quiet! Do whatever you want!"

Even Old Man Li, the sternest representation of old China, can modernize when pressed by his beloved country's modernization.

On the bright streets, Jiexi took strange and instant effect. The Chinese media wrote that Jiexi, "with her blond hair and blue eyes," stole the hearts of Chinese men everywhere. Next to such articles were pictures of me, with dark hair and green eyes, looking bewildered, looking like someone else. I did not feel associated with or implicated by the girl pictured in these articles; she was Ruiqiu or Jiexi. I hid back at the office, grateful that my colleagues, who were also watching the show every night, stopped involving me in their conversations about it.

Chinese reporters called daily and consistently asked me, "So, is Jiexi's life typical of a foreign babe in China?" The sarcasm of my reply, "Yeah, most of us are foreign exchange students, home wreckers, and temptresses," was lost in translation. This response was printed dozens of times in the Chinese papers as a basic truth. I began to lose track of what I had said in jest, for real, or at all. Reporters loved to ask, "What's the difference between American men and Chinese men?" I stayed safe and said the differences between men did not, in general, cleave along ethnic lines. Kate did not agree. "It's simple," she said. "Chinese men are sexier." This was, of course, precisely the sound bite the Chinese media would have liked. But I had read *Orientalism* and hated the film *The Lover*. I was not going to answer questions with a fetishist's lack of perspective. Nor did I want to respond to what I suspected were the litany of real, underlying questions, of the "Is it true what they say?" varieties.

Chinese newspapers ran stories with my name as the byline, as if I had authored them. When I asked our media director at the firm, Zeng Min, about this, he said, "They just want you to write an article for their paper. It's friendly! They want to show the foreign view of the show."

"But why don't they ask me to write the articles? Or for permission to use my name? How does that show the foreign view of the show? Please tell the ones you know that I am used to my Western customs and they cannot use my name as if I wrote articles I wasn't even consulted about. And please, no more pronoun 'I' in third-person accounts."

This was confrontational, and he was embarrassed. "Well," he said, "they think it will be hard to communicate with you, so they write your view themselves."

I was speechless. Kate, on the other hand, loved the show and wanted to talk about it constantly. She memorized and hummed the songs. "Have you paid attention to the one that plays over the love scenes?" she asked. She sang the chorus, *"Ni bu yinggai, ni bu yinggai."* You shouldn't, you shouldn't. Then she sighed. "It stops my heart!" she said. "It reminds me so much of Peter Pan, and the message of the show is great."

"What message?"

"That Chinese men are sexy and strong-willed. I mean, Tianming and Tianliang are hot like the heroes of war propaganda films. It's just what modern TV needs. All we have to do is try to export it to the West, and teach Americans a lesson about how Chinese guys really are."

"You really should have been Jiexi," I said to Kate.

"We're all Jiexi, aren't we?" she laughed.

By all accounts, the Chinese audience loved *Foreign Babes in Beijing.* So did my dad. Of course, according to an article published in the *Washington Post* in the spring of 1996, Chinese had loved *The Bridges of Madison County,* too, because they were "thirsting after a tale of sex, love, maternal devotion and filial piety."[32] Critics raved about *Madison County* that it emphasized not only love and romance, but also family and social responsibility. One viewer interviewed by the *Washington Post* said, "Chinese people can relate to the movie because seven out of ten Chinese marriages are loveless. People here get married for other reasons."[33] The article quoted a poll in which nearly 40 percent of Chinese said that love was not the "basis for marriage." People wanted to watch stories in which real lovers make a break for it, leaving tradition and lovelessness behind.

In *Babes,* there was someone for everyone. Not just the unhappily married, hoping to be swept away by sexy vixens, could succeed in life. So could the old-school doting mother, stern but forgiving father, and the virtuous Chinese heroine. (She gets promoted and is professionally successful after Tianming and Jiexi leave.) Obviously the stars win out in the end: two lovable if scandalous foreign babes, and gorgeous Chinese sons, one true to China, the other to his heart.

The Chinese press raved about *Foreign Babes in Beijing* as a beautiful depiction of the modern struggles of Chinese to adapt to a new cultural and romantic landscape, one that included Western girls and Western-style divorce. Newspapers and magazines all over the country ran articles on multiculturalism and passion.

Given that the divorce rate continued skyrocketing, it was no surprise that Chinese viewers were relieved, rather than troubled, by Tianming and Saozi's divorce. The two had a loveless marriage, and Jiexi and Tianming's true love made up for the split. By 1998, articles in the Chinese press claimed that citizens who chose to get married later did so because they were increasingly aware of education opportunities and career prospects.[34] One law professor, helping to revise the marriage laws to make divorce more accessible, commented that although the liberal sexual activities of young Chinese were an "ideological problem," divorce could often provide a happy ending to a tragic story.[35]

The Western press, when it eventually picked up the story, took a critical view of the show's social implications. For the first time since the *China Daily* had claimed *Foreign Babes* revealed a "foreign view of Beijing," the show actually did: the view of some Western reporters. I opened the *Hong Kong Standard* on July 9, 1996, to a full-page picture of me, looking bitchy, distracted, and caught off guard, sipping from a glass of lemonade. Under the photo was the following caption: "Super Bitch: Tired of the predictable fare, Chinese viewers are switching on to *Foreign Babes in Beijing* and the debaucherous lifestyle of Rachel DeWoskin's character."

The article described me as "single, young and footloose in a new city," and said I was "no Mary Richards, no That Girl. No, she's the pushy, rich supervixen who seduces a good man, destroys his marriage, and shatters the harmony of his honorable family. And China loves her for it." Closer to the truth was the paper's assessment of why *Babes* was so popular: "It stands out against the bleak landscape of formulaic dramas on Chinese television."

The *International Herald Tribune* took a less celebratory stance. On July 25, it printed a story called "Not a Pretty Picture: Foreign Babes in Beijing." Under the headline is a smiley picture of me, in front of a small bust of Mao, holding an antique Chinese hand mirror. Mao's bright white reflection is visible in the mirror. Mine is not. The reporter, who was based in Hong Kong and did not speak Chinese, called *Babes* a "misleading and potentially dangerous portrayal of foreigners that reinforces Chinese xenophobia and feeds a burning nationalism." He wrote that critics of the show included "just about every foreign woman who has ever watched it," but did not interview or quote a single Chinese viewer—or Kate, the only foreign woman I ever heard of who watched the whole show.

Ironically, I became a defender of *Foreign Babes in Beijing*. It wasn't my kind of show, and I wasn't comfortable with it. But I did not think the Western press had gotten its story right. I wrote a letter to the editor of the *International Herald Tribune*, proposing that anyone who buys into television buys into stereotypes, and asking how likely it would be, if we were ever even to see a Chinese character on American TV, that he would be depicted with accuracy or complexity. I also wrote and still believe that it is racist to imply that the Chinese viewing audience can not differentiate between the fiction of a television series and the fact of a foreigner. This sentence was revised to read: "It is wrong to think that the Chinese viewing audience can not differentiate," thereby diffusing the most high-value word in my letter, "racist." The reporter had at least managed to interview Director Yao and ask him about resentment over the show. Director Yao responded beautifully, if predictably: "People don't resent true love."

The *National Enquirer* took a cheerful Western view, claiming that "the hottest TV star in China is an American girl." My mom heard about the story from a woman in her dance class, and ran out to buy a copy and call me.

"My god," she said on the phone, "there's a picture of you on the street, surrounded by people! How are things?" In the picture, I am in the foreground, overexposed and wearing a long cream wool coat. I look like a street lamp, grinning into the flash. Behind me is a crowd of young men and old ladies, pointing and laughing. They appear to be moving forward, toward me. Some are in pedicabs. There is a sweet-potato vendor in the corner.

I was shocked to hear that my mom had bought the *National Enquirer*. "You actually bought it? Why not read it in line?" I asked.

"I bought a hundred copies," she said.

Good Housekeeping ran a picture of Wang Ling and me, in sunglasses on a mountaintop. The *London Times* took the *IHT*'s lead and wrote a story called "Chinese Feed their Fear of Foreigners," using the same bust-of-Mao picture and juxtaposing it with one of a Chinese soldier in Tiananmen Square. The *Washington Post* followed suit with my all-time favorite headline: "Neo-nationalistic China, Suspect of Western Ways, Embraces Foreign Babes."

None of the coverage had much to do with the truth. I wanted to see it reported that we didn't have flush toilets on the set, or that I told a crowd of Chinese people that Columbia University professors castrate their language students. That there was no heat on the set and everyone reminded me to button my coat sixty times an hour. That we were freezing, unglamorous, wearing long underwear, and eating *feirou hefan*, fatty meat lunch boxes, three times a day. Our cultural fights were about fat, flirting, and cab fares, not politics at large or the differences between Chinese and American men or self-referential culture gap problems. That people on the street knew we were actors and loved us.

If *Foreign Babes* was a propaganda machine, it failed. Jiexi's sluttiness and Saozi's virtuousness were moral appendages at best. At worst, they were cynical invitations to Chinese girls to be "more like Jiexi." The press noted but did not analyze the fact that teenage girls began to follow me through stores, whether vegetable markets, Silk Alley or the Friendship Store. Chinese women watched what products Jiexi bought and then followed suit with lipsticks, raw mushrooms, shoes, or tuna. Once, I bought a huge container of fish paste, because Anna's sister had offered to help me learn how to prepare Chinese food and I thought I might need one of every condiment known to man. The women behind me chattered anxiously. "Americans eat fish paste! Jiexi likes fish paste!" Two of them also bought containers. Even my real life had become a surreal advertisement.

In Silk Alley, a group of fourteen-year-old girls surrounded me one day for a picture. I had just bought a gray, fake Prada backpack with a red stripe down the back. They eyed the bag curiously. "We love Jiexi," they said breathlessly. "She is *zhen bang* [really cool]!

Where's Tianming? Is he in America? How much did you pay for that purse?"

"I'm an actress," I said. "The one who acts Tianming is an actor named Wang Ling. As far as my knowledge goes, he's in Beijing. The purse was forty *yuan.*"

"Of course you're an actress," they said. "But are you in love in 'real life'?"

"Unh." I grunted whenever I couldn't think of an appropriate answer.

"That purse should be twenty *yuan*! Will you sign this napkin?"

While I signed, they haggled for Jiexi purses. On the Great Wall, Chinese tourists from outside of Beijing called out, "Jiexi!" and "*Disanzhe*!" in thick accents. Mistress, come and take a picture with us! Nobody I met blamed Jiexi for the pollution of modernization; they certainly didn't seem to blame me.

Decades of propaganda had not been without effect. Especially in major cities, the Chinese audience was full of wary consumers of moral drama; they recognized the hopelessly hackneyed tropes of propaganda, which by their very exhaustion had lost their original value and impact. The audience's appetite for something more flavorful remained intact. In contrast to the usual clichés, the liminal Jiexi and Louisa were outsiders who existed within Chinese culture—distinctly separate from the Japanese invaders or Western-style opium traders of old propaganda. So even if Jiexi was categorically a "typical American," on the streets of Beijing, she stayed beloved, and not only by young people. Grannies came up to me and petted my hair: "It was true love with Tianming, wasn't it?" they asked.

Zeng Min, the media director at the firm, told me he thought I should have a more sophisticated signature for such occasions, and taught me how to sign autographs. He had seen my characters, and they were unquestionably those of a barbarian. So we sat in the conference room and he signed my name again and again, lifting his arm off the paper with tremendous charm and flair. I thought of the name, its strokes coming together and naming me from scratch. Du Ruiqiu, it seemed to me as much Zeng Min's name as mine. I signed it with detachment and watched people on the streets react to the unlovely calligraphy. Some nodded, others joked with each other; many spoke kind lies about it. But the signatures were really evidence of what everyone already knew: Jiexi and Du Ruiqiu were babes in the woods. Of course their script had childlike foreignness to it. The press thought the Chinese audience was unsophisticated. The audience thought the press and the TV characters were unsophisticated. People liked Jiexi because she was unsophisticated and knew how to love openly and with abandon. On the streets, they continued to ask for Ruiqiu's unsophisticated scrawl.

There's a Chinese warning about getting famous: "As a pig fears getting big, so a person fears getting famous." Fame fattens and makes you visible for the roast. Our company headquarters, informed of the Western coverage of the show, wrote a curt note to me requesting a copy of the series. Charlotte shut down that demand by writing back on my behalf that the show was tame by comparison to Western shows, the coverage was inaccurate, and my participation in the show did not in any way reflect the views or goals of our Beijing office. Finally, she said, we did not have a copy to send them. This was true; Wu Jie apologetically told me he could not give me a copy because they had strict rules about selling the show in the West, and some people (although not Wu Jie himself, he assured me) were concerned that the Western actors might sell the show to our home countries' black markets.

His fear wasn't entirely unfounded. Wu Jie called me when he returned from drilling oil. He had had to cut his trip short, he said, because renegade provinces in China were taping *Foreign Babes in Beijing* from television and not paying the royalty fees to Beiying to rebroadcast. In order to sue, Wu Jie had to be present in the provinces when the show was airing and see it with his own eyes. Yet even if he could prove copyright infringement and win a lawsuit, the provinces wouldn't pay. They had no money.

"Then what's the point in suing?" I asked.

"You should know! Americans love copyright. It's the principle!" he shouted into the phone joyfully. "People everywhere love *Foreign Babes,* even if they don't have enough money to pay for the show. It will rerun again and again, Jiexi!"

He wasn't kidding about the reruns. By 1996, only a year after it first played, *Foreign Babes in Beijing* had already rerun six times in Beijing. And it would rerun six more, everywhere in China. The following summer, I traveled south to the border of Tibet on vacation, and was in a remote botanical garden when half of the town's population approached, chewing sticks of sugar cane and giggling a chorus of *"Disanzhe."*

From *Foreign Babes in Beijing*
Episode Three

JIEXI

Raises her eyebrows provocatively at Tianliang.

I know Louisa doesn't love Robert, but he sure has a lot of courage. Tianliang, don't Chinese men have any courage?

列妞传
Lie Niu Zhuan

Biographies of Model Babes Four: Zhou Wen

C*hina Can Say No*, a best-selling manifesto encouraging China to "say no" to the West, came out in 1996 and sold 150,000 copies. The book portrayed America as a superpower interested in containing and stifling China, interfering with China's "internal affairs," and policing the world. Anti-American rhetoric in the official media's campaign against "spiritual pollution" was fever-pitched, and the popularity of the book inspired patriots and authors alike. Song Qiang and Zhang Xiaobo, thirty-one- and thirty-two-year-old writers, poets, and sometimes fruit salesmen, wrote the book with three other friends. Although none of the five had been abroad, all had once looked West for novels, films, and role models. But as Zhang put it, now the West was "disgusting." Song, in an interview with the *Los Angeles Times*, said what China needed was ultra-nationalism, to correct the "imbalance in favor of America."[36] Chinese nationalism and anti-

Americanism were merging into a joint fervor with a joint voice, one that could say no. In the *New York Times,* Zhang summed up his disgust with America in a suggestion that "the Chinese people should have a sense of their own identity."[37]

Several other books came out in the wake of *China Can Say No,* including, *How Can China Say No* and *Why Is China Saying No.* Once a book is a hit in China, variations on its theme flood the market. In 2002, after the huge success of *Who Moved my Cheese?* a management manual that sold 1.6 million copies in China, there was a rush of books inspired by it. Titles included *Whose Cheese Should I Move?*; *Can I Move Your Cheese?*; *Who Dares to Move My Cheese?*; *I Don't Bother to Move Your Cheese*; *Agitating, Alluring Cheese*; *No One Can Move My Cheese! The New Allegory of Cheese*; *Make the Cheese by Yourself!*; *A Piece of Cheese: Reading World Famous Fairy Tales*; *Management Advice 52 from the Cheese*; and *No More Cheese!* Finally, there was my personal favorite: *Chinese People Eat Cheese?—Who Took My Meat Bun?*[38]

The first time I met Zhou Wen and Zheng Yi, two painters from Sichuan, they were praising *China Can Say No.* Anna introduced them to Kate and me in a Japanese bar called Jazz Ya, which means "Jazz Place" in Japanese and "Jazz Duck" in Chinese. Zhou Wen and Zheng Yi were drinking cocktails with paper umbrellas in them.

"Did you two come from Sichuan together?" Kate asked.

Zhou Wen smiled. "We're not gay," he said.

It was the first time I'd heard the Chinese word for gay: *tong-xinglian* or "same-sex love." I was glad to learn the word, but thought the point was a bit labored.

Zhou Wen was in his mid-thirties and stylishly bald, with a tiny reminder of hair fuzzed over his head. His eyes were far away from each other. He was wearing a brown cotton coat with large round buttons down the front of it. Underneath he had on a black T-shirt. Zheng Yi had a full head of dark hair, which flopped down onto his forehead. He wore black glasses and pushed his hair out of his eyes repeatedly. Zheng Yi was two years older than Zhou Wen, extremely handsome, and quiet.

"We were just talking about *China Can Say No,*" Zhou Wen said to us, provocatively. "I love that book."

"I hate that book," I said, even though I had only struggled through half of the first chapter. There was no translation into English of *China Can Say No* and it still took me hours to read in Chinese. But I had brought a copy to my lesson after reading dozens of interviews with the young ideologues who wrote the book and the weathered intellectuals who wrote it off. Critics panned it as a sophomoric rant. Teacher Kang did not approve. "Those authors are young and inexperienced," she told me. "They write from hot emotion, rather than from intellectual depth or experience."

At Jazz Ya, Kate stayed quiet, but I was quick to pretend I had thought of the criticisms myself. "It's a sophomoric rant!" I said. "Those guys know nothing about international relations, and any country that can actually say no doesn't have to write a book shouting about it. Can you imagine a book called *America Can Say No?* Who needs it?"

This itself would of course have been better left unsaid, but my being far away from America inspired patriotic performances, based more on face than on feeling. And what irked me about *China Can Say No* was a personal, more than a patriotic, sensibility. I felt insulted and excluded by the book, as if China were saying no to me personally. I was more American in China than I had ever been in America, so I resented anti-American sentiments more. Zhou Wen said that what was important was being allowed to think what one wanted, not necessarily to say it. It was a polite reprimand, and we both pretended to think he meant China, not me.

As I got to know them over the years, I understood that Zhou Wen and Zheng Yi were patriotic both personally and nationally. Their political views were complex and shaped in part by their alienation from a society that frowned on freedom of expression. Their friends in Beijing were furniture salesmen and businessmen, struggling to get rich. Their families were farmers from rural Chongqing. And the two of them were painters, living a wildly unorthodox life they could never have pulled off before China opened up.

Neither Zhou Wen nor Zheng Yi had received formal training; both were self-taught and proud of it. In the early 1980s they had formed the Chinese Anonymous Painters Association in their hometown of Chongqing and held an exhibition of their paintings. Afterward, they moved to Beijing, the center of China's art world. But when they found modernism roaring there, they stepped sideways away from both the limelight and what they saw as a fad. Each doubled his efforts toward creating a style uniquely his own. Zhou Wen's red slashes of oil paint are unmistakable. His subject's faces look both inhuman and just like Zhou Wen himself; their bodies are often contorted and twisted, sometimes by passion and other times by the horrors and chaos of modernity. Zheng Yi's lithe watercolor figures are filled with romance and shadows. They float freely, naked, in the kinds of vast space nowhere to be found in China.

If Zhou Wen and Zheng Yi's paintings were both representations of and escapes from China, then so were their lives in the capital. Their status in Beijing was made even more peripheral by their somewhat surprising and contradictory connection to the West. Their agent was European. They supported themselves by selling paintings exclusively in Japan and Europe, for thousands of dollars each.

Unlike Anna and Zhao Jun, who looked outward for models and meaning, Zhou Wen and Zheng Yi turned inward and back toward China's history. They refused to participate, at least initially, in China's commercial boom, and were disgusted by what it represented. Zhou Wen argued that modernization was a fad, that China would repent its capitalist ways as soon as the cost became more obvious: the weakening of China's cultural spirit and superiority. He could not accept that China had "so easily forgotten" the Western invasions that had held China back in the first place. His country's reliance on the West to modernize infuriated him. For me, it was difficult to reconcile these views with Zhou Wen's lifestyle and art, which were young, rebellious, and often Tiananmen-centered.

Zhou Wen joked that he and Zheng Yi were "foreigners" in Beijing, too, that China was thinking and saying no to them. Because they were from Sichuan, they had what he called peasant accents, and were cheated by cabdrivers and fruit merchants. Our Chinese was "more standard," and "easy listening" than theirs. We Americans had Beijing accents, meaning we slurred our words with extra *r* sounds. Most of this was humility and flattery; some small percentage of it was true. They were not Beijingers, and for real Beijingers, everything outside of Beijing is *luohou*, or backward. And Zhou Wen and Zheng Yi were in fact outsiders in Beijing, although there are of course varying degrees of outsider status. Those of us who were conspicuously not Chinese were the most dramatic *laowai*. Then there were overseas Chinese, who took flak for being disloyal if they were "too Western" or not fluent enough in Chinese. Then there were non-Han Chinese from China, called "ethnic minorities," who were celebrated in public, at dances and exhibitions, but controlled by the government in private. Zhou Wen and Zheng Yi were Han Chinese, the majority population in China, but from the south; they were as foreign as Texans in New York.

The Chinese idea of self is rooted in a distinction between agrarian peoples and nomadic ones, people with mobility versus those without mobility. Chinese nationalism is not only about dividing what is "Chinese" from what is "foreign," or even what is spiritual from what is material. At its root, the Chinese idea of self is derived from a source no different from that of any culture: the division between self and other. And "other" has not always been (and is still not) fundamentally limited to "Western." In terms of geography in the ancient world, China has always looked like a tic-tac-toe board, with China in the middle of nine continents, the stable center around which the rest of the world moved, the "Middle Kingdom." And Chinese have historically always been sedentary; they built monuments and public works, walls, canals, and rice fields in which they controlled the water. Large-scale public works defined China, and Chinese people derived their ideas of self from their land, through which they were attached to villages, provinces, counties, and finally a country. They were surrounded by nomadic people, who got their addresses by moving, who built no monuments, and whose wealth was articulated in chattel, horses, goats, and herded animals. Ancient Chinese works are about this distinction. *Autumn in the Han Palace* is a defining Chinese story in which a princess is sent off to the barbarians, and

Lie Niu Zhuan, Zhou Wen

everything in the story is about agrarian versus nomadic people. There are people who wear leather versus those who wear silk; people fed by herded animals, who live on milk and cheese, and those fed by agriculture, who eat grain.

I liked to think that I was a combination nomad, a grain-eating vegetarian living in Beijing for a few years. Kate seemed more settled, tied to the city and unlikely to leave. Zhou Wen and Zheng Yi had themselves moved across China, and I would later understand that their move, as much as any other variable or personality trait, had defined them. On my bike home from Jazz Ya after meeting Zhou Wen and Zheng Yi for the first time, I rode the length of South Sanlitun Road out to the Workers' Stadium, curving through back alleys and around the old *hutong*s. The vegetable stands were closed for the night, and rows of auto mechanics' store fronts stood still, lights out. No one was about. The wind was light across my face and the streets were as familiar as if I had been in Beijing forever. Excitement started in my feet and moved all the way up from my knees to my neck. I had loved the chaos and promise of meeting Zhou Wen and Zheng Yi. And I was alone in the middle of the night, pedaling through a city that felt, for a moment, like my own.

Zhou Wen and Zheng Yi invited Kate and Anna and me to their apartment/studio, which they called the "Blue Belly." Worried we'd get lost, Zhou Wen met us at the Beijing Peace Hospital and walked us to their compound. Several Walls brand ice-cream vendors had set up stalls in between identical, short buildings, numbered in red. I bought a haw-fruit Popsicle and trailed behind Zheng Yi to the last row of low-rises.

231

The entrance to their building was full of bikes and boxes. We climbed over piles and onto the cement stairs. Zhou Wen said he and Zheng Yi had liked Kate and me in Jazz Ya that first night because we reminded them of spicy Sichuan food. I had just read on the Chinese newswire *Xinhua* that people from Sichuan have a 68 percent higher risk of getting stomach ulcers. I warned Zhou Wen of this statistic, and he told me that the way to cool the heat down is to eat coagulated duck blood.

At the top of the stairs, Zhou Wen and Zheng Yi had stacked dozens of strung canvases in the hallway. Jars and tubes of colors decorated the stairwell. We walked in and inhaled fresh paint, hot peppers, and incense. The apartment was composed of two rooms straight off the entrance and a narrow cement bathroom to the right. The walls were covered with canvases, some framed and hanging and others propped up, in progress. On the floor were dimly lit lanterns, ancient-looking statue limbs, mostly heads and torsos, and speakers playing Sinead O'Connor's *I Do Not Want What I Haven't Got.*

Zheng Yi was lying on a futon in the room to the right, with an open book on the straw mat in front of him. Next to the book sat a rosewood, marble-inlaid Go table with black and white glass pieces in tidy piles on either side. Zheng Yi stood when we peered in from the hallway, inviting us in. We stared at his watery, romantic paintings, framed beautifully on the walls. Most featured willowy naked women, dancing in swirls. Kate poked me and raised her eyebrows.

Zhou Wen, after putting our coats in the other room, offered us Yanjing beers and a tour. His room was covered with life-sized, firecracker-red oil paintings. They had slashes of black paint through them and round, baby-like characters tossed and spinning in their centers, with their eyes X'ed out. They were not at all whimsical, had none of the dreamlike quality of Zheng Yi's women.

"Are they dead?" I asked, pointing at the X'ed-out eyes.

"No," said Zhou Wen, "but they're lost. They're in China." He laughed bitterly. "China is all about making money now," he said. "Thanks to America. We never even lock the door of our apartment, because in modern China, art is useless and valueless. If someone broke in, they'd steal the speakers and leave the paintings."

"How is that possible?" I asked. "Everyone knows that China has world treasures. I assumed that Chinese were proud of their artistic heritage. That counts as caring about art."

Zhou Wen looked at me unflinchingly. "I mean modern art. Ours, anyway. My paintings are Western," he said, "they only sell abroad."

"Your paintings are Western?" Anna asked.

"They're oil paintings. Oil painting is Western," he said. "But the only Western art technique Chinese people have heard of is impressionism. So when they see my paintings, they say, 'Oh, oil painting! It is impressionism?'" Zhou Wen rolled his eyes.

"But there must be some people who know about art here— what about the people you studied with in Sichuan?" Kate asked.

"I'm self-taught," he said. "And cultured people rarely have money. Just like people with money rarely have culture."

"That's true elsewhere as well," I said.

"Yeah—but here it's especially true. China is nouveau riche, so while people buy Mercedes and washing machines, we sell paintings to Westerners and Japanese."

"You've never sold a painting to a Chinese person?"

"Three in fifteen years."

I was surprised by his cynicism. "What about your affection for *China Can Say No?*" I asked, somewhat irrelevantly.

"That book is right," he replied. "If China spent more time saying 'no' to the West, people here would be more interested in art and less obsessed with making money."

"You blame the West for the fact that Chinese want to make money?"

We were back in spicy territory. Kate, Anna, and Zheng Yi stayed quiet, sipping beer. "Where do you think the influence comes from?" Zhou Wen asked me.

"I don't know," I said, "but it's possible that the desire for comfort and convenience comes from an internal force. And besides, if the West's influence were so overpowering, wouldn't it inspire people to want art as well?"

He laughed. "The advertisements are for electronics and brand names, not paintings."

In a sense, he was right. Western imports came with Western brand names, and those came with fully branded aspirational images and lifestyle suggestions: Marlboro and rugged individualism, M&M's and a carefree love of fun, Pepsi and the Now Generation. Wear Ralph Lauren and be a blond god riding bareback on a pale horse. Drink Coke and have bright white Chiclet teeth. Wear Nikes and you'll appear to have run back from the West, even if they were made in a sweatshop in China.

It's no secret that surface style often suggests dangerous substance and vice versa. Those unnerved by the presence of the West in China in the 1990s, had precedents to support their fear. One subtlety of invasion has always been style by force. Zhou Wen once reminded me of the Manchu takeover of China's Ming Dynasty in 1644. His point was that as soon as the Manchu leadership had executed the last remaining Ming opposition, it began handing down edicts about hairstyles and modes of dress. One day after entering Beijing,[39] the new Manchu leader, Dorgon, decreed that Chinese men must shave their foreheads and wear Manchu-style braids down their backs. This edict met with instant and violent resistance by the Chinese (who associated their long, stylish hair with machismo), and a saying developed: "Keep your hair and lose your head; lose your hair and keep your head."[40] For those who chose to keep their heads, other adaptations were soon enforced as well: Dorgon insisted on the exchange of long, loose-fitting Ming robes for tight and high-collared jackets.[41]

Zhou Wen's fierce theory that the West was polluting China's basic essence with our love of money echoed one of several messages of *Foreign Babes*. Jiexi, in her quest to keep Tianming, sacrifices her inheritance for him. "I don't love money," she tells Tianming's mother, "I love Tianming." It is this declaration that ultimately wins her not only her man, but also the forgiveness and respect of his parents.

I mentioned this scene to Zhou Wen, giving him implicit permission to tell me what he thought of the show, which he and Zheng Yi had chosen not to do, even when various people had approached me in Jazz Ya to ask if I was that "foreign babe in Beijing." As soon as I likened *Babes'* moral message to Zhou Wen's own, Zhou Wen minced no words about *Babes*: it was casual entertainment for empty-minded viewers. And its portrayal of the modern world was not critical; if anything, the show encouraged viewers to be more Western. We agreed on this point.

If Zhou Wen and Zheng Yi worried about the effect of the outside world on China, they were also content to be internal outsiders with Kate and me. Their lives as painters were not only unorthodox because it's hard in any society to be an artist, but also because they had separated themselves from other artists in Beijing, who considered them independent and aloof. Zhou Wen showed me an English-language introduction to their Blue Belly Studio. In the book, in T-shirts and jeans, hands on their hips, staring defiantly into cameras, they looked to me like Western guys. But I couldn't explain that, even to Anna or Kate, because I wasn't sure what I meant by Western guys. I was so tightly bound by my reference points that I projected them onto my friends like a propagandist.

The *Blue Belly Studio Book* introduced Zhou Wen and Zheng Yi as a harmonious couple: "It is almost impossible to speak of either Zhou Wen or Zheng Yi without mentioning the other in the same breath. Their names go together as naturally as the *shui* and *mo* of Chinese painting, as oil and canvas, as water and color." The book was a specific tribute, not only to art and youth, but also to their status as outsiders. "Choosing to make a life in a city not their own, common background, dialect, and experience different from those around them, proved a strong bond."

The funny thing was, I never met anyone, Beijinger or not, who did not seem like an outsider in Beijing. Zhao Jun was an American in China and a Chinese in America. Anna was a foreigner in her own family. Beijing's elders wandered through the city's sleek modern streets like aliens deposited from some other time period.

I was straining through the translated English to Zhou Wen's own words when a Chinese woman came into the studio and dropped keys on a long wooden table in the entranceway. She kissed Zheng Yi hello and nodded at Zhou Wen, who introduced us. "This is Shamei," he said, "Zheng Yi's wife." The book hadn't mentioned her.

It turned out that the three of them lived together, Jack Kerouac and Neal and Carolyn Cassidy style. They were less Westernized than Zhao Jun or Anna, and yet, in some ways, more rebellious and anti-establishment. Zhou Wen, Zheng Yi, and Shamei were untraditional in every sense except their fierce loyalty to China's traditions.

Everyone contains herself and her opposite. In Americans, contradictions were easier for me to understand and accept: I was aware of and privy to the forces that had shaped my American friends. But Zhou Wen, Zheng Yi, and Shamei's dualities came from a foundation it took research to grasp. I asked them endless questions, mainly about the relationship between the Western and Eastern art worlds, which was fraught with tension and complexity. Their understanding of the art world was a metaphor for the way they saw East-West relationships and life in general. And as young modern Chinese artists, they took the tension between China and the West personally. This strain, particularly over art, informed much of both their cynicism—toward an open, Westernizing China polluted by commercialization, and their aspiration— toward creating representations of the beauty, horror, and chaos they encountered. Despite his criticism of the West's influence, Zhou Wen wanted to modernize China's art world in a way that paralleled the opening up of its industry, economy, and government. They were working *for* China, even as they lived against her social mores; they were politicized in a way that none of my young American friends was.

We sat down to Sichuan hot pot. A bubbling pot of hot oil sat on the table, fired by chunks of coal. Legs and tentacles and tripe twisted out, extending themselves generously from the edges of the pot. Kate and I looked at each other in dismay, but Zhou Wen was beside himself with delight. Zheng Yi had to take his glasses off because they were steaming up and greasy. Shamei had left, which I found bizarre. When I asked what she was up to, Zhou Wen said she "has business." Then he turned the conversation inward toward the table. "Genuine Chongqing hot pot!" he said, pointing at the cauldron.

"In Chongqing," Zheng Yi said, "you have to take your shirt off to eat this in the summer, because you sweat so much." It was the longest sentence I'd heard him say.

The food was so hot that we went home with rubbery lips and imaginary ulcers. I wagered I had eaten a pound of pork and enough pig stomach to scare my own with a kind of cannibal recognition. Thus, we offered to host dinner the next time. Zhou Wen and Zheng Yi, nervous about what we would serve, did not accept. Instead, they invited us to the "ghost market," a weekend market in Beijing. Zheng Yi wanted to show us "real" artifacts.

B eijing's ghost market was a chaotic place, a mob of merchants who spread cloth onto a dirt floor and piled up antiques, shards, Mao alarm clocks, boxes, baskets, books, pottery, and whatever else they had. Carved rosewood bed frames leaned against donkey carts. Lines of ceramic vases looked like a celadon horizon. Everything was worth whatever you were willing to pay for it. Zheng Yi browsed slowly and carefully. He was in the market for pottery, and was an expert, avoiding the cheap pieces. He bought a head and part of a neck from a statue he said was hundreds of years old. Kate and I floated down the rows of treasures, wide-eyed and weightless. I bought a framed photo of two young women with bound feet. Both were dressed beautifully, holding their faces straight. On their feet were delicately embroidered lotus slippers. Someone had painted the wooden frame loud, angry colors.

"We learned the history of Chinese art on our own," Zhou Wen was telling me. "China's artistic history is a story about loss. Our goal is to give back, to make up for what's been taken."

By "loss," he meant the literal theft of China's tangible artifacts by the outside world, which has always housed Chinese treasures. For Zhou Wen and Zheng Yi, these losses represented a greater one, of part of China's history and innocence.

There are classic examples of Chinese relics abroad. In 1899, Aurel Stein, a Hungarian-British archaeologist, traveled the Silk Road to the Dunhuang caves, where he found and negotiated for hundreds of Dunhuang manuscripts, which include Buddhist scriptures. The tourism board in Dunhuang now has outlines in the shapes of missing treasures, with plaques beneath reading: "Aurel Stein removed this in 1899."

In May 1999, a translation of Stein's *Serindia: Detailed Report of Exploration in Central Asia and Westernmost China* was published in China. The *China Daily*'s article announcing the release of the translation began: "Aurel Stein removed numerous cultural artifacts from their home in Dunhuang at the turn of the century." Although the English-language daily acknowledged the significance of Stein's work as "undeniable," it also identified the translation of the manuscripts as one "by Westerners—considered 'cultural thieves' by some." Even the translation was theft, and the name Aurel Stein was a bad word in the Blue Belly Studio.

I asked Zhou Wen about what was possibly the most widely debated removal of Chinese art ever, Nationalist Party Leader Chiang Kai-shek's confiscation of the contents of China's Palace Museum, which he took to Taiwan between 1949 and 1950. Chiang's act was one of legitimization; as the leader of the Kuomintang, Chiang saw himself as the ruler of China, and therefore the keeper of its manuscripts, treasures, and art. But Zhou Wen was shocked that I would even ask. "It's stolen," he said. "Do you think Chiang is the ruler of China? *Kai wanxiao*! It's a joke. He took that art in a coup."

The question of ownership is particularly complex in the context of China since the Chinese government itself has historically both expressed a high level of regard for its artifacts and campaigned for their destruction. Many of China's relics were ruined during the Cultural Revolution, fifteen years after Chiang's departure, when Chairman Mao and his wife Jiang Qing encouraged the destruction of artifacts in an effort to reignite revolutionary fervor by removing evidence of class lines. Western art dealers have been known to defend the "relocation" of Chinese art by suggesting the relics would otherwise have been wrecked. Zhou Wen and Zheng Yi's view on the Cultural Revolution was that it was a damaging time for the art world, but that now the relics should be returned rather than sold to wealthy buyers. At the mention of buyers, I asked Zhou Wen about the sale of his own art as relocation. Did he mind that all of it left Beijing?

"No," he said, "this way I can influence the outside world the way it influences China."

"By spreading debauchery, violent images, and sex, you mean?" He laughed. "I hope so!"

In May 2000, Christie's auctioned off two Chinese bronze fountainheads in Hong Kong, in spite of tremendous pressure from Beijing to cancel the auction. The auction house referred on its website to the relics as "dispersed" from the Summer Palace of Yuanmingyuan (the Garden of Perfect Brightness), after an 1860 raid on the garden by Anglo-French troops. The *China Daily* called the monkey and ox heads "two looted Chinese relics," and quoted a Hong Kong official who said the sale "could not be more stupid."

Christie's went ahead with the auction, despite protests by mainland Chinese and Hong Kong residents, a letter from the Chinese Ministry of Culture asking that it be called off, and a report by the *China Daily* stating that the sale would "hurt the feelings of the Chinese people."

Zhou Wen called this story "predictable." When he insisted again that China's treasures should be returned, and not by auction to wealthy private citizens, I agreed. Anna did not. "China can't take care of its treasures," she said. "Why not keep them elsewhere, where they'll at least be preserved? And aren't you the one who's always saying Chinese people don't appreciate art? Why do the Chinese prefer art that's lost to what's here?"

"No one appreciates anything until they've lost it," Zhou Wen said.

Anna and I were interested in Zheng Yi's claim that Shamei was a poet; I was hoping to talk about some of the Tang poems Teacher Kang and I were reading.

"What do you do?" I asked Shamei one night at dinner, waiting for her "I write Tang Dynasty poems" response.

"I'm working for *Motouluola*," she said. Motorola! She was working for Motorola?

Zhou Wen immediately told a story of how Shamei had written a poem and left it lying in the apartment he and Zheng Yi shared. Unaware that Shamei had written it, Zhou Wen had fallen in love with the poet.

"And look," Zhou Wen said. "As soon as she found out I was in love with her, she married Zheng Yi." Zhou Wen roared with laughter and Zheng Yi smiled briefly. Shamei watched Zhou Wen tell his story with a kind of patience I hadn't seen in anyone since my kindergarten teacher. I gathered from her expression that he had told it numerous times before. I wondered what it felt like to live with your husband's best friend.

While I was considering their living arrangement, Zhou Wen and Zheng Yi dropped a social bomb. Kate had just declared her love of *Foreign Babes in Beijing*. "It was like a documentary," she said, "the story of my first Chinese boyfriend."

"What happened with him?" Zhou Wen asked.

"He went back to his fiancée," Kate said.

"That's the trouble with TV," Anna said. "Real life doesn't have a happy ending."

Zheng Yi said, "That's not the only problem with TV," and Zhou Wen finished his sentence: "That's why I don't allow my children to watch it."

Since I knew how unlikely it was that this could be hypothetical, I figured I had misunderstood. Chinese verbs do not conjugate; there is no future tense, only words to imply the future. Zhou Wen had not used any future words.

"Your what?" I asked. He and Zheng Yi looked at each other.

"Our children," they said.

"I thought you weren't a couple," I replied. Zhou Wen, studying my expression and deducing that I had been trying to make a joke, laughed politely.

"My youngest daughter is in Finland with her mother," he said.

"Your youngest daughter," I repeated. Finland? He was married to a Finnish woman? Was this the ultimate connection between them and the outsiders to whom they wanted to say no? And if so, what did it mean for all the conversations we'd ever had?

There was silence. Kate set her glass down.

"His other daughter is in Sichuan with *her* mom," Zheng Yi said.

"Zheng Yi, you have kids too?" Kate asked.

Anna appeared not to find it weird that they had never mentioned this.

"Yeah," Zheng Yi said. "I have two." He offered no further information. The fact that Zhou Wen and Zheng Yi had families struck me as important information, the kind one might gather about a friend within ten minutes of meeting. We'd been hanging out constantly for close to a year. Had I not asked? Should I have asked? I raced through my mind. What did Shamei think of Zheng Yi's kids? Were they her kids? Did she think about them at all? Did she have her own kids? What did I know about any of them, actually? Anything? I asked if I could see a picture.

"I'll show you pictures," Zhou Wen said cheerfully. "Sadly, my daughters look just like me. They have giant noses and no hair!"

"Are you sad that they're far away? Have you been suffering over this the whole time we've known you?" I asked.

Zhou Wen looked at me strangely, his expression softening. "What a question. I never thought you were sensitive," he said. "I considered you a *lihai* [hard-core] businessperson."

I felt my jaw unhinge. What did it mean to be a *lihai* businessperson? I had been promoted at the office to a director, a role I found increasingly loathsome. I was responsible for the time and activities of more "team members" than ever before, but could not bring myself to care how much time they spent promoting American cars in China. Maybe I had mentioned the promotion but not the loathing part to Zhou Wen and Zheng Yi.

"A hard-core executive?" I asked. "What in the world gave you that idea?"

"You are successful at work, confident, and organized," said Zhou Wen.

Shamei was watching me. Could I talk about my disillusionment with my corporate job without insulting her job at Motorola? Maybe she loved being a businessperson and Zhou Wen had complimented me.

"I liked the idea of my job when I started," I told them, articulating the truth of it for the first time, even to myself. "Like acting. It was fun to play this role, I guess. But I resent the work, and I don't care about the end product."

"What's the end product?" he asked.

"Selling cars or washing machines or donuts in China," I said.

"Come on," Anna said, "foreign business in China is opening China up. It gives people like me—and Shamei—good jobs. And it means that people like you guys can live here. This was never true before."

"Maybe," I said. "But all my energy is being channeled to my clients, so they can sell products in China and make more money—I just can't get into it. And I can't stand the stilted language of client service."

"Why don't you quit?" Kate asked.

Here was the hard part. Why didn't I quit? I was too scared to live in China without my own work unit? "It's my iron rice bowl," I said.

"Your iron rice bowl?" Zhou Wen laughed. "*Laowai* don't need iron rice bowls; those are for people who don't have freedom. What's important to you?"

"I don't know," I said. "Poetry." My pre-Beijing life flashed before me, in its indecisive undergraduate splendor. I had pored over poems and tried to write my own. I had studied, mainly, and preferred that. "Account executive" had reminded me of bank accounts and executions. I had liked the *c* sounds. Shamei looked skeptical. She thought I was flattering her by claiming to want to be a poet, like her.

They had their own story about who I was, just as I had one about them. The Chinese saying goes: *"Dangjiuzhe mi, pangguanzhe qing."* The players of a chess game can get confused, whereas onlookers see things clearly. When my friends told me who I was from the outside, I was as often persuaded as I was stunned. It's hard to know who you are when all your familiar reference points have vanished. I thought I could see who everybody else was, so maybe they could see me better than I could see myself. Maybe I was a hard-core executive.

Zhou Wen, Zheng Yi, and Shamei bought a house in the suburbs together in the summer of 1998. The suburbs in Beijing panned a vast map, with freshly painted compounds every ten miles. Matching pastel roofs and walls were visible from the highway. The suburbs were advertised on billboards with photographs of Western families smiling by the sides of duck-filled ponds, or Westernized Asian families playing sports on electric-green lawns. When Zhou Wen threw a house party, Zhao Jun drove us out there crazily, and Kate and I quietly watched the compounds and Nokia billboards stream by. The compounds were called Dragon Villas, Purple Jade, King's Court, and River Garden.

The house was in a nondescript neighborhood of identical buildings. We parked and walked up a stone pathway to their front door, which was flanked by bushes. A bike rack at the entrance to the building held so few bicycles that it looked like a prop from some city other than Beijing. As soon as we neared their house, the smell of food, paint, and incense rushed out at us. Inside, wooden screens with glass panels partitioned the rooms. The white walls were hung evenly with framed paintings and scrolls. In the bathroom, I turned the shower on and it trickled over heated stones into a waterfall. It was not a modest house, and I laughed at Zhou Wen, pleased that he was indulging a bit. They had kept the Blue Belly Studio intact, but would use that only to paint.

I located each of Zheng Yi's treasures from the ghost market in various bedrooms. We stayed for hours, eating Chinese snack mix, vegetables, dumplings, and sunflower seeds. Their *ayi* was in the kitchen, chopping and stir-frying hot dishes, which we picked at from a long, slim table. On the way home, Kate, Zhao Jun, and I marveled over their triangle and how happy and easy it seemed to us. But that fall, almost immediately after the party, Zheng Yi and Shamei suddenly moved back to Chongqing. Zhou Wen stayed in Beijing and promptly sold the house, which they had owned for less than a year. Kate and I went to see him, and he was pale, floating through the studio, alone. He looked like one of his own paintings, eyes crossed out.

"Shamei insisted that they move back," he said.

"Why?"

"She wants to have a normal life, not with artists, not with me," he said.

"But Zheng Yi is still an artist, even if he lives in Chongqing, no?"

"He's going into the furniture business," he said. "Zheng Yi and I have lived together since we were teenagers. He's changed, is all. He wants to be wealthy." I thought about our conversation about

Western influence. What is it that drives people toward lives that are comfortable?

Zhou Wen talked instead about his bird, a *bage*, or mynah bird, who shouted, "Hello!" in Chinese and laughed whenever we walked into the room, by fluffing itself into a poof of feathers and then deflating in short bursts of squawking breath. Zhou Wen was featuring the bird in a series of oil paintings. Each painting held boxes inside boxes. In one painting were four boxes containing fish bones, portraits of Marx, the mynah bird, and a book. The frameworks were like the Li family courtyard in *Foreign Babes*: four families around a central garden or theme. The bird and Marx and books had become Zhou Wen's family, now that Zheng Yi and Shamei were gone. In the second painting in the series, the contents were the same, but the boxes rotated upside down. Zhou Wen was organizing, cleaning house in his mind. The lines were stark, clean and painful, no trace left of his early wild brushstrokes. The *Blue Belly Studio Book* had described his young brushstrokes as "naive and clumsy, in contrast to his solemn themes." Now even the brushstrokes themselves seemed solemn.

"Bage can't make any progress," Zhou Wen said of the bird. "He's perfectly happy with his one word." The bird exhaled a few excited *nihao*'s to me.

"He likes pretty girls," Zhou Wen said.

"Just like you," I joked. "Except you know more than one word."

"I'm old," Zhou Wen said, as if we would both know what he meant.

"What does that mean?" I asked him.

"I have a better understanding of life business than I used to," he said.

"Life business? You mean women?"

"Women are like the sun. When you want them, they disappear and become clouds. Or they're like water. When you try to catch them, they slip through your hands."

"How's Zheng Yi?" I asked.

"Totally different," Zhou Wen said. "For one thing, he and Shamei are divorced."

"Divorced? But they just moved back! Why are they divorced?"

He shrugged. "Everyone gets divorced in China now. Everything is different, except me. When I'm eighty, you will find me here, painting and talking to the bird. It's a certain kind of life in this apartment. One guy, one bird."

And a lot of paintings. He had finished a collection of black and white oil renditions of himself as a baby. He was dressed in a Mao suit in all of them, and as the series progressed, his face became the Chairman's. In one, the baby had Mao's face and was sitting on a gleaming rocking horse. Facing Baby Mao were two paintings of old men, bending out of shadows. The paint feathered out, making the old men blurry and unformed.

"Even though I'm old, China is still young," Zhou Wen said. "China is the girl next door, cute, but not too sexy, not threatening. She will shout when she's ready. I'm waiting, and I'm not modern anymore. To be a modern artist in China now you have to eat people as an installation. I'm old because I think if art isn't humane, then it isn't art. I was modern before Tiananmen."

He took out the photograph he'd promised to show me: a black and white picture of his half-Finnish daughter—a blond, alert, miniature version of him. "Her mother brings her back once or twice a year now," he added. "When she first left, I was worried about how often I would get to see the baby."

"*She* left you?" I asked. Zhou Wen grinned at me. "Yeah," he said. "What did you think? I exiled her to Finland? She left, just like my first wife in Sichuan."

"She left you, too?"

Zhou Wen was laughing now. "Zheng Yi is the heartbreaking playboy," he said. "Not me. Women leave me because all I do is paint. Who wants to live with an artist and a bird? I've always been like an old man; I paint all night, and by the time I go to bed at four in the morning, the bird is up, shouting *nihao!*"

If Zhou Wen's conflict was embodied in his two little girls, one the child of a Sichuan rural woman, the other an international private school student, then it was also manifest in his relationship to China. He himself summed it up best: "If I criticize China, I am criticizing myself. Whenever I object to some topic or problem, I immediately realize that the problem is both external and internal; if it's a problem with China, then it's a problem with me. The younger generation—like Anna, and even your Zhao Jun—they don't understand this connection between themselves and China. They don't realize they are Chinese, that they *are* China." He smiled sadly. "They think McDonald's was a Chinese invention."

From *Foreign Babes in Beijing*
Episode Two

Jiexi and Louisa sit in the dorm, gossiping.

LOUISA
I love Chinese people. I love their families. I love the way
they love their families. I love China.

JIEXI
I'm just jealous that you've found the perfect guy.

SEVEN

模范工人
Mofan Gongren

Model Workers

uring the first run of *Babes*, random people began coming to Fangzhuang, where the elevator girls gave out my apartment number. Friend-seekers knocked on my door and, before I stopped opening it, said, "We'd like to make friends with you, Jiexi." People called me on the phone my landlord had secured immediately after watching the show. Wu Jie was giving out my phone number to anyone who called the studio.

"Please don't give away my phone number," I asked him.

"Why so unfriendly, *yang niu*? They just want to be friends!"

"I know," I said, "but I'm used to my Western customs and need some privacy."

"Don't you want Chinese friends?"

"Of course, but I came from New York. I can't have strangers coming to my door. What if they have bad intentions?"

"Our Beijing is safe! Not like your New York."

"All the same, could you not tell people my number?"

"How about only people I like?"

"But Wu Jie, that's everyone."

He sighed. The phone calls dwindled for about a week and then picked up again. A woman who worked at Rémy Martin began sending me cognac samples. A Chinese man who had moved to America wrote me love letters and enclosed shirtless pictures of himself. *Laowai*, mostly men, wrote to ask if there were still opportunities to act in Chinese shows. (There definitely were, I said, but they weren't going to get the girl, and would probably get beaten up by Chinese heroes.)

I scheduled extra lessons with Teacher Kang. I was concerned at first about asking Teacher Kang about *Foreign Babes*—for a whole host of reasons, not the least of which was that she was an intellectual and I thought it might be rude to imply that she watched "casual" TV. We were reading a Tang poem about beauty called "The Beautiful Xi Shi," with the opening lines: "Since beauty is honored all over the Empire / How could Xi Shi remain humbly at home?" Perhaps this reminded Teacher Kang of Jiexi, because she said, "*Wo kanle nide dianshiju.*" I've seen your TV show.

"You've seen it? *Ai yo!* Oh, no. I'm worried. What do you think?"

"It's casual," she said. "You are not fat in real life, and your accent in the show is not as good as the one I taught you!"

I decided to address only the accent question. "I know! I know! But it's not my voice, Teacher Kang. It's someone else, you know? I don't know how to say . . ."

"*Peiyinle,*" she said. Dubbed. Now I knew how to say dailies, scenes, cut, take, action, chicken, ants climbing a tree, automotive component, constant velocity shaft, drop your pants, media briefing, castrated eunuch, key message, and dubbed.

"Why did you not do your own dubbing?" Teacher Kang asked me.

"I said I would come back to work full-time when we finished filming. I have no time for this *peiyin*. Must work here."

"Even though you hate business?"

"Even though."

"Who did your *peiyin*?"

"Another American woman," I said.

"Why is her accent so much worse than the one I've taught you?"

"I think Beiying asked her to do a bad accent."

"Why?"

"It's clear," I said. "They want her to be a *ke'ai de yang niu*." Adorable foreign babe.

Teacher Kang cocked an eyebrow at me. Was I being ironic about the show? Did I have a perspective that was different from Jiexi's? I was annoyed at her surprise. How credulous did she find me?

"Do you understand my meaning?" I asked.

"Of course," she said. "Producers think a foreign woman's voice should be like this."

"Right," I said, "but not only her voice. Her whole person, yes or no? My meaning is—her face, her body, her dialogue."

"Study well these two words," she said. "*Ti* and *yong*."

Ti and *yong* were Teacher Kang's way of describing to me a distinction between spiritual essence and material achievement. China wants to enjoy the material achievements of the outside world without compromising the cultural attainments of China. China is rich in *ti*, spirit, but needs the West for *yong*, material gain.

"Perhaps," I said, "but why TV shows about American girls, then? Why not just keep the imports limited to American cars and electronics?"

"TV shows are a way of making Chinese people want material gain. They see what other countries have and want China to have those things, too," she said.

"And what if China gets them?"

"Then China gets spiritual pollution, too. Do you know this expression, spiritual pollution?"

In the context of *ti* and *yong*, life at the company didn't vary vastly from that on the set or in the script. The agents of spiritual pollution were the same as those who import material gratification. Jiexi and Louisa *were* Ford, GM, Coca-Cola, and Mars; all offered tempting (if corrupting) products to an audience of willing consumers.

China faced spiritual pollution through two main channels: brute-force remonstrations from politics, and the lurid temptations of popular culture. Western culture was seeping into Chinese life via a predominately Western global media, one to which increasingly large numbers of Chinese had access. Other carriers of pollution included the internet, the flow in and out of Chinese students, and a diaspora of over fifty-seven million. Interface between Chinese citizens and green-card-toting *laowai* also contributed to a loss of control and surge in toxins.

"Aren't you the foreign babe in Beijing?" a cabdriver named Wen asked me.

"Nowadays there are lots of foreign babes in Beijing."

"Do you act on TV?"

"Uh-huh."

"My wife loves that show."

"Thank you. Don't be so polite. You are too kind."

"I never have time to watch, myself."

I did not ask how he could recognize me if he hadn't seen the show.

"Really? Why not?"

He sighed. "I have to work twelve hours a day to make money. Cabdrivers in America don't eat bitterness, do they?"

I considered this. Cabdrivers in America work hard and keep brutal hours.

"I think so," I said. "A lot of them are *laowai,* and work hard."

"Enh. And how much money do cabdrivers in America make?"

I guessed somewhere around twenty-thousand a year.

"American dollars?" he gasped.

"Well," I said, "living expenses cost more there."

"Food?"

"Even food."

"Do you like Chinese food or American food?"

"Both."

"How much money do you make in Beijing?"

I always told cabdrivers my studio salary, which was $80 per episode of *Foreign Babes.* I was embarrassed to mention what the firm paid me, lest I confirm that Westerners made exorbitant amounts of money working for our own companies in China.

"U.S. eighty dollars per episode."

"How many episodes?"

"Twenty-one."

"How many months of work?"

"Close to five."

He thought for a moment and then shouted, "Cheaters!"

"Really?" I asked. "Have I been cheated?"

"I make more than you in a month," he said, glee entering his voice. "And I'm a one *yuan* cabdriver!" His cab was the least expensive of three varieties.

When I told Wang Ling what Sophie and I had been paid, he made me write the numbers down, thinking I must be missing a digit in my pronunciation. That's when I found out that his salary was U.S. $20,000 more than Sophie's and mine. I had assumed when Beiying told me they had no money, that it was true. In fact, the show made a small fortune. I told Wang Ling not to worry, that I made more money than anyone else at the company; it all evened out. He looked at me. "Why do you make more money than the Chinese staff?" he demanded, furious at the unfairness and uninterested in the parallel between it and Beiying's.

In the office, life after *Foreign Babes* was more chaotic than ever. Charlotte, nervous that I would quit forever, promoted me repeatedly. Our gas client suffered a factory crisis and put me in charge of "damage control," which meant writing releases about "doing everything we can to remedy the situation" and bragging about "world-class" safety standards. More and more, I resisted client angles and half-truths, which finally made me an impossible candidate for success in the world of corporate PR. Anna told me that "PR" in English sounds identical to *piyar*, the Chinese word for "asshole." This seemed irrefutable proof of what I had suspected all along.

The social world at the office remained in constant upheaval. When Charlotte suggested that we have a company Thanksgiving,

Anna reported to me, off the record, that the staff did not want to come. Charlotte had proposed Thanksgiving dinner at an American dining club for wealthy expatriates. Visitors had to be accompanied by a member, a rule that technically applied to all nonmember guests, but was selectively enforced. Every time we scheduled an event there, the office was filled with dreadful anticipation of getting dressed up and still feeling underdressed, being treated to a meal that was unfamiliar, expensive, and not tasty. Anna said everyone in the office was "terrified of the clients" and Charlotte. It only punctuated the misery that Thanksgiving would be a long, ceremonious meal, and turkey at that. Chinese hate turkey.

"Thanksgiving?" my colleagues asked. "You eat turkey, right? So dry! No flavor!"

I tried to explain the historical significance and failed. I didn't want to tell a story in which Americans oppress and kill people and then spin the story into a patriotic holiday, even though China has the same tendency. Every celebrated monument in China is a burial ground for the destitute workers who created it. I mentioned in passing to Charlotte that maybe we should have a Chinese banquet for Thanksgiving, as a kind of "hands across the sea" gesture.

"It's an American holiday! Can't they try one of *our* traditions?"

"Well, I'm not sure everyone feels comfortable at an expat country club."

This was a miscalculation. She knew it wasn't a conclusion I had reached on my own, which meant that everyone talked behind her back.

"I offer to host Thanksgiving and no one wants to come?" she asked, too loud. The office was silent and the staff had gathered just outside the door to the conference room, in time to hear:

"Well, if they don't want to celebrate one American holiday all year, then fuck them." Her voice had dropped an octave.

"No, no," I lied, closing the conference room door. A framed picture of the staff karaoake'ing rattled by the door. On the table was a white cake, decorated with brightly colored fruit, for a secretary's birthday.

I felt bad. "I was just guessing about Thanksgiving, and it's a lovely and generous idea. My mistake," I said. Thanksgiving was important to her; she was far from home, and it *was* a generous gesture. She was going out of her way to build bridges; they were just the wrong ones. I attributed her foibles to the difficulty of living out of the language in Beijing. She was a VIP, one of the highest-ranking female executives in Beijing's expatriate community, well connected, well paid, and busy with American Chamber of Commerce events and business efforts. It was easy to be famous in Beijing, even as an executive. If Charlotte had been an executive queen in any American city, she would have seen her same self violently scaled down: less autonomy and power, no chauffer, fewer maids and wishes granted. And so would I. My Beijing self was larger and more absurd than I was; Rui Qiu and Jiexi were presentations I wore in outrageous ways because I could.

Thanksgiving went as if scripted, a terrible and inevitable farce. At dinner, we each sat before plates of cardboard-dry food. My colleagues found it unfriendly that Americans did not eat family-style and share dishes. "Too much of one thing," they said, looking dejectedly at their plates. Charlotte and I were not at the same table. She asked Gary and me to host one table and she hosted another. When the subject of Judaism came up at ours, I looked around to see whether anyone else was potentially implicated. We were all busily pushing food around on our plates when Zeng Min said he had not liked a journalist at a recent media briefing.

"He was aggressive," Zeng Min said.

"Yes," said Xiao Li. "He's a Jewish person."

I swallowed. I thought I should mention I was Jewish, but I waited, hoping the topic would die out before I had to do anything moral or upstanding.

"Jewish people are cheap," said Xiao Li.

"Yes," said Zeng Min, nodding. "Jewish people are great at making money."

Our Asia Pacific president, in town on a visit, looked around pleasantly. He didn't speak Chinese, and came rarely, only if a VIP client was in town or we had some kind of huge meeting. Anna was seated next to him, translating, but she was giving him general paraphrases rather than translating all the conversations word for word. I was grateful.

I cleared my throat, thinking of the time in sixth grade when I had to sing "Dreidel Dreidel" by myself at the public grade school Christmas sing-along. No one else had known the words, and I hadn't realized I'd be singing solo until I had already started. It was too late to backtrack without shaming all my ancestors. I didn't want to make this into a drama at the company, especially in front of our Asia Pacific president, but I was tortured by guilt.

"I'm Jewish," I announced.

"Great!" Zeng Min said. "It makes sense. Jewish people are not only good at making money but are also smart." He said this in English, so that our Asia Pacific president could nod politely in response and wonder how we had possibly arrived at this place in the conversation. He was Japanese-American, and I ruled out the possibility of his being a Jew. Anna exhaled, relieved to have a minute to take a bite of food.

"Well," I conceded, trying not to be contentious, since I thought my contentiousness gave Americans a bad name, "some Jews are smart. Like everyone, right? Some people are stupid; some Jews are stupid. Not all Jews are the same." I was pleased with the sharp logic and grammar of this statement in Chinese.

"How can you say this terrible thing about your own people?" Xiao Li asked.

"Besides," said Zeng Min, in English. "They're all good at making money."

In the spring, I quit. I hadn't found another job, but suddenly could not work in the office a moment longer, and resigned. And once free of my iron rice bowl, I received dozens of offers for "cooperations" and "projects." Some were more tempting than others; all of them involved acts of exhibition on stages I had never imagined existed. My main criterion was weirdness; the more bizarre, the better. I turned down beer commercials (including an offer to be a "live" beer runway model who wore a cowboy hat and lassoed Chinese men from the audience). And I turned down offers from China Central Television to host English-language programs and variety shows. Right away I accepted a job as Avon's master of ceremonies for a perfume branding event, one the woman who called me described as a "combination beauty and poetry contest."

According to the *Biographies of Model Women*, beauty is a virtue. In the biographies illustrating the correct deportment of mothers, the book reads: "If your outer appearance is resplendent and beautiful, you must cultivate virtue and be proper." The governess who gives this good advice about the parallel between external and internal beauty composes her thoughts into a poem: "A splendid woman and upstanding / Brocade she wore, over an unlined coat."

As Avon's emcee, I would introduce the contestants, flatter their poems and outfits, and then announce a winner. The manager faxed me an agenda and "slogan," which Anna shrieked over. "So ugly!" she told me. "*Gaogui bufan yuanzi yongyou?* I can't even translate this—it's about beauty and elegance and wind in high fake language."

"Wind?" I asked. In order to stave off hysteria, I wrote a script, a *pinyin* guess at what I might have to say (thirty single-spaced pages) and convinced Anna to spend hours a night for six days practicing the script with me.

At the contest, Anna and Kate sat in front. The room was filled with audience members: Avon customers, pyramid businesspeople, and friends of Avon ladies, doing favors. I climbed into an Avon suit and clunky yellow jewelry and the manager gave me a hand-held mike. "When the music starts, you will shout the slogan of Avon Rare Gold," she instructed, and I nodded grimly. Music boomed from loudspeakers, crackling and noisy. I walked down the aisle and a spotlight followed me hotly; necks craned around. The music dimmed and I cleared my throat audibly. "*Gaogui bufan yuanzi yongyou!*" I shouted into the hand held mike. I could feel my mouth twitching, threatening to laugh and ruin the event.

Onstage, squawking out a welcome to honored guests, I thought of joint-venture signing ceremonies and the endless string of Chinese events I had attended for work. There was the funeral of an automotive journalist who died while test-driving an electric car. People were wailing in a ritual fashion over his coffin. There was the YiLi-Nabisco joint-venture signing ceremony at which an executive had shouted into the microphone, "The banquet is over!" and guests had leapt up and run out of the room without finishing their food. There were ribbon-cutting ceremonies, ground-breakings, and banquets. What did emcees say at such events? The lights were so hot I had sweat pouring down the inside of my suit, and we were only two minutes into the show. A Chinese woman came from backstage to rescue me.

"Now, we will introduce the contestants," she said. "Du Ruiqiu, what do you think?" There were eight contestants, an auspicious number.

"Eight contestants! Too good!"

The first appeared onstage in a pink dress, a reimagined prom affair. There is no prom in China; this was an appropriation of a Western image. Teacher Kang's teenage daughter was not allowed to leave the house to do anything but study. She wanted to attend college in the U.S., and would have to compete with literally hundreds of thousands of other applicants for visas and spots. What time did that leave for taffeta or dating?

The Chinese emcee introduced the first contestant, who lowered her eyes modestly. The contestant was wearing the iridescent lipstick and pink eye shadow she normally sold. Modeling them, she was turning product.

"You look pretty in that dress. What a graceful dress," I said, using up two adjectives, and immediately regretting it. Seven more women! I had needed to save the dress comment.

"It is an honor to work for Avon and Rare Gold!" the contestant said, so loud that her voice shot through the mike wires. "I have written a poem in honor of Avon's Rare Gold!"

She began to read in a shrieking singsong about beauty,

makeup, and Rare Gold. When she finished, weak applause and a blur of other contestants followed. And as each revealed her far-away hometown, the high stakes of the contest crystallized in my mind. This pageant was a once-in-a-lifetime trip to the capital on business; each girl's hometown knew she was here. It was a chance to be recognized, to advance in a global company.

It was also glamorous to be an Avon lady in China. This was not a contest among door-to-door salesladies of the type Americans associate with Avon. Cosmetics were cutting edge. Avon had come to China in January 1990, its CEO ecstatic that there were "500 million women in China, more than the U.S. and Europe combined."[43] The company had invested U.S. $1 million in a joint-venture production plant in Guangzhou.[44] This competition, according to the manager, was meant to "build Avon as an inspiring brand name among Chinese women who are looking for independence, aggressiveness and successful career development." It was a Chinese Avon Star Search.

Each contestant glowed in her poem about how much she loved Avon and Rare Gold. I imagined them lounging in the gardens of a beautiful Chinese city like Suzhou, writing Avon verse, *Dream of the Red Chamber*–style. I made comments Anna had written.

"Deep and moving poem; rhythmic language; the reading voice of an opera star; music in your words; traditional flavor; uh, deep and moving poem."

The girls' facial expressions vacillated between frozen smiles and serious gazes. I thought of Miss America and Dick Van Dyke. What if these girls came out in bathing suits? When the winner was to be announced, all the girls came out and thanked Avon in high, squeaky voices. But they *were* Avon; they represented Avon. They had been transformed by Avon from occupants of their hometowns into inhabitants of a middle world. And I had been transformed by Beijing into an occupant of that middle world, too. Perhaps none of us would return to our roots; they would follow the lead of the perfume branding contest, an ornate display of Westernized beauty ideals and makeup. They might move to California, as Teacher Kang's daughter eventually did, wear taffeta, and e-mail their mothers in *pinyin*. And I might stay a Beijing hybrid, speaking Chinglish, wearing costumes, and continuing to be unrecognizable as the person I had once been.

A Tang poet named He Zhizhuang once wrote a poem called "Returning Home," in which he leaves his village as a boy, only to return as an old man with gray hair. The village children don't recognize him, because he has become a stranger. The poet was turning in his grave now, spiritual pollution leaking into his spirit's residence. Yet his final lines reminded me of how both the Avon girls and I would feel years from now: "And my children when they meet me, do not know me / They smile and ask: 'Stranger, where are you from?'"

Finally, the winner descended gracefully from the risers, waving and crying. I wondered whether she had ever seen the Miss America pageant, or whether crying when one wins a beauty contest is an innate, universal response. Most likely she was responding to a set of implications distinct from the ones I observed.

The music started up. "*Gaogui bufan yuanzi yongyou!*" I cried out. "Thank you all for coming to the launch of Avon's Rare Gold. Congratulations to our beautiful winner, and to all of our honored audience members! Good night!" It was three in the afternoon. I rushed from the hotel into sunlight. Anna and Kate greeted me and hailed a taxi.

"You looked great," Kate said.

"Maybe a little sweaty, though," Anna said. "My God," she said, an expression she had picked up from Kate, "those poems about how beautiful spring is, or life is, or women are! They were the most cheesy things I have ever heard. They gave me a *rouma* feeling." *Rou* is "meat" or "flesh," and *ma* is "numb." They gave Anna disgusted willies. I wrote *rouma* down; it remains my favorite Chinese expression.

The Chinese beauty industry was blossoming all over China with a vaudeville appeal. As China reformed, to be rich was apparently not the only glorious thing. Beauty roared back into the life of Chinese, freed by rapidly liberating social practice and fueled by the commerce of cosmetics, fashion, and coiffeur. Chinese and foreign girls alike were on stages, acting out explorations of the same story of transformation.

Yun Li, a modeling agent who represented aspiring and newly minted Chinese models, called me after the Avon event, where she had been recruiting. "That Avon thing was not a sophisticated beauty project," Yun Li said scornfully, "but I would like to meet with you and talk about possible cooperations."

She worked for Beijing's New Silk Road Modeling Agency, and called beauty in China a "pioneer process," just the way Charlotte liked to describe PR. Yun Li had been involved with the New Silk Road Modeling Agency since it started up operations several years before. The modeling industry was world-class in Hong Kong but still in its infancy in China. New Silk Road represented more than two hundred models, and worked not only on sending clients to the United States and Europe, but also on developing China's own fashion industry. According to Yun Li, the agency's main goal was to find Chinese supermodels, since Western countries were "more interested in Asian women."

"More interested in Asian women than Eastern countries are, you mean? Or more interested in Asian women than they are in Western women?"

"Both," she said.

I asked how she accounted for the success of *Foreign Babes in Beijing*, and she said, "Television is unsophisticated, and that show was about TV love, not reality."

"The fashion world is sophisticated and reflective of reality?" I asked.

"Well, styles are becoming more Asian everywhere, so the world wants models to match those designs." She looked me over. "Maybe in China the fashion is becoming both more Western and more Chinese. Foreign models who wear Chinese styles show that the clothes are global."

"Or that the women who wear them are global," I joked.

"Right!" she said, surprised that I would agree with her. "For example, the reason Chinese people think you're pretty is because you look Chinese."

"I look Chinese?"

At work, my colleagues had told me I looked both like Whitney Houston and Brooke Shields. Apparently the features they constructed as "American" were so widely believed and deeply held that they overrode distinctions unmistakable to Americans.

But Yun Li thought I looked like a Chinese commercial. "You don't look totally Chinese," she revised, "but you have white skin and dark hair, so if Chinese women were Western, they would look like you."

She invited me to her office, in the middle of a space-age building straight down Jianguomenwai on the edge of Third Ring Road. From the entrance, the first visible wall was covered with headshots of dramatically made-up Chinese women. Their faces appeared to have more dimensions than those of mere mortals.

"These are composite cards," said Yun Li, taking several out. "This model will be famous overseas, I think." She showed me a picture of a severe-looking woman with black eyebrows painted in pointed arches over her eyes. "She is the kind of Chinese beauty that overseas clients like. Especially Eastern-looking. With cherry lips."

"Cherry lips, huh? What kind do Chinese clients like?"

"Various kinds," she said, "but mostly like this." She pulled a different card out, of a moon-faced, babyish-looking Chinese girl. There's a traditional, poetic literature of beauty metaphors in Chinese: duck-egg face, moon eyebrows, cherry lips, melon-seed face, almond or apricot eyes, willow-leaf eyebrows. A melon-seed or sunflower-seed-shaped face is round and tapers smoothly at the chin. Cherry lips are small and bright red in the middle of such a face, with leafy eyebrows wisping across a high forehead.

Yun Li asked if I would like to be in a runway show for a real estate company. "They want to celebrate with some international women because they will have a new residential complex in Hangzhou," she said.

"Why a fashion show?"

"Maybe they want to show some ethnic fashion, the costumes of various places—China, foreign countries, everywhere."

"I'm too short."

"No matter. They need some overseas girls. Hangzhou is a famous city known for beautiful Chinese girls and romance, but the prettiest *laowai* are all in Beijing."

Apparently, the company was having press events in order to woo clients, and then a fashion show that featured a few Western girls thrown in with Chinese models. As far as Yun Li was concerned, this was public relations, no weirder than the clients at my old firm hiring "protocol girls" to sign in guests at the entrances to banquets.

Beauty contests were illegal in China during Mao's reign. But in March 1979, Pierre Cardin, in the market for silk and cashmere, staged a fashion show at Beijing's Nationalities Palace on the Avenue of Eternal Peace. Cardin's show featured scantily clad Parisian models and two Eurasian models, who wore conservative outfits and were distinctly *not* Chinese. The Chinese audience, dressed uniformly in blue cotton suits, sat unsurprised.[45] The show simply confirmed their suspicion that Western women are often half naked.

Nine years later, in 1988, Italian fashion designer Laura Biagiotti presented a fashion show of classic styles in China, also in the hopes of signing a joint-venture agreement to manufacture cashmere.[46] Her China dreams were put on hold after Tiananmen, but in 1993 she signed a joint-venture deal to open four shops in China, then flew home and decorated her mansion in Rome with Chinese objets d'art. Biagiotti spoke about China as an economic paradise, full of untapped potential and innocence.

"We signed the deal because we felt there are enough millionaires in China now to buy designer clothes," she said in interviews, adding that "everything is so new" to the eager Chinese, whereas in Italy, "no one feels rich anymore. We have too much food, fashion, religion, politics, movies, books, everything. This is like going back to 1972."[47]

By 1993, China's beauty industry was no longer like going back to 1972. The 1993 "Miss Beijing" contest offered U.S $14,000 in prize money, and one of the contestants, an architect named Liu, said her goal was to "contradict the many Chinese who still think that a pretty face stands for an empty brain."[48]

Yun Li hired four overseas girls to take part in the Hangzhou real estate fashion show: two French girls named Virginie and Jeanne, a Russian girl named Nadja, and me. She paid us each over $1,000, more than ten times what I made per episode of *Foreign Babes*. We all met at the airport in the airport tax ticket line, where Jeanne glanced at the rest of us, clucking her tongue. She was a shred of a person, tiny and compact, with miniature features and limbs. She was wearing Capri pants and a tank top that didn't cover her stomach.

"My sister is a real supermodel," she said, swinging her hips around to face us. "She does the shows in Paris."

The other French girl, Virginie, was plump with long thick straight hair. She looked punk, like she might be heavily tattooed. She wore combat boots and carried a duffel bag.

Nadja grabbed her bags from the floor. She looked younger than the rest of us, with thin blond hair and a Kewpie doll face. It occurred to me that we were all vaguely cute, but none of us would have been a model in her own country. We weren't stick-thin or angular, our skin wasn't flawless, and we weren't put together. No one looked like she worked out twenty hours a day, and in spite of our scrunchies and best efforts, we did not have shampoo-commercial hair. Everyone was sticky, schlepping bags through the airport. It was hot, and our clothes clung to us like fruit peel.

There was nothing glamorous about it. No one was anywhere near as tall as Yun Li herself, and Nadja joked that she should be the model. "Too boring," Yun Li said, with no irony. I was the only one who laughed.

In Hangzhou, a slippery man named Mr. Xu greeted us, licked his lips, and looked at Nadja. "She's the prettiest, with her yellow hair and blue eyes!" he declared. Then he fed us salted cuttlefish in bags and drove us to the runway venue, where we found groups of emaciated Chinese models devouring buckets of Kentucky Fried Chicken.

The models were unreal. The stereotype is that Chinese are short, but anytime a population exceeds a billion people, some of its inhabitants will be amazons. Apparently, New Silk Road had collected everyone who was seven feet tall, under one hundred pounds, and not already reserved for China's National Basketball Association or the NBA. The models were giraffes. Their cheekbones were wide and high, and their legs and necks were so thin they vanished when the girls turned sideways. None of them showed even a remote interest in the *laowai*, which I took to be arrogance and rather liked. They were proud, tall girls, and professionals. Some arrived on the backs of motorcycles driven by rugged Chinese guys. Many wore acid-washed jeans, either a retro success of 1980s clothing or a fashion faux pas.

The Chinese models saw us, in our shorts, Capri pants, cotton T-shirts, and rice-colored skin, as unfashionable wrecks. Cultural superiority is a quality that transcends culture; everybody indulges. And when the four of us arrived at the stage, waddling fluffily behind a gazelle-girl, the "big boss" announced that we would wear African clothes. African clothes? Was this going to be offensive?

Beijing was not a racially sensitive place; I heard outrageously racist things about Africans and African-Americans while I lived there. Many of the ugly stereotypes came from movies exported from the West, others from oversimplified narratives about historical tensions between African expatriates and Chinese officials. And now, about to model whatever the Chinese idea of "African clothes" was, I was suddenly reminded of the Hong Kong toothpaste brand, "Darkie," which features a smiling black man in a top hat as its logo. The Chinese characters for the name were originally *Hei Ren* Toothpaste, or "Black Man" Toothpaste. The English version on the tube was "Darkie." When Colgate bought the company that produced "Darkie" in 1985, there was a predictable uproar. The company immediately changed the English translation to "Darlie" and bleached out the minstrel logo. But the Chinese characters remained the same for many years. I recently found a tube in New York's Chinatown on which the Chinese reads *Hei* and *Ge*, or "Black" and "Brother." The new English translation reads simply, "Brother." To my mind, "Brother" is still an offensive name for a toothpaste brand.

"Let's see the foreign girls walk," said the big boss. I walked.

The big boss shook her head. "Not okay!"

"Cat-walk!" Yun Li shouted from the audience, in English.

"Right," I said. I walked toward the edge of the stage again.

"Li Li!" called the big boss. "Take her backstage and teach her to walk."

Li Li walked up to me and gestured with her right hand that I should follow her. Her fingers were so long and thin they looked like arms. She stood with her hands on her hips, waiting impatiently. When I did nothing, she waved in front of her. "Walk here."

I pointed out my chicken legs and watched them as I thrust myself across the floor. "No, no!" said Li Li, poking her chin up toward the sky. It was so high above me I could barely tell what her point was. Was it a facial expression? Or did she just mean not to look at my feet when I cat-walked. Cat-walking? Who thought of this, anyway? I clomped back toward Li Li with my chin jagged upward. She nodded dismissively.

When we got back, the big boss drove her gaze over each *laowai*, and finally arrived at Virginie. "She's too fat. She will fit into nothing," the big boss said. Yun Li, in the audience, waved at Virginie, softly, as if she understood that this comment, in front of dozens of Chinese supermodels, might have embarrassed Virginie. I winced but didn't turn to look at Virginie, because I wanted to afford her privacy in whatever her response was. The big boss repeated herself. "The fatty can get down from the stage," she said, and Yun Li spoke in English to Virginie, raising my hopes that Virginie perhaps had not understood the Chinese description of herself. No such luck.

"Yes," Virginie said when Yun Li asked her sit in the audience, "I heard her. I am too fat for the clothes, no?" She took a seat next to Yun Li. The process continued, although not without bitter complaining by the big boss that there were only three foreign girls now, an odd number that could not be choreographed properly. I couldn't bear the idea that Virginie had to remain in Hangzhou for three more days.

The "Chinese costumes" were of the imperial and traditional varieties; the only "ethnic minority" costumes were the ones from Africa, which turned out to be giant orange tablecloths that dragged on the floor when we cat-walked. This made for a strange portrait of world fashion. There were one or two "Western costumes," composed of scraps and ropes tied over models' bodies. I asked Yun Li in what country the ropes had originated, and she said, "Xidan," a shopping district in Beijing.

The show was choreographed with a staggering combination of detail and chaos. But when the performance began, giant Chinese models twirled and clicked with enough flair and professionalism that the show might have seemed real, if the smoke from the dry ice hadn't obscured the runway and caused us to stumble over the edges of our tablecloths, and if the flashing neon lights had borne any relationship to the music, and if the clapping audience weren't made up of real estate executives and local government cadres, some accompanied by wives dressed in red. Everyone sat so stiffly and uniformly that they appeared to be models hired to play audience members. The house was well lit enough for me to make out faces, all frozen in polite smiles, not registering or not acknowledging the ludicrousness of the show.

Cat-walking in hot pants, I might have been a deer, slamming toward the headlights. I grinned nervously. None of the other models moved her face at all on the runway. Chinese models bring out the opposite side of Chinese performance from the "hot emotion" of television actors. The cold modeling drama played like a parody. The components of the show were Chinese: the makeup echoed that of Peking Opera, the clothes were "traditional," the hairstyles were distinctly Chinese. But the overall effects were exotic and exhibitionistic with unmistakably Western overtones. The models were role-playing, acting out images of their middle ground selves, somewhere between *zhong*, center, and *wai*, outside; revealed and hidden, Western and Eastern. And everything about this imported, staged, generic presentation of "global" women—

was new. And it had all the predictable side effects: overstatement, tacky flair, and eclectic misappropriations of style and design.

At a seafood dinner following the show, the real estate executives commented happily that models from the West were less professional than those from China. We were more *kaifang*, open-minded, they said, and therefore our style was more *luan*, chaotic, and *suibian*, casual. Jeanne was infuriated. "We didn't have adequate time to rehearse!" she said. "Which is your fault because this totally unprofessional event was so badly organized."

Mr. Xu tried to diffuse the tension by laughing politely.

"And the costumes were stupid and ugly," Jeanne added.

Everyone was silent for thirty full seconds. Seafood shells cracked against plates, and then Yun Li asked Mr. Xu to describe the history of West Lake.

"Our Hangzhou is more historical than Beijing," he said. He raised his eyebrows at Nadja. "And definitely more romantic!"

In 1998, a magazine called *Beauty* ran an eight-page spread, "Foreign Beauty Prepares to Celebrate the Chinese Spring Festival." The pictures are of a foreign girl, played by me, curling her hair, painting her toenails, exercising in sporty outfits by Esprit, wearing glasses, and taking them off. She even jumps rope. Finally, she puts on the outfit meant to represent the height of true beauty and the realization of her preparation for the Spring Festival. It is an ankle-length, long-sleeved *qipao*, a traditional high-collared Chinese dress, red with gold trim. She wears red dress shoes. In the full-page, glossy final photo of the spread, her hair is completely straightened, darkened, and slicked back, her skin is powdered white, and her lips are small and painted bright red. Her ethnicity is unidentifiable; she is the Chinese version of Western beauty, a transnational alien. Yun Li said that in the pictures my face looked "more melon-seed shaped than ever before."

While I was having my hair straightened and eyeliner slathered on, Anna's sister was getting a nose job.

"Her nose is taller and straighter now, more like a Western one," Anna told me.

"She had this surgery only for cosmetic reasons?" I asked. What was I hoping for, the "deviated septum" excuse?

"To look prettier," Anna said.

"Prettier? But Chinese people call Westerners 'big nose.' How is that prettier?"

"The nose is taller, not bigger," Anna clarified. Her sister had paid $70 to have the operation at a local hospital, and as far as Anna and her parents were concerned, Li Na looked prettier and would therefore be more confident.

I was astonished. "But surgery! It's such a big deal, for a small thing!"

"Being beautiful isn't a small thing. It's easy for you to say so, *yang niu*. And in China beauty is becoming more important now, the way it's always been in the West.

From *Foreign Babes in Beijing*
Episode Twenty

Tianming and Jiexi sit in a park on campus.

JIEXI
(Beginning to cry)
Yes, but I love you more than ever. More than ever, I can't leave you.

TIANMING
Don't cry. I understand the chaos in your heart. For me, you've already sacrificed a lot. I don't think you should sacrifice anymore. We must break up.

EIGHT

二蛋

Er Dan

Two Balls

On summer weekends, Kate and Anna and I biked through Beijing's *hutong* alleys, and went to the Observatory with tools for viewing the heavens. By May 1995, China had instituted a five-day workweek, so people were free on weekends. The city filled with kites flown by children and their fathers. The highway overpasses were full of families staring up at man-made birds: long, billowing dragons, pointy bats, wooden tigers.

Weekend nights, I busied myself setting Kate up on dates with Shi Wei. Initially, she hated his pirate scar. "Did you see that terrifying thing?" she asked me.

"That's why I set you up," I joked.

But after only two dates, she reported, "That scar is from a knife fight!" and continued to date Shi Wei, with increasing enthusiasm. By then I had doubts that both Shi Wei and Zhao Jun could have been in knife fights, but it was possible. Everyone has an image he or she wants to project to the world. It was only in China that I was sometimes unable to separate people from the screens they put up. While this meant that my perceptions of people were hindered by nuance paralysis, the effect was also that life felt as fast and edited as a movie. Beijing was event-packed; I met people in glamorous flashes, briefly usually, but constantly, whether it was working on projects, drinking in nightclubs, or walking through the city. Life's in-between moments and down times were hard to find. This sensation, a kind of high, increased once Kate and I were spending all of our free time with Zhao Jun and Shi Wei.

The four of us spent over a year together, hammering out our culture shock in what might have made a good sequel to *Foreign Babes in Beijing*. Our conflicting desires, to know and hide from each other, informed our conversations. Anna advised Kate and me on how to have Chinese boyfriends, even though Kate argued that Anna had less experience with Chinese men than anyone else Kate knew.

"I still know more about them than you do," Anna said. "My father is one, for example. You and Shi Wei and Rachel and Zhao Jun have big cultural gaps. And it's not just surface things, it's the way you guys think. I can understand Chinese guys. These two are extremely charming, but you will not marry them or have babies."

Anna wasn't wrong about the differences between the four of us; they ran the gamut from taste buds to philosophies and modes of expression. But we lived in the gap; those differences made us amusing and interesting to each other. Anna found the whole scene a bit naive, just as I had seen her lingering affection for Khalid.

Shi Wei's favorite food was hot pot, which he insisted we eat every night. Hot pot restaurants have cauldrons built into their tables, filled with spicy oil and broth. A fire under the table heats up the pot until its garlicky soup boils. Diners dunk and cook mutton, mushrooms, cabbage, brains, fish, tofu, and noodles in the broth before dipping them in a sauce made of sesame oil, garlic, and gloppy nut paste. Shi Wei loved to take raw meat sliced so thin it was barely visible, dangle it into the hot oil, and watch the cooked color crawl up. But vegetarians ruin hot pot for people who love it, and Kate ate no meat. Shi Wei asked her every night whether she ate meat. Kate asked him every night, "Are you joking? Do you think I've changed my mind since yesterday?"

"I wished for it," Shi Wei responded, as he ordered a separate half of the hot pot for brains, lamb, pork, and various bleeding, squiggling treats for himself and Zhao Jun. It was only half true that he would have liked Kate to eat meat; her vegetarianism was exotic, Western, and cute. We thrived on our distinctions: Kate and I liked Zhao Jun's and Shi Wei's histories, sufferings, and edges. She even found Shi Wei's carnivore habits attractive. What Zhao Jun and Shi Wei liked about us was precisely the opposite: our American privilege, clean slates, and freedom from harsh histories. To them, we seemed carefree and free, fresh if shallow qualities.

Kate and I ate tofu, noodles, and mushrooms from our half. "When I eat with you guys, there's only one meat dish," Shi Wei griped.

"When we eat with you, there's only hot pot," we reminded him. I showed him the Tang poem from my lesson that day, Wei Yingwu's "Entertaining Literary Men in My Official Residence on a Rainy Day," in which he writes: "Though we have to go without fish and meat, / There are fruits and vegetables aplenty / We bow, we take our cups of wine / We give our attention to beautiful poems.'"

Shi Wei rolled his eyes and suggested I turn my attention to a bowl of raw garlic cloves, which he insisted were good for our health, given the deficiencies our bodies suffered from not having meat. When I asked whether he minded tasting and smelling of garlic all the time, he gave it some thought. "No," he said, "it's better than smelling like milk." When I asked what he meant by that, he said, "That's what Westerners smell like."

"Really? My god," I said. "That's incredibly gross."

"Really? My god!" Shi Wei said, laughing. They were the only two English expressions he ever memorized. He spoke no other English, and all of our four-way conversations happened in Chinese, as did his entire relationship with Kate.

Zhao Jun and Shi Wei told us frequently that they "had *shi,*" or business, and left for hours. Anna translated "I have business" as "everything from 'I have a meeting with President Jiang' to 'I have to go to the bathroom.'" She also pointed out, with a meaningful glance at me, that the word for "business" is also used interchangeably with the word "sex." If you and someone else "have had business," then you've had sex.

"So every time they say they have 'business' they're out with *disanzhe?*" I joked.

"Very possible," Anna said.

"Business" was only one word in a series of incomprehensible expressions that introduced us intimately to Chinese slang and, to a certain extent, to Zhao Jun and Shi Wei. They referred to each other as *erdan,* or "two eggs." Zhao Jun said, "It's like you and Kate calling each other 'girl.'"

"Except it means 'balls,'" I said.

They coined the "two balls" nickname that summer at Miyun, Beijing's drinking water reservoir. It was a scorching Beijing summer, although the thermometers posted on city buildings never rose above 40 degrees Celsius (104 degrees Fahrenheit), so it's hard to say how hot it actually got. Beijing has a law that when temperatures rise above 40 degrees, work must be canceled. So even when Beijing swelters, the government says it's still 40 degrees. When there are strings of 40-degree days, no one can bear to stay inside. That summer, the streets were packed with children and old people, all in undershirts and sandals, eating watermelon and Walls-brand Popsicles. Melon trucks drove through the city stacked to the sky with cold green fruit. Kate, Zhao Jun, Shi Wei, and I sat in air-conditioned cafés and shopped for pirated CDs and VCDs, video CDs, a precursor to DVDs. The discs cost less than 10 *yuan*, a dollar per disc, and we collected hundreds of movies. The VCDs provided authentic home theater experiences; when people stood up, threw popcorn, or walked in and out of the theater, it was recorded.

All summer the air stood still, holding us in, making us crazy. On especially suffocating Saturdays, Zhao Jun, Shi Wei, Kate, and I drove out of the city, watching the buildings spread out until the road turned into dirt and hills sloped away from its edges. The air lost its Beijing texture and the sky cleared. Once we stopped at a remote-access site to the Great Wall, called the "Wild Wall," where we hiked the broken rocks and picnicked in a fortress built on the bones of workers. We camped there that night, watching the wall snake off ten thousand *li* into the distance, until the sun sank and we saw nothing but stars. It is not true that the Great Wall is the only man-made creation visible from space. But it is the only place I've ever stood from which every bit of space seems visible.

Looking out from the Wall, we had a charged feeling that everything was different, changing, alive. China felt as young to us as we felt to ourselves. We talked about hope, movies, and China's future. Within a hundred years, China would be the world's leading economic and cultural force. The world would be Sino-U.S. and bilingual, with Beijing at its center. In the morning, when light filtered down in shards through the cracked bricks of the fortress, we brushed our teeth over the side of the wall, climbed out to our cars, and drove to the reservoir at Miyun, where the swimming was glass-clean. The swimming hole was flanked on either side by steep banks, and we parked on one of them, at the house of some local farmers. A family came out to greet us, and offered to make us a lunch of stir-fried grasses and local vegetables. Their daughter hung near the table, listening to our Chinglish conversation shyly, sometimes running inside to get tea or napkins.

Shi Wei had brought a net to refrigerate drinks underwater. When he took his shorts off to leap in the water and plant the drinks, he exposed a startling blue Speedo. Zhao Jun called out, "hey, *erdan*! Why are you wearing that swimming suit? My god!" The trunks-versus-briefs conversation, it turns out, is a universal cliché. I remembered Wang Ling and Director Yao, in matching tighty-whities during the *Babes* love scenes. I tried to imagine translating the Speedo jokes for the family who had just made us lunch. Zhao Jun was wearing trunks, which he kept gesturing at. "I got these in L.A.," he said. "No one wears Speedos." Shi Wei turned to Kate and me for confirmation.

"Some guys do," we said.

"Yeah, but what kind of guys?" Zhao Jun asked.

"Maybe European guys," Kate said.

Zhao Jun dove in and thrashed around in the water for a few minutes and then hung on to the side of the metal boat Kate and I were paddling around in. Shi Wei swam to the other side of the reservoir and back to us, over a mile. We were stretched out on land again when he arrived. "If you're going to swim for real," he said, "you need this kind of bathing suit. Of course, if you can't swim, it doesn't matter." He looked at Zhao Jun, who couldn't swim well and was clutching the side of the rusty boat. Shi Wei dived back into the water. Kate and I raised our eyebrows at each other. "Damn!" she said. "He can swim."

"Cute Speedo," I said.

On the ride home, Zhao Jun got stuck behind a blue peasant truck and picked a fierce game of chicken with its driver. "Calm down," I begged, clinging to the handle above the Jeep window. Instead of responding, he called Shi Wei on the cell phone.

"Slow down and cut this guy off," he said. "When I get there, I'm going to get out and teach him a lesson." He waved a fist out the window and laid on the horn.

I pitched a fit about safe driving. "What did Shi Wei say?" I asked.

"He said of course," Zhao Jun said. "He understands this kind of thing."

"What kind of thing? What's the point of it?" I asked him. "Just don't do it."

"But this guy is fucking with us," he said.

We were still fighting when I realized that Shi Wei had let the guy pass and turn. He was gone. The phone rang.

"Yeah," Zhao Jun said. "He must have gotten scared." Then he said something I couldn't follow, from which I picked out the word "henpecked."

"Don't use that word," I said. He smiled and hit the off button on his phone. "Then don't nag me like an American wife," he suggested. I thought about his American ex-wife, what her life in China must have been like. In spite of what Hollywood movies imply, that Americans get harassed as soon as they step into China, the opposite is true. Westerners had a profound, unspoken diplomatic immunity in Beijing, particularly in our personal behavior. Zhao Jun forgave and in some sense even enjoyed my American outbursts. And as much as my behavior infuriated him and his enraged me, we got to practice on each other all the people each of us might want to be. And ultimately the more we each learned to act like and appease the other, the less interesting we found our affair.

"You're like the dragon in the backseat," Zhao Jun said in Chinese, "the one who also wants to drive and also breathes on the driver."

"Except I'm in the front seat," I said in English. When we argued, we retreated into our native languages. Fluent arsenals are better equipped with bitter phrases. Now we were quiet for two or three minutes and then he said, "I would have beat the shit out of that guy if Shi Wei hadn't let him go."

I watched the highway go by. The trees along it were painted white halfway up their trunks so they would glow in the dark like street lamps. Fruit merchants had set up stands along the sides of the highways, only feet away from traffic. The white trees reflected headlights, lighting up the stalls. Some had folding cots with children snuggled into them. I thought of how dangerous it was to play or sleep or trade along the road to Miyun. Our own lives seemed suddenly not only decadent, but also dangerous in a way I found hard to pinpoint.

"Do you think our life is shallow or immoral?" I asked Zhao Jun in Chinese, using *zanmen*. I had never used an inclusive "our" to describe a shared life. We both heard it.

He sighed. "What do you mean?" I knew why he sighed, and I

felt for him. What I liked both most and least about being with Zhao Jun was the space he allowed me. Chinese reporters had asked me about differences between Western and Chinese men, and I eventually understood at least one as a difference not in the men themselves, but in the kinds of partnerships they expected. Zhao Jun did not demand explanations of my internal world; he did not ask, "What are you thinking?" hoping the answer was "About you." He did not ask much. I delighted in the ways Zhao Jun let me keep myself secret, even though I resented the ways he stayed secret from me. The only practical, non-face-loss solution was to agree that we each had our own "business"; if he did not mind mine, then I would not mind his. The cost of this arrangement was obvious: we were furious and jealous, and each knew far too little about what the other thought, did, and felt. We were the way I had imagined Wang Ling and his wife, during the conversation about his French mistress. Sometimes, whether out of sheer habit or a particular loneliness, I asked Zhao Jun questions he resented.

"What does our caravan of chattering couples on cell phones have to do with the rest of China? Or with anything meaningful?" I asked.

"What does anyone's life have to do with the place they live?"

"Right, but on a practical level our being in China and acting the way we do is especially disgusting. What could that family who cooked roots and leaves think of us?"

"Do you think I can speak for every Chinese peasant?"

"Come on, Zhao Jun, you know that's not my point."

"Don't feel guilty about poor people here; it's condescending. The guys who fed us at Miyun were glad we paid them, just like any restaurant owner."

"Okay," I said, "but what about on a larger scale than that? Do they think we're privileged and obscene? Do you feel bad for the way you were able to live in L.A.? Or for the way you're able to live here?"

"Poor people don't think of it that way. It's a luxury for you to have these ideas and talk about them, which is one of the reasons they're condescending."

"What are the other reasons?"

"Because you're a guest in China."

"Yeah? Do you think I wouldn't have this conversation about poverty anywhere?"

"*Bu qingchu.*" Unclear.

"Well, I would, and I wouldn't lead a life in which I displayed the difference so grotesquely, either."

He shook his head. "You've never been to L.A."

We arrived at the Metro Café, a new and crazily popular pasta place, and waited for Kate and Shi Wei. But Shi Wei called Zhao Jun's cell phone to say they were not coming, and then called again to remind Zhao Jun of some additional "business" they had later. I was embarrassed that the cell phone had rung twice. We were seated in intense proximity to the next table, where a blond couple was having a romantic dinner. I suggested quietly to Zhao Jun that we turn off the phone. The man at the next table, an Australian with cropped platinum hair and an earring, said, "Yes, turn the thing off. You've used it enough fucking times."

It was as if a traffic light had changed. The man's wife leaned forward nodding, and Zhao Jun's veins tore up his neck. I imagined him going dark green like Lou Ferigno, shredding his shirt and killing the blond couple, but before any of that could happen, the man took it an amazing step further.

"You must be really important," he said, "you ignorant asshole."

Zhao Jun threw his chair backward and stood up, sending silence like a shock wave across the restaurant.

"Zhao Jun, don't even bother," I said.

But he leaned over to their table and free-flowed Chinese *maren hua*, or curses, a good choice. People are always better off swearing in their own languages, even when they're as bilingual as Zhao Jun. If I shouted a Chinese curse word at someone, there is no way it would inspire any response other than raucous laughter. But then Zhao Jun switched to English and said, "I'll kick your face in, you piece of shit," and it came out electric fluent, no one laughed.

"How dare you call him a piece of shit?" the man's wife shrieked.

"I'd call anyone a piece of shit who acted like one," Zhao Jun said, "you racist bitch. Would he call anyone ignorant? Or just a Chinese?"

He spun and stormed to the bathroom. The restaurant thawed; people returned to eating. I turned to the couple to say we'd had an emergency on the phone. The wife shrugged, and already hating myself for half apologizing, I added, "Besides, it's a public place and you're in China. Everyone uses cell phones."

"I'll have you know I've been here five years," she said.

"So you're a slow learner."

"Fuck you."

I felt sick. Good American girls don't like confrontation with strangers. Zhao Jun came back from the bathroom and did not glance at their table again. We all stayed and ate our whole dinners, each couple refusing to lose face and waiting for the other to leave first. We twisted single strands of clammy spaghetti on our forks and stabbed at wisps of lettuce. My chest was tight. In the

Jeep, I tried to steer us to safety by asking about Shi Wei's Speedo. Feeling wretched, I asked the mild, "Why did you tease Shi Wei about his bathing suit? Don't most Chinese guys wear them?"

"Is that what you're thinking about so quietly?" Zhao Jun asked, watching me sideways. "I told Shi Wei to get some trunks because he shouldn't show so much *erdan*."

I never found out whether he knew I had half apologized to the couple. And yet we were momentarily safe again, in the way we were always safe, a thin, euphemistic, dangerous way.

S hi Wei told Kate that his life story had a tragic pallor. His parents were sent to the countryside during the Cultural Revolution in 1973. He was ten years old at the time. His maternal grandmother, a wealthy landowner, was stripped of all her wealth and moved into one bedroom. She could only afford to take in one of the two boys, and Shi Wei's older brother went to live with her. Shi Wei himself stayed in the courtyard house his parents had occupied in Beijing. Three other families lived there as well, and offered to watch over him. "But nobody there loved me," he told Kate. "There was nothing my parents could do. I lived alone." He had gobbled an entire bag of sugar one day, because he was "a little kid," and the neighbors had screamed at him for wasting the sugar they all needed to use for weeks.

Shi Wei had been married, and had a six-year old son whom his parents were raising with his ex-wife. In part, this was recompense for their absence during Shi Wei's own youth. When I asked Kate whether his parents resented having to raise Shi Wei's child or felt critical of his divorce, she said they blamed themselves. Shi Wei was a drinker, and they worried, but they worried quietly, since his *shi* was his *shi*.

Shi Wei and Zhao Jun had both served time in jail. According to Shi Wei, he went to jail when he was sixteen, for taking pictures of a pro-democracy movement and "Democracy Wall." He did not provide details about the incident, and when we asked to see the pictures, he looked incredulous. "Do you think I still have them? They were taken immediately!" This was somewhat plausible, and asking probing questions seemed accusatory. When we asked Anna what she thought, she shrugged. "He wants Kate to think he's an outlaw," she said.

"That doesn't mean he isn't one," Kate said.

"Of course. But there are lots of things you guys don't know about each other."

"And lots we do," Kate said.

"Does he know your last name?" Anna asked.

"What does that mean?"

"In English."

"He doesn't speak English," Kate said.

"Right," said Anna. "I know."

"You date tons of people who don't speak Chinese," Kate pointed out.

"I make sure they know how to pronounce my last name in Chinese," Anna said. "He should ask things about you. And you should ask things about him. About his son. His divorce. His ex-wife. His family. If you're as serious about him as you say you are, these are things you should research."

The one topic Shi Wei and Zhao Jun were forever open to discussing was each other. Shi Wei told me that Zhao Jun had always wanted to be American. "Ever since he was young," Shi Wei said, "this is what he wanted. Not just to go abroad, but to *be* an American." This was a certain kind of baiting. Unwilling to be disloyal, I deflected. "And you?"

"No," Shi Wei said, "I have traveled to the U.S. only to buy movies. I have never wanted to be American, because I am truly Chinese."

"What does that mean?" I asked.

He did not answer. Instead, he said, "You and Kate think you know more than you do." He smiled. I was surprised to hear him admit this; we knew so little that it should have awakened us from our lives with a start. It seemed a risky thing to bring up at all.

He and Kate had been fighting horribly about Shi Wei's "I have business" evenings, and Shi Wei had stopped by my apartment. We were sitting on my couch when he told me he was writing a book about Kate and me. He had moved into her apartment, which complicated their fights. Every time they argued, Shi Wei said, "But we already have a household. These things we disagree on are small matters. It's our life together that matters." Kate said that they had never discussed moving in together, that it had just "happened." I would have found this hard to imagine if I hadn't found myself in the same situation. Zhao Jun stored a few things at my place, which grew in number and volume until they included him as well.

When Shi Wei told me that day that he wanted to talk about Kate, I said I thought he should probably talk to her directly. "I can't really speak for her," I said, and then joked, "despite the fact that we *laowai* are all the same."

"I'm writing a book," he said.

"About Kate?"

"About the things you two are always saying and doing. About American girls."

"Really? Do you know enough about us to write a book? *Is* there enough about us to fill a book?" I smiled.

"I know a lot," he said, "about American girls and love."

I was flooded with affection for him. "What are you going to write?"

"Stories about you and Zhao Jun and me and Kate."

"Stories about me and Zhao Jun?" I didn't like the sound of it. "What about us?"

"What the troubles are."

"And what are they?"

"Zhao Jun is concerned with himself and you need someone to pay more attention to you. You guys have communication problems. And you're both passionate and American."

"Zhao Jun is Chinese," I said. "And that hardly makes a book. You and Kate, *ne*?"

"It's complicated."

"I figured. But why write a book about *aiqing di shi*? Won't it be self-indulgent?"

"I want to write it so I can keep us all from breaking up."

"In that case, you better hurry up and write it," I told him.

It interested me that Shi Wei thought that making our "stories" public would prevent us from breaking up in private. I thought of Anna and all the other young Chinese I was meeting, flaunting their beautiful, individual selves. Of Zhao Jun's and Shi Wei's chicken shows on the highway. Of Kate's and my reluctance to admit, even to each other, how little we understood about the connections we were forming. Now I know we stumbled blindly through Beijing, even once we were fluent in its language, trying to read details that might make us clear to ourselves and each other. And even now I wonder, from what realities does public display shield our private selves? I can still understand Shi Wei's feeling that if he either knew enough or pretended to know more, he might have been able to halt fate.

B ut he could not. He and Kate broke up a month before Christmas, and we all saw each other at a Christmas party in the Beijing suburb of Shunyi. Shi Wei and I ate close to a pound of imitation Tootsie Rolls and talked about cowboys. I thought of the bag of sugar he had eaten while his parents were being reeducated. The party was held by an American named Bob. Bob owned a candy company, and wore cowboy boots and a hat every day. His suburban house was decorated with Chinese furniture, and had an office in the back where he kept boxes of candy samples. Shi Wei and I sneaked away into the candy sample room. Shi We was talking in Chinese about whether *liumang*, hoodlums, or *niuzai*, cowboys, have more *nanzihan di fengdu,* machismo. We were drunk, slurring our words. Shi Wei was wearing his Harley-Davidson belt with the huge silver buckle.

"Harley Davidson is macho," I told him, laughing. I looked up at him; he was drunk, flushed and grinning. "So," I added, "is your scar."

"I miss you guys," he said.

"I miss you, too," I said. "But the hot pot is better without us, right or not right?" Kate and I hadn't seen him in over a month. It was the longest I had gone without seeing Shi Wei since I'd met him the first time. When we emerged from the candy storage room, he and Kate had an argument. He wanted to talk about their breakup, but was too drunk to handle a conversation, and she said so, angrily. He was overwrought and miserable. She suggested to me that we leave. It seemed like a reasonable idea. I collected my hat and boots and began to say good-bye to everyone, but as I did, Shi Wei slipped out the door. Kate gestured to me to stop getting ready, hoping to avoid another painful encounter in the driveway.

"My reason for leaving just left," she said. "Let's not go outside yet."

"Okay," I said, turning to her. "Sit for a minute and chill."

I have often considered that moment and wondered why I didn't turn to look at the door as Shi Wei left, and whether it would have made a difference if I had. I don't know whether he was planning to leave, or had seen us preparing to go and was hoping to talk to Kate. It has occurred to me that when we didn't go outside, he eventually left to avoid coming back inside and losing face.

We left forty-five minutes later in Kate's car. Zhao Jun was ahead of us; we were to meet him at a club called Poachers. As soon as Kate started the engine, my stomach clamped with panic.

"Was Shi Wei driving?" I asked her.

"I don't know," she said.

"He was really drunk," I said, and then again, stupidly, "Was he driving?"

The Cui Jian tape she had in her car stereo jumped on, playing a song called "The 90's," in which Cui Jian sings: "Words are not precise already. Can't express this world clearly." We had heard only those two lines when Zhao Jun called my cell phone from his Jeep.

"Go home and wait for me to call you," Zhao Jun said. "We found Shi Wei's car over the side of the road."

Over the side of the road. Kate pulled under a bridge and we sat for a minute, trying to calm down. I called Zhao Jun back to ask what was going on, but he didn't pick up. We drove the rest of the way home. Inside my apartment, the light was offensively bright. Everything looked grotesque: the shiny floor, the woodwork around the edges of my living room, paper lanterns. We sat on the couch. We said, "He'll be fine, right?" and "Let's not panic until we have news." Time stalled, draping over my house and choking us.

I called Zhao Jun again and again, and finally got his friend Yao Hua on the line.

"What's going on?" I asked him. "Where's Zhao Jun? Have you found Shi Wei?"

"Yes."

"And?"

"He's in the hospital."

"Is it serious?"

At this, Yao Hua paused. Zhao Jun explained to me later that they didn't want to scare us; they knew we "wouldn't understand" and couldn't help. I asked him what he meant by "wouldn't understand" and he just looked at me.

"No," said Yao Hua, "he should be okay."

I was silent.

"Actually, yes," said Yao Hua, "it's serious."

"Which is it?" I asked.

"Which is what?"

I asked for Zhao Jun.

"What's going on?" I asked him when he picked up the phone.

"Shi Wei has to have surgery," he said in English.

"What kind of surgery?" I asked in Chinese.

"For the head. Maybe he hurt his head."

"Do you mean brain surgery?"

"Maybe."

"Maybe he has to have surgery or maybe it's brain surgery?"

"Yes, he will have brain surgery."

I could hear my breathing. I tried to think. "Where are you? How can we get there?"

"No," Zhao Jun said. "Best you don't come. Let me call you back."

I didn't know whether this meant we would be a nuisance or that he didn't want to inconvenience us.

"No, wait, don't hang up. Is he okay? What happened? Did you guys find him? What hospital is he at? How did he get there?"

"Someone else found him and took him to the hospital. When we got there, he was already not in the car."

I had seen enough car accidents in China to know that people were reluctant to stop and help, because anyone who got involved, even an altruistic stranger, was likely to be stuck with hospital bills. I wanted to find and thank whoever had risked himself to take Shi Wei.

"We'll know by tomorrow if it's okay," said Zhao Jun finally, eager to hang up.

"If what's okay?" I asked, "the surgery or Shi Wei?"

"Let's talk when I get there," Zhao Jun suggested.

I set the phone down, surprised to find that my hands were numb. Kate was sitting on the couch, folded up into an origami version of herself.

"What should we do?" I asked her.

"Wait, I guess. There's nothing else to do, right?"

"Maybe we should call our parents."

We did that. It was three in the afternoon in the U.S., so they knew it was three in our morning and were horrified to hear our middle-of-the-night voices. I was sitting on the floor, thinking how odd it was that I was in my own house but felt like I didn't know where I was. The floor was cool and I leaned onto it, imagining Michigan. There's something American about cold tile. It suggests first world bathrooms. I wanted to go home so much that I could feel planes taking off in my stomach.

We turned on *Men in Black*, because the VCD was sitting on the coffee table. It played over and over on a loop for hours. Zhao Jun came to the apartment at five and said, "Still in surgery." We all passed out and then woke up. The world paused for a minute before I remembered it with an ice-cold surge.

Zhao Jun was on the phone in the kitchen. Kate and I got in her car and went to a Japanese place, Sansilang, and ordered rolls of sushi. When they arrived, we stared at them in disbelief. It was nine A.M. We called Yao Hua and couldn't understand anything he said. The vocabulary was impossible, and we couldn't tell what details and realities he was sparing us. We called Anna and asked her please to call Yao Hua and translate what everything meant. When Anna called us back, she minced no words. "I think there's no hope," she said. "But maybe you should go over to the hospital. If you want me to, I'll meet you there."

We drove back to Zhao Jun, carrying the Japanese food, which I would throw away twenty hours later. "Please take us," we said, and he agreed. When we arrived, there was a group of our friends outside the hospital gates. We were not allowed in. I asked Zhao Jun why.

"A rule," he said.

"The hospital's?"

He shrugged, and I tried to supply answers that felt acceptable to me.

"Because he's in intensive care?"

"Maybe," said Zhao Jun. He put an arm around me.

"Are you allowed in?" I asked.

He shrugged. "Maybe," he said. Yao Hua started to go into the hospital and then caught sight of Kate and me and gingerly suggested we go to a restaurant next door. Then he disappeared into the hospital. Zhao Jun escorted us over to the restaurant.

We stood in its oily doorway, utterly bewildered. No one was crying; no one was talking about the details. I called my parents from a cell phone. When they asked me what was happening now, I had no idea.

"Do you know what happened last night?" My dad asked.

"No."

"Will he be okay?"

"I don't know," I said. "I don't think so."

Kate and I tried and failed again to get into the hospital. I knew only American hospitals and their particular information tactics, how we seek refuge in the details of our loved one's illnesses, surgeries, progress. American doctors tell patients and families more than we can understand, in language we learn for crisis occasions. Chinese doctors and families do this as well, but the details were not available to us. Shi Wei's male friends, including Zhao Jun, kept them from us in an effort to protect us from feeling pain. At the time, I thought there were no Chinese words for such crises, as ludicrous an assumption as the one by my client who imagined

Chinese had no word for "prowess." Eventually, Yao Hua said to us, "Don't cry in front of Shi Wei's parents," who had just shown up. We stared in disbelief at this suggestion.

"We don't want to make them sad," he said. "Oh," he added, "and don't mention the party." His voice had dropped to a whisper.

He meant the drinking. We would lie to each other about it, to protect ourselves from the misery of having let him leave. We would save group face by not mentioning it. We subscribed to the lie that it was a sheer accident, so no one would be embarrassed. I did not ask whether they ever planned to tell Shi Wei's family the truth. I did not ask what they thought the truth was. Everyone had his own story, and maybe Shi Wei's friends were right. Maybe it was less horrible not to collage our versions, and Americans are gluttons for punishing, irrelevant details.

Yao Hua, sensing our distress, gestured to Zhao Jun to get us out of there. Anna had just appeared, and Zhao Jun pulled her aside and asked her to take us somewhere.

"We'll know by eight tonight whether Shi Wei will be okay," he told us. "You should go home and wait."

Zhao Jun stayed. Kate and Anna and I went to the Friendship Store and wandered among crowds of people and Chinese souvenirs. Everything was red and electric; there were shelves of merchandise imported from a life I was no longer in: approximations of Christmas cards, stuffed animals in Chinese zodiac lineups, amber rings, watches, brass door knockers shaped like lions' heads. Kate turned to me, "We're waiting to see if Shi Wei lives or dies," she said, amazed.

Just before eight, Anna went home and Kate and I went back to the hospital. This time we waited in the garage. It was freezing. Shi Wei's mother was in the garage, too. When she walked up to us, I felt like a tiny particle of something unidentifiable, landed on a planet I knew nothing about. I was at a stark loss for what to say to her in this situation. Was the rule still that I had to say nothing that might make her sad? I wished for a script. Her hands were holding each other, white at the knuckles. I thought of her life in the countryside, her relationship with her grandson, the years she had missed of Shi Wei's life. What could she have thought of the life he was leading recently, his expensive car, Hollywood movies, trips to L.A., swim trunks, Kate, me? Had Shi Wei's mother and father been pleased at his conventional success, and if so, what about the values that success represented? What would she tell his little boy?

"Would you like these?" I asked, holding out my gloves. I was peeling them off, but she shook her head.

I didn't know whether she was politely declining the offer or hadn't understood me. I stood still, thinking. I spoke Chinese. In fact, I knew several ways in which to say, "I'm sorry about Shi Wei," but also knew I couldn't be sure I would choose the best one. If I said it, I might accidentally use words that meant, "I regret it" or "Please excuse me." A flutter of heat spread into my stomach and fanned out into my chest. I was in a panic to say something, anything, to make her feel better. As it turned out, I picked something strange and inappropriate.

"We really love Shi Wei," I said truthfully.

She stared at me, and then looked over at Kate.

"Are they still together?" she asked me.

I inhaled. Had I been insanely literal? Did the word "love" only mean romantic love? What to say now? No, they've broken up, Kate left him? No way.

"Yes," I lied, nodding. "We're all still close."

She smiled with such relief and graciousness. And I stacked betrayal upon betrayal.

It was only seconds later that we heard Zhao Jun's cry. It came from the hallway between the garage and the hospital, but sounded like it came from a tunnel. When Zhao Jun came outside to tell me, he had to say it three different times because I couldn't understand the euphemisms. Finally he just said, "*wandanle*," finished. I thought of numbers. First the time, 9:20 P.M. Then the twenty hours it had taken since the accident. Then nothing.

Zhao Jun, Kate, and I sat in the car for hours, not speaking. The next day, I flew home to Michigan and Kate went to Maine; it was Christmas, and we had both been planning for months to go home. Shi Wei's funeral was scheduled for ten days later, but our parents were hysterical and insisted we not change our plans. Out of Beijing, I floated through the days in a haze of shock. I hardly talked about Shi Wei or anything else; I didn't have the correct words for what happened, even in English. I tried again and again to reconstruct the night and find comfort in the details, but I found neither details nor relief.

Ann Arbor, the opposite of Beijing, gave me hope that the Shi Wei story was simply locational, and that his death depended on Beijing as a set. Maybe this was a scene in the movie Shi Wei was writing, and when I got back, he would be intact.

I was having dinner with my parents when Zhao Jun called me. The funeral had just ended. His hand on the gearshift that night came shooting through the phone wires. I could see the Jeep, parked outside the hospital, Zhao Jun's knuckles wrapped over the steering wheel. It seemed strange to me that they were the same knuckles he had had the day he and Shi Wei played chicken with the blue truck on the way back from Miyun, and impossible that

Zhao Jun and I would ever see or know each other again. I was agitated to hear his voice, confirmation that even home wasn't off-limits from the misery. I wanted to be driving away, safe from Beijing and the endless fact of Shi Wei's absence.

"It's over," he said in English.

"The funeral, you mean," I said.

We were both quiet. When he started talking again, his voice had sped up; its pitch was higher than usual.

"It's too bad you and Kate weren't there," he said. "I bought flowers and put your name on them, too."

This was the first event, action, activity, or conversation, since Shi Wei's death that I actually understood.

"Thank you for thinking of it," I said. "How was the funeral?"

"Terrible," he said.

We were back in familiar territory, since I was not sure what this meant. I didn't want to ask. My stomach was turning.

"Painful, I guess," I said.

"Well," said Zhao Jun. "We saw him."

"Saw him," I said.

I could hear him nod. What Zhao Jun had seen he later called "the ashes from Shi Wei's bones."

"It's too bad you and Kate weren't there," he said again.

This time, I understood better. "You're angry about it?" I asked. "Should I not have flown home? My parents were beside themselves. And also, it was my only chance to go home this whole year," I argued, defensive. I did not add that this wasn't the real reason I hadn't stayed, since he knew that. I wasn't brave enough to make it through the funeral and had wanted to escape.

"I know you couldn't cancel," he said. "It's okay for you."

I asked nothing about Kate; I didn't want to hear it. When we got off the phone, my stomach was cooking. We had been excluded from Shi Wei's death and then judged for missing his funeral. We spent his death in a restaurant doorway, noncomprehending and with no translator. We spent his funeral in Western countries. Our retreats seemed metaphorically apt. Of course it makes sense that Zhao Jun was furious. If Kate had died in the U.S. and Zhao Jun had been back in China for her funeral, I would have been enraged. He and I never discussed it. We didn't know how. And as accustomed as we were to not talking about most things, we never recovered from not talking about Shi Wei's death. Our romance froze in those moments and stayed there.

I saw Shi Wei's friends only once more. Kate and I ran into Yao Hua, the one who found Shi Wei's car with Zhao Jun, in Beijing's new Ikea. As soon as I saw him, my eyes heated up. I felt like tears were pouring upward from underneath my eyes. None of us mentioned Shi Wei. The tip of everything I said was an apology. I wanted to apologize for missing his funeral, for not knowing how to act in the hospital, for not having seen any of our mutual friends since the minute I heard he was dead, and for not wanting to see them again. Any acknowledgment of that night would have broken the Beijing rules for restraint. I had trashed those protocols happily before, but no longer felt like I could do that in good faith. I felt respectful, if not of the social code itself, then of Yao Hua's position in it. The places we did not go in our conversations represented comfort zones; why do Americans risk tearing each other out of those? Restraint, which I considered Chinese and which didn't come naturally to me, had begun to come in handy as a bandage after Shi Wei died.

Wrapped and safe, I said only, *"Ni maile shenme?"* What have you bought?

"Yizi," he said. Chairs.

We all nodded. Kate managed a line of polite questions about lives, related people, and movies. I wondered, if we calculated and distributed percentages of blame, how many each of us would accept, and how many we'd assign each other.

For a long time, Kate and I almost never mentioned Shi Wei's name; we were sick with guilt. Sometimes we brought him up, but usually only as a marker of time. "It's been five months since," we said.

When it turned hot again, Kate and I went driving into the country. We drove by a long stretch of flat, burned-out ground. Kate pointed. "That's where Shi Wei's buried."

"You've been there?" I asked her.

"Yeah," she said.

I was quiet for a minute. The landscape looked to me like nothing.

"Who'd you go with?"

"I went alone," she said.

I wondered what she had done at his grave. Stood still? Spoken?

"There's a picture of him on the tombstone," she offered.

"Zhenda ma?" Really?

"I know the picture, too. It's cropped on the grave, but in the original, he was holding a drink, *gan bei*'ing." Bottoms upping.

Zhao Jun described the cemetery to me once by saying, "I hate his grave. It's crowded." He and Shi Wei's other friends go once a year and sprinkle *baijiu,* booze on the site. A toast of sorts.

When Kate and I talk about Shi Wei now, we talk about "what happened," whether Shi Wei meant to drive that drunk, and whether there is a genuine difference between suicide and an accident, if the risk one takes is serious enough to cost his life. Shi Wei, like the rest of us, was spending parts of his life in a fantasy zone. The night he left that Christmas party, maybe he wanted to make a dramatic statement just by leaving. Kate and I do not believe that he wanted to die. If he risked death knowingly, it was because he had no idea that unlike in the movies, his death would last past the credits. The night Shi Wei died was the moment when we all crossed an unacceptable boundary—forgetting what's real for long enough to lose it permanently.

I am a plot-lover, a literalist, and I never understood what happened. If I gained experience or context as a result of losing Shi Wei, then I also lost confidence in my belief that any language can cover the bases. The only words that filled the impossible leaks between what we felt and what we could say about it, were the ones that acknowledged their own brevity, lack, ambiguity: *wandanle,* finished.

And when I think about the night of Shi Wei's accident and the tumble of years that have followed it, the moment that rings in my ears is still Zhao Jun's: *wandanle,* finished. It's the Chinese past tense participle *le* that locks the box of that clause. We don't have one in English. It indicates a change in the status of something, a completion of something that was previously unfinished, and a surprise.

From *Foreign Babes in Beijing*
Episode Twenty

Tianming and Jiexi face off in the courtyard garden.

TIANMING
Go.

JIEXI
No.

TIANMING
You must go! Immediately!

JIEXI
No! I'm not leaving! I can't be without you!

NINE

无能的力量
Wuneng di Liliang

Power of the Powerless

By the end of the 1990s, Beijing was beginning to feel more like Hong Kong than Beijing. No longer forbidden, the city became increasingly attainable fruit, yet stayed as delicious as ever. Throngs of *laowai* arrived. Beijing became modern enough to be unrecognizable as the place I moved to in 1994. There were no more donkey carts. Street kiosks made way for sleek boutiques and cafés, where Chinese and foreigners lounged together, drinking lattes and Italian sodas. The city flaunted brilliant sushi, served in loftlike raw bars with full-wall water fountains and names for Beijing's specialty rolls: 911 dynamite, Beijing duck and roll, sweet pea. Latino's Club offered salsa lessons and The Big Easy served up fried chicken with New Orleans Jazz belted out by a St. Louis singer named Jackie.

Jenny Lou's Grocery Stores spread across Beijing's neighborhoods and put gourmet cheese, cold cuts, and nonnegotiable vegetables on sale. Beauty salons opened, and Carrefour, a French Wal-Mart, imported Clairol Mousse. The real estate market softened so much for foreigners that Beijing became inviting to wealthy executives, backpackers, and lost graduates alike. It had everything from sprawling suburbs and Montessori schools to summer raves on the Great Wall, complete with tiki torches, neon jewelry, and designer drugs.

By 1998, foreigners were already less likely to get kicked out of privately owned Chinese apartments. Foreign ghettos rose up in neighborhoods including Maizidian'r, where a massage parlor called Love Heart Blind Massage Parlor opened up and gave massage by the blind for 60 *yuan* ($7) an hour. Poor students lived in the neighborhood's no-frills cement block apartments for less than $200 a month, and pool tables on the streets provided inexpensive social opportunities. Maizidian'r had a seedy appeal and flaunted a hint of danger: sometimes police raided the *laowai* quarters and fined everyone for living illegally. The fines were negligible, understood by both tenants and police to be part of the arrangement. Beijing was more open than ever.

During this time, Kate, Anna, and I had all quit our relatively prestigious jobs and moved into slower, weirder, and better ones. My friend at the metals and minerals company left to do graduate work in psychology. The naked-booty freelance reporter moved back to Europe with a Chinese photographer. All of the expatriates I knew were gone, moved on to other, Western works. A fresh crop of young China lovers arrived, desperate to find newly competitive jobs, corporate days, and sultry, international nights. *Newsweek* ran an article on "our generation" in Beijing and called the piece "Kids Going Global." Jiexi was the lead. I had been in the city for close to five years, and was happily cobbling together projects: acting in an art-house film called *Bitter Herbs*, acting in an American film called *Restless*, producing segments on influential Chinese women for an Australian TV station, freelancing for nonprofits, and writing. But I decided in 1999 to leave Beijing, and applied to graduate school in poetry in the U.S. I believed that writing poetry in English would be a paradise of repatriation; I would relearn English from a fresh vantage point and translate Tang poetry in the off hours. And I'd be back.

Kate, who had wound down her crazy life following Shi Wei's death, left for a journey down the Yangtze River, which China was damming in its biggest engineering project since the Great Wall. The dam was a hugely controversial project, rumored to have terrifying environmental implications. It would submerge thousands of factories, destroy ecosystems, and uproot millions of people. China's leadership, particularly hard-line premier Li Peng, who had supported the attack on students in Tiananmen Square in 1989, argued that the dam would tame a river that terrorized China with floods, as well as harness enough power to fuel the new China's boom. Environmentalists and critics compared Li Peng to Emperor Qin, famous for burning scholars and libraries.[49]

Kate came home raging about engineers who said that if the world worried too much about environmental impact, then nothing would ever get built. She pondered and finally loathed the Chinese argument that America had done its polluting while it developed in the twentieth century; why couldn't China have its turn? A truism among Chinese was that China walked into a room full of smoking countries and was told, "The room is already smoky; you can't light up." Kate said she could not remain a journalist *pangguanzhe*, peripheral observer. So she quit her job, took a 50 percent pay cut, and went to work for an environmental nonprofit.

Anna quit the PR firm and traveled to Italy with her father, who was taking his children's' chorus there. In a pizza parlor in Rome, she fell in love with a young Italian man, who followed her back to China, where Anna joined Kate at the environmental group.

My friends and I had found jobs and lives that seemed to fit, and we settled into a quiet groove. Zhou Wen was painting; Zheng Yi was a successful businessman in Chongqing. Zhao Jun's script was finished and he would circulate it successfully on the festival circuit. Anna and Kate were working in jobs and a world they cared about; they would work together for years before Kate moved to New York for graduate school and Anna moved to Italy to marry her Italian love.

All over Beijing, optimism was soaring in 1998, following Clinton's visit. But if we were lulled into a false sense of calm, it was momentary. Sino-U.S. affairs were about to take the deepest and nastiest plunge I saw while living there. Anna thought it might be the open-door apocalypse when in May 1999, NATO bombed the Chinese embassy in Belgrade. She had predicted a ten-year swing of the 1989 pendulum, and cited China's decade-long cycles of chaos. The bombing happened in uncomfortably close proximity to the ten-year anniversary of Tiananmen. China was tense anyway, and NATO lit the country's short fuse.

It was a Friday night and Kate, Anna, and I were eating dumplings and drinking Dragon Seal wine to celebrate my acceptance into grad school and their new apartment. Our shared Beijing lives were winding down, and the dinner was a good-bye party of sorts. Suddenly we saw people gathering outside, and walked out to investigate. Hundreds of people began to converge around the U.S. embassy. The pieces of story we heard from bystanders were incoherent, so we ran to the China World Hotel to watch CNN. But cable TV was off the air. In spite of myself, I hoped it was a coincidence, that there was a technical problem with reception. More likely, the Chinese leadership turned off imported television news while strategizing their response to events. We headed back to the embassy, where we heard from bystanders that America had bombed the Chinese embassy in Belgrade; several Chinese civilians had been killed and others injured.

Saturday morning, CNN was back up in the China World Hotel. From a treadmill in the downstairs gym, I watched Clinton issue an apology to China. He said, "I apologize. I regret this," and added that he had contacted Chinese President Jiang Zemin to offer condolences. He called the embassy bombing "an isolated, tragic event," and opposed it to the ethnic cleansing of Kosovo, "a deliberate and systematic crime." The CIA had used a four-year-old street map to "guess" its target. It was stupid, but not malicious. I was vaguely persuaded. Countries at war bombed hospitals and kindergartens accidentally all the time; why not a Chinese embassy?

Zhou Wen called to invite me to the Five Colors Earth Studio to make T-shirts. As soon as I arrived, he told me an American friend of his had called him to confirm that the U.S. had, in fact, "done it on purpose." She was a student at Beijing University and would not, I thought, have access to international media. I was tying a cotton T-shirt up in knots, dipping it in a blue vat.

"How does she know that? They don't even have CNN at the universities," I said.

"What does CNN have to do with it?" asked Zhou Wen.

"Clinton apologized. Did she tell you that?"

"No," he said. "What did Clinton say happened?"

"It was a tragic, isolated accident," I said. "They had an old map and thought the Chinese embassy was a Yugaslov arms agency." Even as I said it, it sounded implausible.

"An old map? Aren't they a high-tech army?"

"Yes, but mistakes like this happen all the time."

"How many missiles hit the building?" he asked.

"I don't know. Why do you ask?"

"Well, how many missiles is it possible to shoot accidentally?"

NATO had shot three missiles at the building, which was, to my Chinese friends, irrefutable proof that the bombing could not have been an accident.

"Maybe they want to help Milosovich," Zhou Wen said.

"Why? What purpose could that possibly serve?" The pottery teacher, Old Liu, who shared the studio, was listening. I had taken pottery classes with him the summer before.

"Americans do whatever they want," he said, braking the wheel where he was spinning a wet bowl. "Americans are like the 'world police.'"

Zhou Wen waited for me to respond on behalf of Americans.

"What do you mean by 'Americans?' " I asked.

Old Liu smiled, embarrassed. "I mean the government. The government and the *laobaixing* are not the same." He gestured at me to let me know that I was one of the common people, not to be blamed for my government's actions.

"I appreciate the distinction. How do you know what the American government thinks?"

"Look what they do! They bomb Chinese buildings and violate Chinese sovereignty! They spill Chinese blood!"

It was straight from Chinese TV, just like my CNN language. Zhou Wen nodded.

"Come on," I said to Zhou Wen. I was more willing to be confrontational with him than I was with Old Liu, who was not only my elder but also my teacher. Zhou Wen was pulling a red T-shirt out of the dye. He had tied it up and stained the ties blue. Maybe the T-shirt would present itself as an American flag.

"That's straight from Chinese TV," I finally said. "Don't you ask questions?" He smiled. "And you? Do you take CNN's word for it?"

"People could make informed decisions if they were given a chance to see the footage," I proposed. The "they" filled the space around us.

"Even if it hasn't been broadcast," Zhou Wen responded, "how much stock are you going to put in a political apology? Maybe we just won't buy it."

He was right. As soon as Clinton's apology was broadcast, China was indignant about the details of it. Both the Chinese media and my friends argued that Clinton's apology was insincere, that the term "regret" was insufficient, and sounded vague, like "excuse me" when pushing past someone on a crowded bus. They also thought that the apology had come too fast, that Clinton had issued it without mulling over what had happened or actually deciding to take responsibility. American apologies were all about expediency.

We hung the T-shirts to dry, and I headed back to the embassy district. There were thousands of people now, many of them Chinese students. Buses were lined up politely along the streets, fancy ones with dark windows and air-conditioning. The students could not have paid for them, and I doubted the universities had. There was a group of students carrying a hundred-foot banner, embroidered with Chinese characters and English letters. It read "Down With NATO." There was no way they had prepared that in one night.

The protest had been in the making for weeks. China was angry about any U.S. presence in Belgrade. America was world-policing, causing trouble where we weren't wanted and setting a bad precedent for the rest of the world. The Chinese government has strict ideas about what it means to mind other countries' business. It wants to be left enough autonomy to handle its own "internal issues," namely Tibet and Taiwan. So the government tries to support the efforts of other countries to keep their own internal affairs internal. China had been preparing to protest NATO anyway; when the embassy bombing ignited public rage, the government sanctioned and controlled the protests. People's Liberation Army soldiers stood in front of the U.S. embassy, ducking as protestors threw Molotov cocktails, rocks, and paint balls. International news reports had it that American Ambassador Sasser was holed up in the basement, eating freeze-dried ice cream.

That seemed to me to be a good PR move. Freeze-dried ice cream reminded Americans of astronauts, progress, and sacrifice. It had been one full day now and the protests were raging. There were students on podiums, shouting through megaphones about capitalism and world police. There were soldiers in the crowds, cheering. For the first and only time since I had lived in China, I felt genuine fear. I hailed a taxi.

The driver rolled down his window. "Where are you from?" he asked.

"Why?"

"Because if you're American, fuck your mother's cunt."

I hailed another cab. The driver pulled up to the curb and I got in before he could ask me anything. He turned to me before starting the car.

"I'm Swiss," I said, looking down. He drove me home in silence.

In the mouth of the alley that led to my apartment, I stopped to buy some mineral water at a kiosk. Behind me, someone said, "There goes that American girl, Jiexi. What is she doing living in this neighborhood?"

I went home and locked the door, thinking it might be melodramatic, but not confident enough not to do it. I called Anna. "What's going on?" I asked.

"My god," she said, "it's like a nightmare. Where are you?"

"I'm in my apartment."

"Good. Maybe you should stay at home."

"Seriously? You think it's that bad?"

"Three people were beaten by the embassy and now the students are marching everywhere. Can you hear it?"

She put her phone to the window and I heard crowds. "Vaguely," I said. "I hear something. What do you think of this whole thing?"

"I don't know yet. The Chinese students are brave, though, don't you think? I am proud!"

"Brave how? For standing up for what they believe, you mean?"

"Yes," she said. "I think the protest is a beautiful story for China. But I'm also worried that maybe it will be like 1989 again and China will close its doors. Too much anti-Americanism won't be good."

"Do you think NATO bombed the embassy on purpose?"

"The Chinese news says it's on purpose. Maybe the U.S. warned everyone to leave, but there were still people in the Chinese embassy."

"Maybe," I said. "And maybe the individuals were targets of the U.S. Were they spies?"

"Unclear. Let's wait a bit, *manman lai* [take it slow]. I think it's hard to say right now what happened."

314

When I had first arrived in China, I believed that propaganda was a tool used by the Chinese government to persuade people of the government's view. Later, though, after *Foreign Babes in Beijing* and the Belgrade incident, I considered a wider framework for the Chinese word *xuanchuan,* propaganda, which does not have the 100 percent negative nuance of its English equivalent. Public education, whether about health, environmental protection, or world events, also falls under the rubric *xuanchuan* in China, and much of it is positive, both in its aim and its manifestations. And after my own soft-soundings research into the reactions of my friends to news stories, entertainment, and government edicts, I came to think that even the negative brand of propaganda, which promulgates half- or non-truths, is less about convincing people of falsehoods than it is about showing them just how preposterous an explanation officialdom can concoct and disseminate without anyone challenging it. Chinese audiences understood the tropes of *Foreign Babes in Beijing,* and knew that the *People's Daily* was a sheer display of official theater. But no one dared contradict official lines. After Tiananmen, Chinese were more reluctant to criticize media or leadership openly, so people kept private their understanding that press was not gospel. News everywhere has to be read with perspective on its sources, creators, and funders. America is no exception to this rule. The China on American news is not a place I've ever been.

When Kate came over, she was crying. "I'm furious," she said. I pulled her into the apartment, where she slumped onto the couch. Her posture reminded me of the night Shi Wei had died; the couch behind her reminded me of the way he had looked the day he told me he wanted to write a book.

"Are you okay? Why are you so unhappy?"

"Guess who I just ran into at the protests? Zhou Wen and Cui Jian and his whole band. All my friends. I can't believe it." Cui Jian had remained her favorite musician, and Kate had just started spending time with his saxophonist.

"Did you talk to them?"

"Yeah, but it was useless. None of them can understand why I'd be unhappy that they were there."

"Were they throwing stuff?"

She shrugged miserably. "I couldn't tell. But I told them I need my friends to support me. I mean, do they want to be part of a protest in which Chinese are shouting, 'Down with Americans'? Does Cui Jian want to be the poster boy for a new era of anti-Americanism? No one has any idea yet what happened. Is everyone going to buy the Chinese party lines without asking questions?"

"I don't know," I said. "But Zhou Wen asked the same thing about us."

She blinked.

"Did you tell those guys that your feelings are hurt?" I asked her.

"Yes, and they asked me why. They said I'm not the American government, and that they're opposed to any U.S. activity in Kosovo, since China and Serbia were allies during the Cold War. Mainly, they said they object to war in general; how can I criticize any of them for that? And they also kept saying if we were in the U.S., and China bombed our embassy somewhere, I'd protest it, too."

"You don't think that's persuasive?"

"No. If it were an American protest about China and Americans were yelling, 'Down with Chinese,' I wouldn't go, because my best friends are Chinese."

"What if the guys from the band, like Cui Jian, turn up in all the papers tomorrow as an advertisement for China's new Anti-American youth?"

"I asked them that," said Kate. "And they said there's no possibility of it, since he just went to *kan renao.*" To "look at what's hot and noisy," rubberneck.

On the roof of an alley bar called Jamhouse, we fought it out that night. Press reports warned that everyone should avoid hanging out in the bar district because tensions were high, and rumors raged that some *laowai* had been beaten up there. But we all decided to go out anyway, angry that there should be any limitations on our movement around the city. When I realized everyone else was out, I agreed to join them. I biked to Jamhouse to meet Kate, Cui Jian, Zhou Wen, and some of Cui Jian's musician friends. Zhao Jun appeared; he and I were working on a post-breakup friendship.

We all sat in a tense circle. Zhou Wen was furious. "This is just one of the many outrageous activities of the world police country," he was saying as I walked up. "At least China is standing up now."

"Do you think this NATO bombing was an intentional, cold-blooded killing?" Kate asked him, hoping he would pick up on her substitution of NATO for America.

There was vigorous nodding around the table. Kate looked at me unhappily.

Zhao Jun put his hand flat on the table. "That's absolutely fucking stupid," he said. "Today I saw this moron riding his tricycle and shouting, 'Down-With-America!' Everyone here is so quick to believe the bullshit. There's no way America did this on purpose. People here have nothing to believe, so the first chance they get to believe in something, they grab it. Even if it's something this stupid. The people I know who have gone to America and fail there—they try to get Ph.D.s or Western girlfriends and they fail in the U.S., they come back bitter and become patriots. Patriotism is about bitterness. Sour grapes."

There was a chill over the table. I tried to smooth us out. "There are other possibilities," I said. "Maybe this was somewhere between a complete mistake and a joyful slaughter—I mean, there might be internal reasons for China's presentation of this event."

"What internal reasons?" Cui Jian asked, his voice turned low.

I answered with questions: "That it gives conservatives in the government an excuse for slowing reform? That China is angry about a whole host of things and this is a lucky way to bring them all to a head? China wants to deflect attention from the upcoming Tiananmen anniversary?"

"No Chinese believes that this was anything other than an American attack on China," said a musician named Wang Nan.

Zhao Jun pushed his chair back and stood up to leave. "I'm not even going to bother with that," he said, and stormed off.

I mentioned Anna, who had wisely stayed home. "No Chinese?" I said, "Come on. I know at least two; one is Anna. And at least she's open to discussing it," I said.

"Yeah, but she's just *kang yang qiang*," Wang Nan responded under his breath. She "carries a foreign gun." I had never heard this before, but all its obvious meanings flooded the table, suffocating the conversation for a moment before I recovered. I tried to keep my face straight, give nothing away. I didn't want to acknowledge the obscenity behind the saying, lest my reaction validate it. I wished for a fractured second that Zhao Jun had stayed.

"You can really talk," I said. "Let me ask you: does that make her more or less sophisticated than you about international events? Have you ever considered the possibility that interacting with foreigners makes someone more likely to understand the foreign way of doing things?" I asked.

Time dropped out from under me, rushed back to 1995 on the *Foreign Babes* set. There was no foreign way of doing things. And if what I meant was the American government's way of executing foreign policy, then I had no business with this conversation. I did not want to promote the idea that the American government's "foreign way of doing things" had any direct relationship to the things we were saying, doing, or thinking on the roof of the Jamhouse Bar.

"*Kang yang qiang* makes someone less Chinese. She's a traitor," Wang Nan said.

"Well, on behalf of Anna, fuck you."

I got up. Kate motioned to me to sit down. "I carry Chinese guns," she offered sweetly, referring to her string of Chinese boyfriends. Everyone laughed with difficulty.

Downstairs, the first two cabdrivers I hailed refused to pick me up. Finally, I flagged down a third and said I was from Iceland. *Zhen leng,* I said, really cold in my hometown. *Nar dou you bing.* Ice everywhere. We sped away. I looked at the driver's ID.

"Mr. Li, trouble you to ask a question," I said.

"No problem. Ask *ba.*"

"Are you angry at America?"

"Of course! America spilled Chinese blood!"

"Wasn't it NATO that bombed the embassy in Belgrade?"

"Unh! America is a world police. It controls everyone and listens to no one. America wants to get its way all the time, just like Americans do."

So now the distinction between the government and Americans

was melting. "America is not the same as NATO," I pointed out. "It's not the only country. What about the UK?"

"The other countries just listen to America. No one else has a say."

"In the whole word? No possibility of that. No country is that powerful."

"Americans citizens don't even have human rights."

This was new. "What are you talking about?"

"Your American president, *Kelindun,* can't even have a mistress! Tell me, Jiexi, what kind of human rights is that?"

Beijing demanded that the U.S. issue a condemnation of the bombing, but that was impossible, since the U.S. wasn't ready to admit that it was an "act" at all. Then U.S. Defense Secretary William Cohen announced that people involved in what he called the chain of errors might face disciplinary action. Those errors, though, were "institutional," rather than mechanical or human. Chinese were understandably irate at the words "institutional error," since such vocabulary implied that no one would pay. What government institution faces disciplinary action?

Movie theaters in major cities including Beijing, Guangzhou, and Shanghai, canceled screenings of *Saving Private Ryan* and *Enemy of the State,* two of the eleven American films allowed in China that year.

The media had it out on their editorial pages. The *International Herald Tribune* printed an editorial in which it accused China of reacting to the mistaken NATO bombing "suspiciously like a total-itarian nation. . . . The state-controlled media, which is to say, China's only media, whipped people into a fury with inaccurate and incomplete reporting. Newspapers failed to report U.S. explanations or apologies."

Beijing called the three journalists who were killed "revolutionary martyrs"; there were parades in support of them, and their pictures were all over the morning newspaper cases, sunlight shooting off their images in halos. The *People's Daily* focused on the three missiles and the three journalists. According to the *People's Daily*, "Three missiles blasted the embassy from different angles, which completely exposed the aggressors' evil intentions and spilled Chinese blood."

Meanwhile, in America, Larry King had Tom Clancy on air, and Clancy said that if the U.S. had wanted to bomb China, it would have just "sent a nuke" to China. U.S. Undersecretary of State Thomas Pickering said people would have to be "certifiably loony" to believe NATO could have done this intentionally, implicating almost all Chinese citizens.[50]

The protests gained momentum. The Chinese government postponed talks with the United States on human rights, nonproliferation of nuclear weapons, arms control, and international security. It was unclear just how fevered a pitch this might reach. But sanctioning protests has historically backfired in China, since any protest against the outside world inevitably turns into a critique of the government's response to oppression. Demonstrations in China invariably turn inward. Knowing that, China decided to channel all unrest away from Chinese subjects and targets, and, finally, away from its capital city. As quickly as it had whipped up the rallies, China squelched them. There were no more buses, banners, or roaring broadcasts. The government simply flipped a switch that cut off power to the protestors. They said stop, and the protests stopped.

Some of the same students who had been marching now lined up to apply for visas. The foreign press corps covered this irony with an unusual dose of rage. Chinese youth complained bitterly that the consulate was closed, even though it was closed for cleanup after the destruction in which many had participated. The press pointed out that the protesters now applying for visas were wearing Levi's and Nikes. To me, there was something poetic, rather than enraging, in that. If America supplies other countries with glamorous exports, it should also welcome an engagement that includes harsh criticism of its policies. While I thought the violence had been out of hand, I hoped the embassy would still give generously of visas. I did not think there was an irreconcilable contradiction between criticizing America and wishing to go abroad to study or conduct business there.

I had been to the American embassy visa consulate twice, once to help Shi Wei get a business visa to the U.S. and once to try to help Teacher Kang's daughter get a student visa. Both times my presence allowed us to skip the six-block line and enter the embassy "like an American," as Shi Wei had put it. He got a visa easily; Teacher Kang's daughter applied repeatedly and desperately before securing one. She was a flight risk, and had to provide documentation of every penny she would need, and of her love of her parents. If filial, she would return.

For the Belgrade incident, the CIA fired one employee and disciplined six. China's leadership remained furious, but on the ground, young people tried to reconcile. Cui Jian's band played on the Fourth of July, two months after the NATO bombing, a concert that took place between the lines drawn by the Belgrade incident.

Wuneng di Liliang, Power of the Powerless

The Independence Day celebration, sponsored by the U.S. embassy and American Chamber of Commerce, was an official annual event. In 1999, it took place in a netherworld, at a global shipping company's warehouse on the outskirts of Beijing, mainly because the crowds had grown too big to remain safe at the embassy. The venue change, from the embassy to a warehouse, also indicated a kind of progress; the year before, Chinese nationals were allowed in only if they had registered in advance and had to be invited by individual Americans. Then, I had had to register Anna in advance; now she was nobody's guest.

The Fourth of July crowd, armed with giant plastic squirt guns, danced and sang along with Cui Jian. Anna, Kate, and I wove between cotton candy and antique stands, joking about *kang*'ing *butongdi qiang*, carrying various guns. Across from the stage was a lawn covered with water tanks, children's games, and corporate booths: McDonald's, Baskin-Robbins, Pizza Hut, the Shangri-La Hotel, and Mrs. Shannon's Beijing Bagels.

Right in front of the McDonald's booth, we faced the stage and sang Cui Jian's title song, "Power of the Powerless." In it, he sings: "I do it all and accomplish zero. / I can't be calm or free. / I still daydream of changing an era. / But I'm still powerless and you have to wait. / And if I fail, will you still want me? / You watch me silently, / say nothing—wordlessly. / Drop your hand to catch my hand, / and hold it soft and tight. / Then you make it a fist, raise it to your lips. And bite."

It seemed especially apt that his almost-metal song should be fundamentally about silence and contradiction. For me, it was also a political song about China, as well as a personal song about *Foreign Babes in Beijing*, Anna, Jiexi, Louisa, Kate, Director Yao, Wu Jie, Sophie, Zhou Wen, Zheng Yi, Zhao Jun, and Shi Wei. As I watched the other *laowai*, dancing to Cui Jian's music at an embassy-sponsored party at a Beijing warehouse, I knew I had as little and as much access to them as I had to the Chinese man dressed as Uncle Sam. U.S. flags flapped on their poles. I thought of the Chinese and American flags that decorated all the business scenes in *Foreign Babes in Beijing.*

I left Beijing that summer, certain that my years there had been worth every weirdness, shock, and awkward moment. I had spent half a decade in struggling to understand people I loved or might love, and taking stock of myself in an unfamiliar context. Luckily for anyone who wants an adventure, the new Beijing is still leading itself, its citizens, and its resident *laowai* in the wobbly search for self we call culture shock.

In the airport that summer, after I had kissed Kate, Anna, and Zhao Jun good-bye, a customs official flipped through the worn pages of my passport. He gave me a serious look.

"Can I ask you a question?"

"Of course," I said.

He paused carefully, as if he were auditioning the words he would use. Then he asked, "Are your teeth real or fake?"

"Really? That's the question?"

He nodded.

I tapped on my teeth, the way merchants bite down on genuine pearls or slice glass with diamonds. He waited. I sighed. "They're real."

"They're so white!" he said. "Americans have white teeth and big jaws." He flashed his own toothy grin at me, stamped my passport, and waved me through the line. But as soon as my back was turned he said in Chinese, "Say hello to Tianming for me, Jiexi!" He switched to hard-studied English to add, "Jiexi, you are welcome to come back to China forever."

From *Foreign Babes in Beijing*

Episode Twenty

Jiexi and Tianming are about to leave for America.

OLD MAN LI

Tianming, good boy. I raised you to be this old. You're leaving.

Your old father's heart is broken. But you're all grown up.

You're mature. Fly! Fly!

TIANMING

(To Jiexi)

Call him Father.

JIEXI

Father! You and Mama are the greatest elders I have ever met.

I will miss you.

OLD MAN LI

(To Tianming)

Don't let China lose face.

NOTES

1. Faison, Seth, "Chinese Are Happily Breaking the 'One Child' Rule," *New York Times*, August 17, 1997.
2. Becker, Jasper. *The Chinese*. New York: Oxford University Press, 2002, p. 186.
3. O'Hara, Albert. *The Position of Women in Early China, Translation of* Lieh Nü Chuan. Taiwan: Mei Ya Publications, 1971, p. 190.
4. Seto, Doug, "China's Historic Jews, Synagogue Honored in 'Silk Road' Exhibit," *Jewish News Weekly of Northern California*, October 3, 1997. http://www.jewishsf.com/content/2-0-/modul/displaystory/story_id/7136/format/html/displaystory.html.
5. "China population growth slows in 1995." Reuters, April 1996.
6. Ibid.
7. Wang, Robin R. *Images of Women in Chinese Thought and Culture*. Hackett, 2003, p. 3.
8. "China's First All-Woman Rock Band Breaking New Ground." *Christian Science Monitor*, April 17, 1992.

9. Ibid.
10. "Women Poised to Shake off Skirts of Feudalism," *South China Morning Post,* April 19, 1992.
11. "China: Equality for Women Has a Long Way to Go." Inter Press Service Global Information Network, April 3, 1992.
12. "When the Sky Falls on Women." *The Economist,* March 13, 1993.
13. "Marriages Between Chinese and Foreigners." *Jiefang Ribao,* September 8, 1997.
14. Poole, Teresa. "China Discovers Adultery and Divorce." *Independent on Sunday,* (UK), September 7, 1997.
15. "China: Survey Reveals Problems with Marriage Law." *China Daily,* October 31, 1997.
16. From Yale-in-China Archives, Hume to Palmer Bevis, Shanghai, January 10, 1925. Quoted in Spence, Johnathan, *To Change China: Western Advisers in China 1620–1960.* New York: Penguin Books, 1980, p. 177.
17. Spence, Jonathan. *To Change China: Western Advisers in China 1620–1960.* New York: Penguin Books.
18. "China Prepares to Launch Physical Fitness Program for Young City Dwellers, Fatty Food and Sedentary Lifestyles Have Begun Taking a Toll on Health." Associated Press, October 2, 1994.
19. Cernetig, Miro. "In China, Fat Ain't Where It's At: Childhood Obesity a National Problem." *Toronto Globe and Mail,* December 5, 1998.
20. Ibid.
21. "China Prepares to Launch Physical Fitness Program for Young City Dwellers, Fatty Food and Sedentary Lifestyles Have Begun Taking a Toll on Health." Associated Press, October 2, 1994.
22. Parker, Jeffrey. "Global Forum Faces China to Face Women's Plight." Reuters, August 9, 1994.
23. "When the Sky Falls on Women." *The Economist,* March 13, 1993.
24. "Is it an NGO or a GONGO? New Chinese Body Rebuts U.S. Report on Human Rights." *Far Eastern Economic Review,* July 7, 1994.
25. Parker, Jeffrey, "China Slams U.S. 'double standards' on Rights." Reuters, June 8, 1994.

26. Xinhua News Agency. June 1994.
27. Ibid.
28. "Facing Threat of Sterilization, Women Given Refugee Status." *Toronto Star*, April 1993.
29. Wang, Robin R. *Images of Women in Chinese Thought and Culture.* Hackett, 2003, p. 329.
30. Zha, Jianying. *China Pop.* New Press. April 1, 1996, p. 28.
31. Ibid.
32. Mufson, Steve. "Madison County Bridges Cultures." *Washington Post*, April 30, 1996.
33. Ibid.
34. "Marriage Slows, Divorce Grows." *China Daily*, October 13, 1998.
35. Poole, Teresa. "China Discovers Adultery and Divorce." *Independent on Sunday* (UK), September 7, 1997.
36. Tempest, Rone. "China's Youth Find it's Cool to Be Seen as Anti-American." *Los Angeles Times*, July 8, 1996.
37. Tyler, Patrick. "Beijing Journal: Rebels' New Cause; A Book for Yankee Bashing." *New York Times*, September 4, 1996.
38. "We've Created a Muenster." *Harper's*, March 2003.
39. Spence, Jonathan. *The Search for Modern China.* New York: W. W. Norton, 1990, p. 38.
40. Ibid., p. 39.
41. Ibid., p. 38.
42. O'Hara, Albert. *The Position of Women in Early China, Translation of Lien Nu Zhuan.* Taiwan: Mei Ya Publications, 1971, p. 29.
43. "Avon Calling in China." Associated Press, January 1990.
44. Ibid.
45. Fraser, John. "Cardin Circus Hits Peking." *Globe and Mail*, March 20, 1979.
46. Costin, Glynis. "Laura Biagiotti's China Syndrome." *Women's Wear Daily*, 1993.
47. Ibid.
48. Agence France-Presse, May 19, 1993.

NOTES

49. Browne, Andrew. "China Finally Moves on Massive, Controversial Yangtze River Dam," Reuters, December 24, 1992.
50. Lavin, James. http://www.futureresearch.com/PlanetPath/PPChinese EmbassyBombing.txt, 1999.

ACKNOWLEDGMENTS

I owe a boundless debt of gratitude to the following people:

My teachers and mentors, for their generosity, brilliance, integrity, and time: Robert Pinsky, Derek Walcott, Rosanna Warren, and Sven Birkerts.

My smart and savvy agent, Jill Grinberg, for the limitless advice and energy she gave this project—and gives me.

My editor at Norton, Alane Mason, for the unique combination of autonomy and intense reading she provided.

My beloved Beijing friends, to whom I owe at least this book: Chen Shanying, Chen Daming, Hei Yang, Mu Shi, Erika Helms, Wang Tong, Alex Xie, Saskia Trotzer, Cui Jian, Teacher Kang, Ye Hui, Joelle Permutt, Christopher Mumford, Jason Overdorf, and Colleen Ryan.

My readers, for poring over this manuscript repeatedly and uncomplainingly, and for the insight and pages of ink: Donna Eis,

Julia Hollinger, Thai Jones, Greg Lalas, Lara Phillips, and Heidi Schumacher.

My support system from Butler, Boston, and beyond, for being ever-present in their wisdom and patience: Harriet Beinfield, Bear and Efrem Korngold, Christine Bauch, Kirun Kapur and Jamie Cash, Fred Speers, Molly Metzler, Susanna Rosenstock and Philip Angermeyer, Kathy Boudin, Mona and Rashid Khalidi, the faculty at Community High School, and my writing students at Boston University.

My living heroes, for smashing stereotypes of China, of genre, and in general: Anne Carson, Ha Jin, Tony Kushner, and Yao Ming.

My family, for providing everything from unconditional love to China travel services and dangling modifier corrections: Judith and Kenneth; Jacob, Aaron, Melissa, and Adam Hunter DeWoskin; the Silvermintzes; the Kaufmanns; Gail and Isaac Handley; Bernardine Dohrn; Bill Ayers; Chesa Boudin; and Malik Dorhn.

And last and most, Zayd Dohrn, who would be my baby daddy and favorite person even if he hadn't read and edited this manuscript literally a hundred times.

60033728

12/05 - 5 (12/06)
10/07 - 11 - 01/08 (2/09)